Bristol Studies in International Theory

Series Editors: **Felix Berenskötter**, SOAS, University of London, UK, **Neta C. Crawford**, Boston University, US and **Stefano Guzzini**, Uppsala University, Sweden, PUC-Rio de Janeiro, Brazil

This series provides a platform for theoretically innovative scholarship that advances our understanding of the world and formulates new visions of, and solutions for, world politics.

Guided by an open mind about what innovation entails, and against the backdrop of various intellectual turns, interrogations of established paradigms, and a world facing complex political challenges, books in the series provoke and deepen theoretical conversations in the field of International Relations.

Also available

Care and the Pluriverse
Rethinking Global Ethics
By **Maggie FitzGerald**

I0136036

Praxis as a Perspective on International Politics
Edited by **Gunther Hellmann** and **Jens Steffek**

The Civil Condition in World Politics
Beyond Tragedy and Utopianism
Edited by **Vassilios Paipais**

Snapshots from Home
Mind, Action and Strategy in an Uncertain World
By **K.M. Fierke**

What in the World?
Understanding Global Social Change
Edited by **Mathias Albert** and **Tobias Werron**

The Idea of Civilization and the Making of the Global Order
By **Andrew Linklater**

Find out more

bristoluniversitypress.co.uk/
bristol-studies-in-international-theory

International advisory board

Find out more

bristoluniversitypress.co.uk/
bristol-studies-in-international-theory

BROKEN SOLIDARITIES

How Open Global Governance Divides and Rules

Felix Anderl

BRISTOL
UNIVERSITY
PRESS

First published in Great Britain in 2024 by

Bristol University Press
University of Bristol
1-9 Old Park Hill
Bristol
BS2 8BB
UK
t: +44 (0)117 374 6645
e: bup-info@bristol.ac.uk

Details of international sales and distribution partners are available at bristoluniversitypress.co.uk

© Bristol University Press 2024

British Library Cataloguing in Publication Data
A catalogue record for this book is available from the British Library

ISBN 978-1-5292-2021-6 hardcover
ISBN 978-1-5292-2022-3 paperback
ISBN 978-1-5292-2023-0 ePub
ISBN 978-1-5292-2024-7 ePdf

Cover design: blu inc, Bristol
Front cover image: 'Solidaritas' (Solidarity) scuplture by artist Dolorosa Sinaga

Contents

List of Figures and Tables

Figures

Tables

Acknowledgements

This book would not have been written without the generous help of many people and institutions. Financially and intellectually, my work was supported first by the project *No Alternative? Social Protest in the Alter-Globalisation Movement between Opposition and Dissidence* funded by the German Research Foundation (DFG). I want to thank Nicole Deitelhoff for enabling me to travel to Southeast Asia and conduct lengthy and costly field research. The cross-fertilization of the project-related work and the research for this book was an invaluable asset, and I therefore also want to thank Priska Daphi for her companionship and advice, and Jannis Gebken, our student assistant, for his support over the years. Further student assistants who helped with the transcription of interviews were Wahyu Hadi Pradana, Laura Leschinski, and Theo Kassaras.

After the end of that project, I worked as a research associate at the Cluster of Excellence: The Formation of Normative Orders. Thanks to Nicole Deitelhoff for granting me the privilege of this position with few obligations, an inspiring environment, and enough time to work on this study which was initially a PhD Project at Goethe University, Frankfurt. In Frankfurt, I worked with a fantastic crowd of academics who supported me and this book enormously. Thanks go to the 'Gangstas of Excellence', Janusz Biene, Lisa Bogerts, Maik Fielitz, Regina Hack, Holger Marcks, Daniel Kaiser, Victor Kempf, Max Lesch, Nele Kortendiek, Jannik Pfister, Sebastian Schindler, Martin Schmetz, Eva Ottendörfer, Philip Wallmeier, Tobias Wille, and Jens Zimmermann.

I received a travel grant by the Vereinigung von Freunden und Förderern der Goethe-Universität to travel to Washington DC where I spent three months at the Elliott School of International Affairs. I want to thank Barbara Miller and Martha Finnemore for hosting me there, and for kindly discussing my research. My time in DC was enriched by Patrice Wangen and Christine Andrä, who also organized an inspiring workshop with great discussions and mediocre red wine. Furthermore, I want to thank Jonathan Fox, who discussed my thoughts on the World Bank Group with me in my favourite bookshop, Kramers, where I also conducted several interviews.

For the final stages of this work, I was lucky enough to get hired by the Centre for Research in the Arts, Humanities, and Social Sciences (CRASSH) at the University of Cambridge. Inanna Hamati-Ataya has created an unparalleled intellectual environment in the Centre for Global Knowledge Studies (Gloknos), where I was lucky to work on the global as an artefact, putting my work on global governance into perspective. Inanna has become a dear collaborator and inspired me to think differently about the world and its politics. At CRASSH, I also met Rosie Worsdale with whom I started the Research Network 'Solidarity across difference' (co-funded by King's College Cambridge). Thanks to everyone who attended weekly; I learned so much about solidarity in this context, from too many people to name here.

In Cambridge, I was lucky to find 'the Cambridge Cool', who are all brilliant minds and who I miss as friends now that I've moved back to Germany. Federico Brandmayr, Thandeka Cochrane, Rob Gruijters, Ryan Heuser, Sophia Hornbacher-Schönleber, Olga Löblová, Tobias Müller, Tejas Parasher, Josh Platzky Miller, Julia Rone, Lucia Rubinelli, and Laura Traijber Waisbich. You have all deeply shaped my thinking about politics and everything else. Around the same time, two very special colleagues, Audrey Alejandro and Paul Beaumont, suggested starting an online writing group. Everybody thought this was going to be short-lived, but for over two years now, the three of us have been meeting online to talk and write every week, and I have no idea how I would have finished this book otherwise.

I presented this research at various stages in the process and was privileged to receive comments and discussions from many people. Early on, I described my idea in Kassel at Aram Ziai's PhD Colloquium. My initial proposal, as well as the introduction, were discussed in Christopher Daase's and Nicole Deitelhoff's 'RiesiKo'. I want to thank Julian Junk, Stefan Kroll, Jannik Pfister, Sebastian Schindler, Philip Wallmeier, Tobias Wille, Antonia Witt, and Lisbeth Zimmermann for their engaged discussions of my drafts. An early version of the project was furthermore presented at the PhD Workshop 'Resistance. Subjects, Representations, Contexts' in Oldenburg. Chapter 7 was presented at the 'Colloquium from below' by the Institut für Protest- und Bewegungsforschung (IPB) in Berlin. Chapter 8 was presented at the 3rd European Workshop in International Studies (EWIS) in Tübingen, and at the School of Government and Public Policy in Depok, Indonesia. The Conclusion was presented at the Joint PhD Workshop of the Berlin Graduate School for Transnational Studies and the Hebrew University of Jerusalem. The Introduction was presented at the colloquium of the Peace Research Institute Frankfurt, and DVPW thematic group Ethnographic Methods in Political Science, both of which have become an intellectual home in the meantime. Later versions of the overall book were presented at the International Studies Association in San Francisco, the European International Studies Association (EISA-Pec) in Prague, and the European

Consortium on Political Research (ECPR) in Hamburg. Out of many helpful and constructive contributions, I want to thank those who thoroughly read and discussed my work at these occasions: Paul Beaumont, Karen Buckley, Ben Christian, Catherine Craven, Lisa Dellmuth, Micha Fiedlschuster, Jannis Grimm, Eva Johais, Julian Junk, Franziska Müller, Tobias Neidel, Nicholas Onuf, Thomas Risse, Mariam Salehi, Florian Spissinger, Simon Teune, Tobias Wille, Aram Ziai, and Michael Zürn. Their input has been of utmost importance.

The lion's share of counselling during these years lay with Nicole Deitelhoff and Aram Ziai. I am highly indebted to both for their support, patience, and trust. This work has, furthermore, profited immensely from the feedback of many gifted scholars who took the time to discuss my arguments with them, among them Amitav Acharya, Janet Conway, Klaus Dingwerth, Jannis Grimm, Patrick T. Jackson, Nicholas Onuf, Hanna Pfeiffer, Leon Schettler, Gianna Schlichte, Jens Steffek, Jonas Tallberg, Jürgen Rüland, Katrin Uba, Antonia Witt, and Ayşe Zarakol. Finally, the folks at Bristol University Press have done an excellent job. Stephen Wenham, Zoe Forbes, and Annie Rose steered this manuscript towards publication professionally and with great care. The series editors, especially Stefano Guzzini, have provided very detailed feedback on two full drafts, and four reviewers have transformed this into a better piece of research, particularly one 12-page review report by Nicholas Onuf, which should be published as an essay itself. With gratitude, I acknowledge the cover artwork by Dolorosa Sinaga. Her sculpture 'Solidaritas' and her important artistic activism in Indonesia are a true inspiration.

The biggest influence on this work cannot be reconstructed from the program of conferences. I want to thank Johannes Haaf, Sophia Hornbacher-Schönleber, and Laura Gorriahn for their friendship and support during these years. Moreover, I owe a lot to Dorothee and Philip Anderl, as well as to my father, who unfortunately is no longer around to read this. Thank you Niklas Beckmannshagen, Jana Borusko, William Callison, Claudia Duppel, Jean Enriquez, Katharina Hoppe, Nilda Inkermann, Thomas Lindner, Martin Petry, Hannah Pfeiffer, Marius Piwonka, Andrea Sempertegui, Elias Steinhilper, Philip Wallmeier, Antonia Witt, Anna Wolkenhauer, and Rosie Worsdale who have shaped this book, maybe without their knowledge of it. Solidarity can only be achieved together. During the time of writing this book, I have come to experience a form of togetherness that I could have never imagined. I am therefore very grateful to Julia Leser whose love and solidarity gives me hope and purpose every day.

My utmost respect and gratitude go to those activists and professionals who took the time to discuss their struggles with me. These conversations were not only the foundation of this research, but they have also been so enriching that they are at the core of why I decided to do this for a living. I sincerely hope to have produced something of value to them. Thanks to

Martin Petry who gave me the initial inspiration, Knud Vöcking and Korinna Horta of *Urgewald*, who opened the doors to transnational activism, as well as Emil Salim who took the time to extensively talk to me in his home. Throughout the research process, I was touched by people who fight for global solidarity every day, and who continue to do so when their goals are termed 'unrealistic'. The following is dedicated to them.

Berlin
January 2022

Introduction

In May 2016, a group of about 50 global justice activists assembled for a meeting in a youth hostel in Frankfurt am Main. Hailing from all continents, they met to discuss a strategy for their protest and advocacy work against destructive development projects. In Frankfurt, the meeting was scheduled at the occasion of the Asian Development Bank (ADB) annual meeting which, perhaps oddly, was held in this European city. The place, with its wooden architecture choices of the 1970s, was desperately needing a makeover. But it was cheap, and its location proved convenient. Residing just on the quay of the river Main, the attendants could see the European Central Bank (ECB) across the river when turning slightly to the right, and the banking quarter with its luminating Commerzbank tower on the left. The activists sat cramped into a stuffy room and talked for hours without interruption. They were specialists in transnational finance, using terms and abbreviations from the technical repertoire of their adversaries, the multilateral development banks (MDBs). But the worn-out furniture, participants' khaki shorts, and a leftist common sense made it easy for me not to forget which side of the Main I was on.

These activists have been collaborating for a long time. The older ones among them were once the leaders of the infamous Global Justice Movement which mobilized against the capitalist development model epitomized by the MDBs, particularly the World Bank Group.[1] Today, this movement is fragmented into numerous local and regional patches, wanting the transnational solidarity that they once brought to the streets. In 2000, for example, they mobilized about 20,000 people at the occasion of the World Bank Group's annual meeting in Prague, a summit that they undermined to the extent that the President of the institution, James Wolfensohn, fled through a hidden tunnel and was forced to hold a special meeting with

---

[1] The World Bank Group is a compilation of five institutions, the International Bank for Reconstruction and Development (IBRD), the International Development Association (IDA), the International Finance Corporation (IFC), the Multilateral Investment Guarantee Agency (MIGA), and the International Centre for Settlement of Investment Disputes (ICSID). I say World Bank Group when I refer to all of them and specify the agency when I refer to one of them. In practice, many use 'World Bank' and 'World Bank Group' as synonyms. In direct quotes I therefore cannot always sustain this distinction.

activists and hear their demands, instead of proceeding with the official agenda. Debt cancellation for poor countries, the end of forced resettlements, stopping the extraction of oil and gas as well as the deforestation and displacement occurring during many development projects – these were the issues raised by the movement which, already in 1994, had claimed that '50 Years is enough', mobilizing about 60,000 people for the dissolution of the World Bank Group in Washington DC.

In 2016 though, such a movement was nowhere to be seen. Although the activists were carrying banners and shouting a few slogans at the summit, their actions did not mobilize anyone beyond themselves. A German activist who organized the strategy meeting (and invited me to attend it) had in fact asked me to spread the word among my students prior to the summit, hoping that some of them might join the mobilization against capitalist development practices. A lecturer at the local Goethe University at the time, I gladly returned the favour, but no students showed up. The activists' actions in front of the ADB meeting were more of an add-on to their work anyway. Their main task during the summit was to sit in conference rooms and lobby for the cause of communities negatively affected by development projects. The outside actions were thus more of a remnant of earlier days, a relict that produced some flashy pictures which they could later upload to the websites of NGOs that they work for.

The group of people assembled in Frankfurt have continued what they have been doing for almost three decades now. They keep a sharp eye on the institutions that finance 'development projects' which – in their opinion – create devastation rather than progress. The most prominent adversary in that regard has been the World Bank Group. It is the cornerstone of a governance and business model which other institutions such as the ADB generally emulate. That is why, in this book, I mainly focus on activists' interaction with the World Bank Group. These activists research the negative impacts of development projects financed by these institutions, publicize, and scandalize them, lobby for better safeguards and standards, protect the communities targeted by projects, and mobilize the wider public to take a stance against destructive development practices. Yet, in 2016, in contrast to the years around the millennium, the transnational activist network did so without a powerful movement to back it up.[2]

---

[2]   I use the concept of the transnational activist network as a modification of Keck and Sikkink, *Activists beyond Borders: Advocacy Networks in International Politics* (Ithaca: Cornell University Press, 1998). Civil society organizations, either in the form of NGOs like Amnesty International, or in the form of foundations or think-tanks, can be part of it, or employ individuals who are. Frequently, an activist network is a core element of a social movement which is more mass-based, less organized, and grounded in local struggles.

Of course, the activists are aware of this situation. They have professionalized and adapted to the discourse of the organizations that they oppose. They know that movements do not last forever, and they know that destructive development is no longer the big public issue that it used to be. They know, but they don't understand. Their puzzlement was expressed by one of the most experienced and well-known activists of the transnational activist network who, during the later hours of the meeting in Frankfurt, raised his hand to ask the following question:

'The big reforms at the World Bank – first and foremost the accountability mechanisms and the transparency initiative, came out of mass movements that were built on massive problems and people who had died, and they transported that to Washington and made a massive splash at the Bank. Still today, there are people massively suffering from World Bank policies, but nowadays we don't manage to bring those local struggles together anymore; the movement is so fragmented. How has that happened?'

The meeting had generally been dominated by anxiety. After some activist successes over the past 20 years, the movement fragmented over time and was unable to react properly to the ongoing World Bank safeguards review which was widely expected to dilute its social and environmental standards in favour of big business and smooth large-scale investment. On top of that dilution, the Chinese-led Asian Infrastructure and Investment Bank (AIIB) had just entered the scene and was widely seen to be ridiculing the safeguards, transparency measures and risk assessments, which the transnational activist network assembled in Frankfurt had for decades been fighting for. Furthermore, shortly before the meeting, a consortium of journalists had published stories from all over the world, detailing the horrific effects of current World Bank Group projects: forced resettlement, environmental degradation, masses of local people indebted and unpossessed of their livelihoods – all of which didn't receive an appropriate response from the institution's management.[3] In short: everyone in the room was expecting regression, and nobody was sure what to do about it, let alone how to mobilize another mass movement. Despite this clear sense of

---

[3]   See the project 'Evicted and Abandoned' by the International Consortium for Investigative Journalists for a comprehensive assessment of the World Bank Group's project failures until 2015, available at: {http://projects.huffingtonpost.com/proje cts/worldbank-evicted-abandoned/worldbank-projects-leave-trail-misery-aro und-globe-kenya}.

urgency, the senior activist's question – *the movement is so fragmented. How has that happened?* – received little response from his exhausted colleagues. But I was animated. So much so, in fact, that I wrote this book to answer the question.

Divide and rule? Open global governance and cooptation

The scene just described is symbolic for a time in which the advocacy specialists who are left of the Global Justice Movement feel increasingly little grip on the international organizations (IOs) that they try to influence. At first glance, this seems surprising, because these IOs have significantly turned towards their external critics after being the subject of hostile protest movements throughout the 1990s. Wolfensohn inviting his critics in to voice their concerns was hence not an isolated incident but part of a bigger shift in global governance which International Relations (IR) scholars have dubbed the 'opening-up' of IOs. This trend is explained by a growing international norm for civil society access, although this is mediated by the issue area (human rights IOs are more open than security IOs), and their membership structure (the more democratic member states an IO has the more open it can be expected to become).[4] IOs like the World Bank Group that face a lot of criticism, furthermore, feel a stronger demand to legitimate themselves publicly.[5] Decisive changes in institutional setups of these institutions came after the protests against them.[6] Empirically, there is a broad consensus on the fact that civil society has a much easier time accessing global governance institutions today than they had before the turn of the millennium. The World Bank Group stands for a type of IO that slowly but continuously opened its doors for civil society after the Cold War, raising civil society involvement from 21 per cent of its projects in 1990 to 88 per cent in 2015.[7] It can therefore be understood as an 'open'

---

[4] Jonas Tallberg et al., *The Opening Up of International Organizations* (Cambridge: Cambridge University Press, 2013).

[5] Sidney Tarrow, 'Transnational politics: contention and institutions in international politics', *Annual Review of Political Science* 4, 1 (2001), pp. 1–20; Robert O'Brien et al., *Contesting Global Governance* (Cambridge: Cambridge University Press, 2000); Jens Steffek et al. (2008) *Civil Society Participation in European and Global Governance: A Cure for the Democratic Deficit?* (Basingstoke: Palgrave Macmillan).

[6] Susan Park, 'Accountability as justice for the multilateral development banks? Borrower opposition and bank avoidance to US power and influence', *Review of International Political Economy* 24, 5 (2017), pp. 776–801; Tallberg et al., *The Opening Up of International Organizations*, p. 138.

[7] Tallberg et al., *The Opening Up of International Organizations*, p. 5.

IO.[8] Its interaction with civil society is an instructive example of what I call *open global governance*.

But for social movements, this opening-up is a double-edged sword; it is likely to trigger 'a spiral of opportunities and threats'.[9] For activists, these opportunities of participation entail a moral and political dilemma which often leads to internal conflicts and division.[10] On the one hand, the temptation and moral pressure to make use of the opportunities for manipulating international politics in such a way is undeniable: if you finally get a chance to have a say on the issue you were criticizing for so long, why would you not go for it? On the other hand, participation can be a trap. The IO may use these interactions as a fig leaf for their policies, covering its traces and coopting its opponents.[11]

Social movements have become coopted by governments time and again. Originally attributed to Niccolò Machiavelli, the strategy to *divide and rule* their opposition has long been an essential tool of governments to stabilize their power and achieve their goals more smoothly. Otto von Bismarck, who is honoured with a monument not far from where the ADB held its summit in 2016, applied this governing strategy with great skill when introducing social relief policies for workers while crushing the labour movement at the same time. Therefore, a few decades later, Rosa Luxemburg (who has not received a monument, but a street named after her in Frankfurt) unsuccessfully warned the Social Democrats not to be distracted by the breadcrumbs that the oligarchy was willing to give to coopt their opposition into the existing system of rule. Such a story could be told about almost any historical context in which leftist social movements and governments interacted.[12]

Given the plethora of examples in which social movements were offered certain opportunities by rulers, and then fragmented as a result of their internal conflicts over how to deal with them, it is surprising

---

[8] Tallberg et al., *The Opening Up of International Organizations*, p. 13; Anders Uhlin and Sara Kalm, *Civil Society and the Governance of Development: Opposing Global Institutions* (London: Palgrave, 2015), p. 12.

[9] Sidney Tarrow, *Power in Movement. Social Movements and Contentious Politics* (Cambridge: Cambridge University Press, 2011), p. 159.

[10] Felix Anderl et al., 'Keeping your enemies close? The variety of social movements' reactions to international organizations' opening up', *International Studies Review* 23, 4 (2021), pp. 1273–99.

[11] Charlotte Dany and Katja Freistein, 'Global governance and the myth of civil society participation', in Berit Bliesemann de Guevara (ed) *Myth and Narrative in International Politics. Interpretive Approaches to the Study of IR*, (London: Palgrave Macmillan, 2016), pp. 229–48.

[12] Frances Fox Piven and Richard Cloward, *Poor People's Movements: Why They Succeed, How They Fail* (New York: Vintage, 1977).

that the activists – well-read about leftist history – were irritated about the fragmentation of their own movement. They know, of course, that integration of movement groups into institutional politics is frequently associated with a de-radicalization of their goals and repertoires, that is, a change from disruptive to more conventional means of protest as an effect of cooperation,[13] and that such processes of participation hold the danger of cooptation.[14] From such a historical point of view, the fragmentation of the Global Justice Movement that occurred just after the opening-up of the IOs that they contested is no surprise at all.

Rulers have long utilized the strategy of 'divide and rule' in order to coopt parts of their antagonist into the ruling order, in effect dividing social movements into those who joined the newly won channels of political influence, and those who radically rejected cooperation with the ruler. The only problem is: there is no ruler in global governance. Due to this absence, decades of scholarship in IR have been dedicated to the issue of governing without a government.[15] It would be easy to ridicule the idea of global governance as a lofty ideal, and indeed the power-blindness in much of the global governance research remains a problem.[16] But the activists' confusion suggests that there *is* a difference between national labour movements being coopted by a central government, and the fragmentation of a transnational social movement with opportunities of participation in global governance: if there is no ruler in global governance, who should have divided them? This book does not give an answer to that question. In fact, I will argue that there is no good answer to it, because rather than dwelling on the '*who*' question, it is more productive to understand *how* the Global Justice Movement was, indeed, divided and ruled. This, first, helps answer the activists' desperate search for the reasons of their own fragmentation. But second, it contributes to the theorization of what rule in the international could mean in the absence of a central government.

---

[13] Hanspeter Kriesi, 'Political context and opportunity', in David A. Snow, Sarah A. Soule, and Hanspeter Kriesi (eds) *The Blackwell Companion to Social Movements* (Malden: MA: Blackwell, 2011), p. 85; Doowon Suh, 'Institutionalizing social movements: the dual strategy of the Korean women's movement', *Sociological Quarterly* 52, 3 (2011), pp. 442–71.

[14] Rhiannon Morgan, 'On political institutions and social movement dynamics: the case of the United Nations and the global indigenous movement', *International Political Science Review* 28, 3 (2007), pp. 273–92; Markus Holdo, 'Cooptation and non-cooptation: elite strategies in response to social protest', *Social Movement Studies* 18 (2019), pp. 444–62.

[15] R.A.W. Rhodes, 'The new governance: governing without government', *Political Studies* 44, 4 (1996), pp. 652–67; Klaus Dingwerth and Philipp Pattberg, 'Global governance as a perspective on world politics', *Global Governance* 12, 2 (2006), pp. 185–203.

[16] Michael N. Barnett and Raymond Duvall, 'Power in global governance', in Michael N. Barnett and Raymond Duvall (eds) *Power in Global Governance*, (Cambridge: Cambridge University Press, 2005), p. 2.

Rule without a ruler

This book reconstructs how one of the most impressive transnational social movements in modern history has fragmented to a degree that warrants the label *divide and rule*, because the movement's most valuable currency – solidarity – has been broken in the process of interacting with the institutional politics of its adversary. Yet, the World Bank Group is not a ruler. How, then, can we speak of 'divide and rule' in this situation? For this question, I build on a concept derived from Luc Boltanski's work: *complex rule*. Boltanski's argument is that, in modern capitalist systems, we cannot see structures of rule as easily because they govern in a veiled and indirect ('managerial') fashion.[17] While 'simple rule' works through oppression in order to totally fragment critique (think Bismarck), complex rule is more difficult to detect because it grants more room for opposition. Critique is legitimate within complex rule, as long as it is expressed in a specific form.[18] Yet, as much as simple ('traditional') rule, complex rule has the aim and effect of fragmenting critique. To rule means to keep critique in fragmentation.[19] Although the mechanisms are very different from simple rule, the effect is still the same: disguising potential entry points of attack, getting rid of issues around which critique was able to cohere and constitute a movement. Moderate critique is included, and controversies are relegated towards symbolic exchanges and interactions within institutions that create and maintain a certain reality as inevitable. By this, a specific form of interaction is presented as rational – within reality – and oriented at progress, while all other forms of critique are excluded and presented as backward and out of touch with reality. Through constant regrouping, the changing of boundaries, the softening and re-interpretation of policies, and the opening-up of rules of selection, institutions create the fragmentation of critique through its disorientation. This can strengthen moderate forms of critique discursively and materially, at least short-term, while radical critique that questions the very institutionalized reality is ruled out.

Complex rule as a concept helps understand why social movements can become divided even in the absence of an authoritarian ruler, when governing institutions make offers of participation to their critics. But not

---

[17] Luc Boltanski, *On Critique: A Sociology of Emancipation* (Cambridge: Polity, 2011).

[18] Luc Boltanski, 'Individualismus ohne Freiheit. Ein pragmatischer Zugang zur Herrschaft', *Westend. Neue Zeitschrift Für Sozialforschung* 5, 2 (2008), pp. 144; based on Daase and Deitelhoff, I call this form of critique moderate and its proponents oppositional, in contrast to radical critique whose proponents I call dissident. See Christopher Daase and Nicole Deitelhoff, 'Opposition and dissidence: two modes of resistance against international rule', *Journal of International Political Theory* 15, 1 (2019), pp. 11–30.

[19] Boltanski, 'Individualismus ohne Freiheit', p. 142.

all forms of cooperation lead to cooptation. Empirically, the effects are rather diverse, ranging from enthusiastic cooperation to increased hostility or indifference.[20] Furthermore, social movements like the one portrayed here are no judgemental dopes.[21] They make conscious decisions and assess the political situation around them. To assume an automatism that leads from the opening-up of IOs to the fragmentation of social movements would therefore be misplaced. What is more, attributing the explicit *aim* to fragment critique, and hence a coherent intentionality, to the World Bank Group would contradict the findings of prior empirical studies on the matter, especially those that engage the institution from an ethnographic perspective.[22] Therefore, I adjust Boltanski's concept in accordance with what I find empirically: where he uses the term complex domination (modalité domination complexe), suggesting an intentional and direct practice of oppression, complex rule describes a dynamic constellation in which power asymmetries come to light. While including strategic practices on the side of the institution and its critics, my main theoretical point is that these practices arise within and collectively constitute a form of politics, the effects of which may or may not go back to intentional action.

I understand transnational rule as an institutionalized relationship of super- and subordination beyond the nation state.[23] With 'complex rule', I denote a specific relationship which is co-constituted by both the drivers and the opponents of this very process of institutionalization. I show how a discursive and practical shift in international politics has been undoing and fragmenting critique by changing governance in accordance with new management practices. In *open global governance*, this form of rule shapes politics with 'networked, team-based, practice-oriented techniques' that are so all-encompassing that it is fruitless to ask who caused them.[24] Instead,

---

[20] Anderl et al., 'Keeping your enemies close?'.

[21] Robin Celikates, *Critique as Social Practice: Critical Theory and Social Self-Understanding* (London: Rowman & Littlefield International, 2018), pp. 1–8.

[22] Jon Harald Sande Lie, 'Developmentality: indirect governance in the World Bank–Uganda partnership', *Third World Quarterly* 36, 4 (2015), pp. 723–40; Jonathan A. Fox, 'Advocacy research and the World Bank: propositions for discussions', in Marc Edelman and Angelique Haugerud (eds) *The Anthropology of Development Organizations: From Classical Political Economy to Contemporary Neoliberalism* (Malden, MA: Blackwell, 2005), pp. 306–33; Dana Clark, et al., *Demanding Accountability: Civil-Society Claims and the World Bank Inspection Panel* (Lanham, MD: Rowman & Littlefield, 2003).

[23] Christopher Daase and Nicole Deitelhoff, 'Reconstructing global rule by analyzing resistance', Dissidence Working Papers 1/2014, 2014, available at: {https://dissidenz.net/wp-content/uploads/2013/03/wp1-2014-daase-deitelhoff-en.pdf}; Daase and Deitelhoff, 'Opposition and dissidence'.

[24] Wendy Brown, *Undoing the Demos: Neoliberalism's Stealth Revolution* (New York: Zone Books, 2015), p. 34.

I carve out the mechanisms that arise in this mode of rule – mechanisms that collectively produce the fragmentation of social movements. This fragmentation, in turn, stabilizes the constellation that I call complex rule. Yet, complex rule is not 'a thing'. It is a descriptive term for a transnational constellation in which institutionalized, hierarchical relationships are enacted in the contestation between a social movement and an IO, resulting in the fragmentation of the very movement that co-constitutes this relationship. Beyond answering the activist's question, the second contribution of this book is, hence, an offer to IR: based on the reconstruction of the Global Justice Movement's fragmentation, I make the case for understanding open global governance as an institutional environment that does not need a ruler to divide (and rule) its opposition.

The following traces the process during which the transnational social movement against capitalist and exploitative development practices fragmented during its interaction with the World Bank Group. I reconstruct how the fragmentation took place by tracing the history of activism against the institution, starting in the early 1980s, showing how the activists were able to gain traction during the late 1980s, and coalesced with what became the Global Justice Movement in the 1990s. During that time, particularly during the Wolfensohn Presidency starting in 1996, the institution reacted to critics by incorporating their moderate parts. This led to the institutionalization of critique, notably in the Extractive Industries Review (EIR), an externally led multi-stakeholder consultation process from 2002 to 2004, and the Civil Society Policy Forum (CSPF), the institutionalized forum of civil society engagement jointly organized by the World Bank Group and the International Monetary Fund (IMF) since 2002. I reconstruct these processes, showing how a new constellation was inscribed into the contested field of global development governance, a constellation that was made possible by and contributed to the fragmentation of critique.

By tracing the decline of the movement against the World Bank Group, I answer the question by the activist: how has the fragmentation of the movement happened? This is important because while we know that 'divide and rule' has been a prevalent method of rule for a long time, we don't know exactly *how* this happens. Otherwise, we could assume that movements might be a bit more effective in designing countermeasures. Furthermore, in the context of open global governance, the ways in which rule leads to fragmentation have not yet received much attention. My answer to the activist's question is that the movement fragmented because of the way in which it engaged with, and thereby co-constituted, an institutional order that I describe as 'complex rule' from the 1990s until today. While it is not surprising that parts of a movement get coopted, my emphasis is on the contingency of these processes and the historically specific ways in which open global governance divides its critics. Transnational social movements can learn from this history, and so can theorists of global governance. The character found in the processes (different from, say, the ways in which Bismarck divided and ruled) can be explained by the specific constellation of complex rule which I theorize in Chapter 2. I argue that the specific character of rule in open global governance is organized alongside three dimensions, normative, discursive, and organizational. Complex rule is:

- governed by a neoliberal rationality;
- reflexive, and hence in constant need of justification;
- organized as a managerial bureaucracy.

Based on the reconstruction of empirical processes, I propose five mechanisms that connect these three dimensions with outcomes alongside which the critique's fragmentation and the resulting decline of the social movement can be understood. It is important to stress, again, that these mechanisms are not the result of top-down institutional politics, but they are co-created by institutions and movements, and hence also observable in practices on both 'sides' of the contention. These mechanisms are: (1) *Economization*, a mechanism that can be observed in the division of global from particular knowledge and the quantification of issues (institutional practices), as well as the usage of economized language and the acceptance of economic ends (practices of critique); (2) *Incorporation*, which can be observed in the opening-up as well as active cooptation of critics on the side of the institution, and the ensuing participation of critics as well as the elevation of particular individuals, mostly from NGOs; (3) *Legitimation*, observable in a specific way of arguing which refers to an objectified 'complexity' and disarms critics (institutional practices), and the willingness on the side of critics to engage pragmatically within the same order of justification; (4) *Professionalization*, which can be observed in a new management style and the formalization of interaction (institutional practices) and the sharing of responsibility as well as NGOization (practices of critique); (5) *Regulation*, observable in the creation of rules, the ordering and disciplining of critique (institutional practices), and the endorsement of institutional rules and self-policing (practices of critique). On the side of the critics, each of these practices is contested, however. It is in the contestation of these processes that fragmentation of critique can be observed.

Fragmentation in interaction: IR and social movement studies

In the following, I look at global governance in interaction with those who resist it, and I observe how the latter are being divided along the way. This endeavour builds on a number of studies which have dealt with IOs' reactions to transnational protest, especially in their attempt to regain social legitimacy.[25] We now know a great deal about the legitimation strategies of IOs and how they try to establish public authority through specific strategies of civil society inclusion,[26] or rhetorical democratization.[27] We also know a lot about social movement strategies on how to disrupt IOs.[28] But these analyses often encounter a trade-off: either researchers focus on the movements, but neglect to theorize and differentiate what they resist: rule then remains an obscure 'alphabet soup',[29] in which seemingly random symbols and institutions float, without any explanation of what the pot is made of, who cooks it, and above all who eats it.[30] Or those structures of rule are extensively theorized, but the dynamic moment is lost from view and the movements that resist it can only be described as 'external shock'.[31] For this reason, within social movement studies, an increasing number of scholars have called for a stronger focus on interaction rather than analysing either 'side' of hierarchical conflict alone.[32] With this interactionist principle, the approach of this book is to combine the two disciplines (see Chapter 1).

---

[25] Michael Zürn et al., 'International authority and its politicization', *International Theory* 4, 1 (2012), pp. 69–106; Lisa Maria Dellmuth and Jonas Tallberg, 'The social legitimacy of international organisations: interest representation, institutional performance, and confidence extrapolation in the United Nations', *Review of International Studies* 41, 3 (2015), pp. 451–75; Jonas Tallberg et al., 'Explaining the transnational design of international organizations', *International Organization* 68, 4 (2014), pp. 741–74.

[26] Monika Heupel et al., 'International organisations and human rights: what direct authority needs for its legitimation', *Review of International Studies* 44, 2 (2018), pp. 343–66; Jennifer Gronau and Henning Schmidtke, 'The quest for legitimacy in world politics – international institutions' legitimation strategies', *Review of International Studies* 42, 3 (2016), pp. 535–57; Steffek et al., *Civil Society Participation in European and Global Governance: A Cure for the Democratic Deficit?* (Basingstoke: Palgrave Macmillan, 2008).

[27] Klaus Dingwerth et al., 'The rise of democratic legitimation: why international organizations speak the language of democracy', *European Journal of International Relations* 26, 3 (2020), pp. 714–41; Jens Steffek, 'Discursive legitimation in environmental governance', *Forest Policy and Economics* 11, 5–6 (2009), pp. 313–18.

[28] Sidney Tarrow, 'Transnational politics'; Keck and Sikkink, *Activists beyond Borders*; Priska Daphi, 'The global justice movement in Europe', in Christina Flesher-Fominaya and Ramon Feenstra (eds) *Routledge Handbook of Contemporary European Social Movements. Protest in Turbulent Times* (London: Routledge, 2019), pp. 142–54.

[29] Alex Veit, 'Social movements, contestation and direct international rule: theoretical approaches', *Stichproben: Wiener Zeitschrift Für Kritische Afrikastudien* 20, 20 (2011), p. 38.

[30] Felix Anderl, 'Kontestation, Politisierung, Herrschaft: Bewegungsforschung und internationale Beziehungen', *Forschungsjournal Soziale Bewegungen* 34, 1 (2021), pp. 122–37.

[31] David S. Meyer, 'Protest and political process', in Edwin Amenta, Kate Nash, and Alan Scott (eds) *The Wiley-Blackwell Companion to Political Sociology* (Oxford: Blackwell, 2012), pp. 395–407; Yves Schemeil, 'Bringing international organization in: global institutions as adaptive hybrids', *Organization Studies* 34, 2 (2013), pp. 219–52.

[32] Eitan Y. Alimi et al., 'Relational dynamics and processes of radicalization: a comparative framework', *Mobilization* 17, 1 (2012), pp. 7–26; Jeff Goodwin and James Jasper,

My motivation is hence to broaden the perspective of global governance literature on the effects of transnational legitimacy politics beyond the IO itself. I will show empirically that the movement's fragmentation is a property of the specific governing constellation of complex rule. The main feature of this book is to reconstruct the paths alongside which that process unfolds. To understand this process, social movement studies, a discipline that has long engaged with questions of mobilization, cooptation, and recently protest outcomes, offers helpful analytical tools. With this lens, I build on prior work in IR which has highlighted the complex processes of subjectification that arise in the interaction of IOs and social movements.[33] What these works have in common is that they highlight the productive character of interaction: the back-and-forth between social movements and IOs is not only an outcome of protest in the sense of achieving a seat at the table, nor is it the basic given of analysis for studying governance processes with multiple 'stakeholders'. Rather, the process of interaction itself is understood as transformative.

The goal of the following is to understand and empirically trace how the Global Justice Movement underwent such a staggering fragmentation. By tracing the process of these reconfigurations from a mass-based social movement towards a fragmented transnational activist network, I show through empirically traceable mechanisms how the interplay between movement and IO created an institutional order (complex rule) which hinges on and contributes to the movement's fragmentation. Both complex rule and the pathways of fragmentation are constantly re-constituted in this process.[34]

The fragmentation that occurred in the transnational movement against the World Bank Group is thus not explained externally by some political event or material change that happened between the late 1990s and today, but it is traced 'internally', that is within the interaction between the movement and the institution itself. Of course, a critical reader will see a danger in

---

'Caught in a winding, snarling vine: the structural bias of political process theory', in Jeff Goodwin and James Jasper (eds) (2004) *Rethinking Social Movements* (Lanham, MD: Rowman and Littlefield, 2004), pp. 3–30; James M. Jasper and Jan W. Duyvendak (eds) *Players and Arenas: The Interactive Dynamics of Protest* (Amsterdam: Amsterdam University Press, 2015).

[33] Catherine Eschle and Bice Maiguashca, *Critical Theories, International Relations and 'the Anti-Globalisation Movement': The Politics of Global Resistance* (Abingdon: Routledge, 2005); Karen Tucker, 'Participation and subjectification in global governance: NGOs, acceptable subjectivities and the WTO', *Millennium: Journal of International Studies* 42, 2 (2014), pp. 376–96; Christopher L. Pallas and Anders Uhlin, 'Civil society influence on international organizations: theorizing the state channel', *Journal of Civil Society* 10, 2 (2014), pp. 184–203; Uhlin and Kalm, *Civil Society and the Governance of Development*.

[34] Thanks to Stefano Guzzini for helping me with this formulation.

tautological theorizing. But I agree with Guzzini that process factors do not need to be 'variables' that cumulatively explain a linear causal chain: 'The input itself needs to be explained, and such explanation is partly provided by factors that the input generates during the process'.[35] Complex rule as a constellation is both effect and cause of the fragmentation of critique in open global governance (see Chapter 4).

While my focus here is not on defending a causal link, I do consider some alternative pathways to my story in the conclusion of this book. In short: there are some possible alternative explanations to movement fragmentation, but none of them seem particularly convincing: one might, for instance, argue that the movement had simply reached its goals and was no longer necessary ('success hypothesis'). But, as I show empirically, within the movement, there was no sense of 'victory' that could explain the overall movement decline. This proposed causal path is insufficient, even if it may apply to some individual actors. Another widely held belief is that the terror attacks of 9/11 made it impossible to mobilize for anything unrelated to the war in Iraq.[36] But I show in detail that the fragmentation of the movement was already in full swing before 2001, 9/11 helping with the demobilization but not explaining the movement's overall fragmentation. These explanations, hence, do not help us understand how fragmentation happened, and therefore we need to look deeper into the process.

Complex rule is a descriptive term for the constellation that triggered the mechanisms under which the movement fragmented. That is, I assume a contingent causal relationship which is accomplished by five mechanisms. These, in sum, give the reader a good understanding of how the process of fragmentation occurred, but I neither claim that these are the only possible mechanisms contributing to the process, nor do I claim that these can simply be applied to other contexts. What I do claim is that the reconstruction of the processes of interaction between World Bank Group and its critics alongside the five mechanisms answer the activist's question: At the end of this book, I hope readers will not only have a clear understanding of 'how that happened' but will also be able to spot similar constellations in the future, understanding rule without a ruler, and knowing a few tricks on how (not) to engage with it.

---

[35] Stefano Guzzini, 'Social mechanisms as micro-dynamics in constructivist analysis', in Stefano Guzzini (ed) *The Return of Geopolitics in Europe? Social Mechanisms and Foreign Policy Identity Crises* (Cambridge: Cambridge University Press, 2012), p. 254.

[36] Sidney Tarrow and Jennifer Hadden, 'Spillover or spillout? The global justice movement in the United States after 9/11', *Mobilization: An International Quarterly* 12, 4 (2007), pp. 359–76.

Plan of the book

The idea of this book is to look at a social movement and an international institution in interaction. For that, I do not privilege either/or, but look at both of these social entities and what they co-produce, hence bringing social movement studies and IR in closer exchange. Chapter 1 will lay the groundwork for that enterprise by sketching the state of the art in bringing these two disciplines together and outlining the ways in which I plan to further this agenda. Particularly, I stress that we are missing a focus on interaction between IOs and movements for understanding either side of the contention. To capture that interaction, I propose rule and resistance as a conceptual framework that draws on and caters to both disciplines. Building on this argument, I ask what kind of 'rule' there is in the international realm. In Chapter 2, then, I introduce an understanding of rule derived from the perspective of its critics who experience it on the receiving end, that is, during a process of their own fragmentation. While the book is about this very process, I need to make some theoretical remarks on the constellation that sparks it off (Chapter 3). This is important for not drifting into an unduly simplified model of power (who rules?), and for understanding the scope and significance of the empirical processes. Building on the concept of complex rule and its three core dimensions, in Chapter 4, I outline the design of the empirical study with the aim of tracing the fragmentation of critique. First, I introduce the general logic by describing techniques of process tracing and how my approach utilizes them, also tackling the concepts of causation and mechanisms and how the constitutive theorization of complex rule fits into this logic. Consecutively, I specify five mechanisms through which critique has been fragmented and how we can empirically observe them. These mechanisms are developed on the basis of the three theoretical dimensions and in iteration with inductively generated observations in Chapter 5 which traces the history of interaction between the World Bank Group and its critics from the mid-1980s until 2001. I show how the World Bank Group reacted to this movement, beginning to take seriously the moderate critics and inviting them in from the mid-1990s onwards. Moderates, in turn, started to defend their newly received privileges by distancing themselves from the radicals. Furthermore, ruptures between activists from the Global North and the Global South are traced with the example of the anti-debt campaigns, leading to a fundamentally altered field of critique after the millennium.

Having introduced the contentious interaction through the 1990s, Chapters 6 and 7 show in detail how it was partly institutionalized and what effects this institutionalization had, both on institutional policies and on the activities of the protest movement. At the peak of the resistance in 2000, a transnational protest movement against extractive industries managed to pressure World Bank Group President Wolfensohn to agree to a review of all activities in this sector. Based on interviews with almost all important participants, I reconstruct that review process. Led by the independent 'eminent person', Emil Salim, many advocacy groups decided to join and debate with other stakeholders, governments, companies, and World Bank Group staff. The resultant review took up many of the critics' complaints and made progressive recommendations to the World Bank Group. These recommendations were strongly contested inside the institution. The official Management Response took up some of the recommendations but watered down central recommendations. Surprisingly, the powerful social movement did not react with protest to this weak institutional reaction, despite being extremely disappointed by the result. During this review, several processes of fragmentation, in accordance with the mechanisms of complex rule, can be found and illustrated, explaining this lack of critical response.

After this in-depth case study, Chapters 8 and 9 make the case that these processes have been continuing until this day. The World Bank Group and the IMF have created public fora which enable 'civil society' to participate in the governance of development. I ethnographically describe the interaction of institutional staff with critics at the CSPF in 2016, the most prominent forum of interaction. I observe panel sessions that illustrate the back-and-forth of arguments and highlight the specific ways in which critique can and cannot be issued. I describe the frustration of some advocates and the disarming air of institutional representatives in light of which the critics are unsure what to reply. Furthermore, I display the mutual critique and incrimination of different parts of 'civil society', specifically highlighting the processes of hierarchization that the institutions initiated by way of a conscious elevation of specific moderate individuals and organizations. All of this shows that the process of fragmentation is still ongoing among the already fragmented group of critics.

Having traced five mechanisms through which the Global Justice Movement fragmented, the conclusion serves two purposes. First, it discusses alternative explanations (*equifinality*) and weighs the identified process up against them. Second, it discusses the meaning of these findings for international theory. I promote a constellational theory of global governance, explicating the subordinating effects of a transnational order without falling into conspiracy traps by overestimating the agency of a single institution.

1

Social Movements and
International Relations

In recent decades, international politics has been heavily shaped by disruptive non-state actors such as social movements. IR theorists have developed an enormous body of knowledge about supranational governance over the last decades, but have often had difficulty grasping the logic and political meaning of the informal actors who contest international institutions.[1] Social movement studies, on the other hand, has accumulated a great deal of knowledge on these informal actors, but has historically focused on national developments or country comparisons and often lacks the expertise to make sense of transnational protests' impacts on international institutions. Surveying the efforts to understand the effects of protest movements, Lorenzo Bosi and Katrin Uba observe that '[c]onsidering the increasing attention to antiglobalization protests, it is … worth noting that we have little systematic research on the ways international organizations like the World Bank or the International Monetary Fund respond to these actions'.[2] IR with its expertise on IOs could make an important contribution to the field of movement outcome research. Combining social movement studies and IR therefore holds a promise for both disciplines, overcoming the formalistic emphasis on institutions in IR and the institutional blind spot in social movement studies.[3]

---

[1] Jan Aart Scholte, 'Beyond institutionalism: toward a transformed global governance theory', *International Theory* 13, 1 (2020), pp. 1–13; Klaus Schlichte, 'Der Streit der Legitimitäten: Der Konflikt als Grund einer historischen Soziologie des Politischen', *Zeitschrift Für Friedens – Und Konfliktforschung* 1, 1 (2012), pp. 9–43; see also Claus Offe, 'Governance – an "empty signifier"?', *Constellations* 16, 4 (2009), pp. 550–62.

[2] Lorenzo Bosi and Katrin Uba, 'Introduction: the outcomes of social movements', *Mobilization* 14, 4 (2009), p. 413.

[3] Felix Anderl et al., 'Introduction', in Christopher Daase et al. (eds) *Rule and Resistance beyond the Nation State: Contestation, Escalation, Exit* (London: Rowman & Littlefield, 2019), p. 5.

There has already been a growing trend in IR to import insights from social movement studies in order to study the transnational challenges to international politics, or in other words, to understand how the politics of the streets impact the politics of global governance.[4] In this chapter, I survey these efforts to apply movement research to international politics, drawing on the opportunity structure approach and the repertoires of contention approach, both of which have been channelled into the concepts of *contestation* and *politicization* of IOs. I show how these have each inspired their own research agendas and emphases, thus giving IR a productive twist. With the example of the literature on the 'opening-up' of IOs, I argue that these approaches, however, often black-box the social movements that demanded such opening-up in the first place. This short-cut mirrors how movement studies have, in turn, black-boxed the institutions that were in the focus of protest, by attributing them to a vaguely defined 'opportunity structure', that is the exogenous factors which limit or empower collective actors. Movement scholars have therefore come up with the principle that protest and resistance should be considered in their dynamic interaction with state and sociocultural institutions. To do this, then, social movement studies and IR need each other, for both have the knowledge about the respective 'outside' of the other's field of expertise. Studying their interaction with tools from both disciplines is hence a promising way forward.

Movements and institutions: mechanisms of contention

The activist's question dealt with in this book (How has the fragmentation of the Global Justice Movement happened?) touches an issue that social movement studies have long been concerned with. To explain the changing behaviour of social movements is at the core of a discipline that typically engages with such questions with a view on changing protest repertoires. Repertoires of contention constitute a distinctive constellation of tactics developed over time and used by protest groups to act collectively to make

---

4 Bice Maiguashca, 'Globalisation and the "politics of identitiy": IR theory through the looking glass of women's reproductive rights activism', in Catherine Eschle and Bice Maiguashca (eds) *Critical Theories, International Relations and 'the Anti-Globalisation Movement'* (London: Routledge, 2005), pp. 117–36; Thomas R. Davies and Alejandro M. Peña, 'Social movements and international relations: a relational framework', *Journal of International Relations and Development* 24, 1 (2021), pp. 51–76; Matthias Ecker-Ehrhardt, 'Self-legitimation in the face of politicization: why international organizations centralized public communication', *Review of International Organizations* 13, 4 (2018), pp. 519–46; O'Brien et al., *Contesting Global Governance*.

claims on individuals and groups.[5] The theatrical metaphor of the concept suggests 'established ways in which pairs of actors make and receive claims bearing on each other's interests'.[6] The concept of repertoires hence entails certain continuities: they refer to a recurrent and predictable toolkit of specific protest tactics. Nonetheless, repertoires have been observed to change. Sometimes changes are small and slow; sometimes they are fast and broad.[7]

Social movements' repertoire changes have for long been explained either by internal goings-on in the movement, or by changes of their environment, that is external (structural) factors. Internal factors come into play because not every protest tactic is suitable for every movement; they need to resonate with the movement's previous tactics and overall culture: its values, frames, routines, and identities.[8] While these aspects are helpful in explaining certain repertoire choices, they do not usually explain why those repertoires change, sometimes rather abruptly, though. Therefore, social movement studies have placed a lot of emphasis on capturing the external environment and its effects on movements' repertoires.

Going back to Tilly's political process approach, changing repertoires of contention are therefore often explained by a change in the political opportunity structure.[9] The opening of opportunity structures is generally expected to lead to less radical repertoires of contention, the closing of opportunities is expected to lead to more radical ones. For instance, a decentralization of the state in terms of dispersed decision-making structures creates more access-points for institutionalized contention and thus typically leads to de-radicalized protest repertoires.[10] Closing opportunity structures,

---

[5] Charles Tilly, *From Mobilization to Revolution* (Reading: Addison-Wesley, 1978); Verta Taylor and Nella van Dyke, 'Get up, stand up: tactical repertoires of social movements', in David A. Snow, Sarah A. Soule, and Hanspeter Kriesi (eds) *The Blackwell Companion to Social Movements* (Oxford: Blackwell, 2004).

[6] Charles Tilly, *Popular Contention in Great Britain. 1758–1834* (Cambridge, MA: Harvard University Press, 1995), p. 43.

[7] Priska Daphi and Felix Anderl, 'Radicalization and deradicalization in transnational social movements: a relative and multi-level model of repertoire change', Dissidence Working Papers (Frankfurt am Main, 2016), 1, available at: {https://dissidenz.net/wp-content/uploads/2013/03/wp1-2016-daphi-anderl.pdf}.

[8] David S. Meyer, 'Protest and and political opportunity', *Annual Review of Sociology* 30 (2004), pp. 125–45; James Jasper, *The Art of Moral Protest: Culture, Biography, and Creativity in Social Movements* (London: University of Chicago Press, 1997); Priska Daphi, *Becoming a Movement: Identity and Narratives in the European Global Justice Movement* (London: Rowman & Littlefield, 2017).

[9] Kriesi, 'Political context and opportunity'.

[10] Herbert Kitschelt, 'Political opportunity structures and political protest: anti-nuclear movements in four democracies', *British Journal of Political Science* 16 (1986), pp. 57–85.

on the other hand, are often connected with processes of radicalization. Hence, in situations where social movements do not have access to political decision making, disruptive tactics are more likely.[11] In particular, limited access to resources in combination with closed political opportunity structures are expected to lead to internal divisions and more disruptive repertoires.[12] Scholars have shown that movements in more subordinate positions – with little possibilities to influence political decision making – are more likely to engage in disruptive protest.[13]

From this perspective, one could explain the fragmentation of the Global Justice Movement in the context of the changes in its opportunity structure, because the opening-up of global governance institutions constitutes precisely such a change. In the recent literature, however, the opportunity structure approach has been criticized for various reasons. Particularly, scholars have stressed that social movements are not just reactive bodies that automatically respond to changes in their environments in predictive ways. They hence warn not to overemphasize structure over agency of movements and to focus instead on contingent dynamics of interactions.[14] Furthermore, next to political opportunities understood as institutional opening, other opportunities are crucial, such as discursive opportunity structures that shape how much a certain issue is present and accepted in public debates.[15] Yet, such a diversification of the opportunity structure approach has also received criticism because in that way, the concept holds the danger of 'becoming a sponge that soaks up virtually any aspect of the social movement environment' by adding various context factors and summarizing them under one conceptual frame.[16]

---

[11] Donatella della Porta, *Social Movements, Political Violence and the State* (Cambridge: Cambridge University Press, 1995); Charles Tilly, Doug McAdam and Sidney. G. Tarrow, *Dynamics of Contention* (Cambridge: Cambridge University Press, 2001).

[12] Tilly, *From Mobilization to Revolution*; Lesley J. Wood, 'Breaking the wave: repression, identity, and Seattle tactics', *Mobilization: An International Quarterly* 12, 4 (2007), pp. 377–88.

[13] Nella van Dyke, 'Protest cycles and party politics: the effects of elite allies and antagonists on student protest in the United States, 1930–1990', in Judith Goldstein (ed) *States, Parties, and Social Movements* (Cambridge: Cambridge University Press, 2003), pp. 226–45.

[14] James Jasper, 'Introduction: from political opportunity structures to strategic interaction', in Jeff Goodwin and James M. Jasper (eds) *Contention in Context: Political Opportunities and the Emergence of Protest* (Stanford: Stanford University Press, 2012), pp. 1–36.

[15] Hans Pruijt and Conny Roggeband, 'Autonomous and/or institutionalized social movements? Conceptual clarification and illustrative cases', *International Journal of Comparative Sociology* 55, 2 (2014), pp. 148; Renata Motta, 'Transnational discursive opportunities and social movement risk frames opposing GMOs', *Social Movement Studies* 14, 5 (2014), pp. 576–95.

[16] William A. Gamson and David. S. Meyer, 'Framing political opportunity', in Doug McAdam, John D. Mccarthy and Mayer N. Zald (eds) *Social Movements: Political Opportunity*

Another critique of the opportunity structure approach concerns the call for more attention to how social movements interpret their environment and opportunities in particular, in order to provide a satisfactory explanation of how political context affects social movement dynamics.[17] Rather than assuming a direct effect of 'objectively' opening and closing opportunity structures on movement dynamics, these scholars have suggested that the way social movement groups perceive the intentions of their opponents is instrumental in shaping their reactions. In a research project with Priska Daphi and Nicole Deitelhoff, we found accordingly that social movements' reactions to IO opening-up are highly diverse:[18] while some social movements react to institutional opening by cooperating with the institution, others reject such offers of cooperation or do not even notice them in the first place. These institutional openings, furthermore, are often a reaction to protests. The way they are being interpreted by social movements in turn shapes the way these institutional procedures get a life of their own (or not). Such interpretation and re-interpretation and successive action and reaction is thus best understood as a dynamic back and forth between movements and institutions.

In social movement studies, it is therefore increasingly established that we should move from conceptualizing opportunities as conditions towards tracing mechanisms of contention in order to account for the dynamic nature of these processes instead of implying false determination.[19] Alimi et al. highlight that it is insufficient to conceptualize changes of repertoires as effects of changing opportunities.[20] They suggest to examine the interplay of various relational mechanisms instead. These mechanisms are additionally contingent with respect to their 'arenas of interaction'.

Mechanisms of contention in global governance

One such arena is global governance, where the opening-up of opportunities can itself be the effect of social movement action.[21] This may be another reason for social movement studies and IR going mostly separate ways so far,

---

    Structures, Mobilizing Structures, and Cultural Framings (Cambridge: Cambridge University Press, 1996), p. 275.

[17] Gamson and Meyer, 'Framing political opportunity'; David S. Meyer and Debra C. Minkoff, 'Conceptualizing political opportunity', *Social Forces* 82, 4 (2004), pp. 1457–92.

[18] Anderl et al., 'Keeping your enemies close?'

[19] Goodwin and Jasper, 'Caught in a winding, snarling vine', p. 14; Jasper, 'Introduction: from political opportunity structures to strategic interaction'.

[20] Alimi Eitan, Bosi Lorenzo, and Demetriou Chares, 'Relational dynamics and processes of radicalization: a comparative framework', *Mobilization* 17, 1 (2012), p. 8.

[21] O'Brien et al., *Contesting Global Governance*, p. 6.

because what looked like the starting point for one strand of research was the end point for the other: while the opening-up of IOs for civil society can be read as the beginning of research (how do movements react to these environmental changes?), other scholars have asked how movements managed to pressure these openings in the first place. Their question is which *impact* protest movements have on formal political organizations. However, similar to the deadlocks mentioned before, this question has not been answered sufficiently and is still one of the most controversial in movement research. The research field of outcome studies has therefore set out a whole range of methods to measure movement effects.[22] However, the search for causalities has proven problematic, as policy changes are rarely attributable to just one specific protest movement and its campaigns. 'The ways that movements make a difference are complex, veiled, and take far longer to manifest themselves than the cycle that covers a single demonstration, or even a whole protest campaign'.[23] The insight that political change is always influenced by a plurality of factors has therefore been used as an argument to discredit the outcome research approach, especially when it comes to the success or failure of movements.[24] Referring to the World Bank Group, Fox clarifies that,

> assessing whether and how public interest campaigns are indeed having an impact is one of the hardest challenges. ... Advocacy impact often needs to be assessed in terms of the terrible things that actually *did not* happen or were avoided – damage control – and this leads one onto the slippery terrain of the 'counter-factual'.[25]

Just like with the study of repertoire changes, factors for movement effectiveness initially discussed in movement research, such as movement centralization and bureaucratization,[26] were mainly internal to the movement,

---

[22] Edwin Amenta et al., 'The political consequences of social movements', *Annual Review of Sociology* 36 (2010), pp. 287–307; Edwin Amenta and Michael P. Young, 'Making an impact: conceptual and methodological implications of the collective goods criterion', in Marco G. Giugni, Doug McAdam, and Charles Tilly (eds) *How Social Movements Matter* (Minneapolis: University of Minnesota Press, 1999), pp. 22–41; Jennifer Earl, 'Methods, movements and outcomes: methodological difficulties in the study of extra-movement outcomes', in Patrick G. Coy (ed) *Research in Social Movements, Conflicts and Change* (Bingley: Emerald, 2000), pp. 3–25; David. S. Meyer, 'Social movements and public policy: eggs, chicken, and theory', in David. S. Meyer, Valerie Jenness, and Helen Ingram (eds) *Routing the Opposition: Social Movements, Public Policy, and Democracy* (Minneapolis: University of Minnesota Press, 2005), pp. 1–26.

[23] David. S. Meyer, 'How social movements matter', *Contexts* 2, 4 (2003), pp. 31.

[24] But see Raza Saeed, 'Conceptualising success and failure for social movements', *Law, Social Justice & Global Development Journal* 9, 2 (2009), pp. 1–13.

[25] Fox, 'Advocacy research and the World Bank', p. 306, emphasis in original.

[26] William A. Gamson, *The Strategy of Social Protest* (Belmont, CA: Wadsworth, 1990).

which in turn led to a wave of research emphasizing contextual, 'external' aspects.[27] However, the more sophisticated these approaches become, the more they lead to a potentially infinite stringing together of aspects to be considered as part of the context. This tendency is 'completely understandable and extremely frustrating'.[28]

Movements and their demands are not homogeneous.[29] This is also true for their adversaries. Complex coalitions of pragmatic parts of the movement with progressive actors in the target organizations can be found.[30] Accordingly, political contexts are so crucial that generalizing, context-independent statements about movement effects make little sense.[31] '[F]ormulating a general and parsimonious theory of social outcomes is in vain and should be abandoned', Rucht argues accordingly.[32] Instead, inductive analyses of intermediate scope should be pursued in his view. In movement studies, such a change has been discussed primarily in the context of weaker and stronger nation states. The weaker a bureaucracy, the greater the gateways for social movements to enter; however, the corresponding executive power to implement any decisions is subsequently lacking.[33] Less is known about the effects of institutional change in the *transnational* political sphere. Bosi and Uba therefore highlight that the transferability of case specific movement-outcome research to organizations such as the World Bank Group has not yet been clarified (quoted earlier).

This is where IR can help social movement studies. In recent years, a large body of research has emerged that examines the response mechanisms of IOs to protest. It is empirically established that the addressees of protest campaigns tend to react with changing procedures.[34] The most prominent approach here is the analysis of the opening-up of various IOs to civil

---

[27] Marco G. Giugni, 'Was it worth the effort? The outcomes and consequences of social movements', *Annual Review of Sociology* 24 (1998), p. 379.

[28] Meyer, 'Protest and and political opportunity', p. 135.

[29] Giugni, 'Was it worth the effort?', p. 383.

[30] Nicola Piper and Anders Uhlin, 'New perspectives on transnational activism', in Nicola Piper and Anders Uhlin (eds) *Transnational Activism in Asia* (London: Routledge, 2004), p. 4; Jonathan Fox and David L. Brown, 'Assessing the impact of NGO advocacy campaigns on World Bank projects and policies', in Jonathan A. Fox and David L. Brown (eds) *The Struggle for Accountability: The World Bank, NGOs and Grassroots Movements* (Cambridge, MA: MIT Press, 1998).

[31] Lorenzo Bosi, Marco Giugni, and Katrin Uba, *The Consequences of Social Movements:* (Cambridge: Cambridge University Press, 2016).

[32] 'Studying movement outcomes: a skeptical view', *Draft Paper at the Conference Outcomes of Social Movements and Protest* WZB, June 23–25 (2011), p. 3.

[33] Donatella della Porta and Marco Diani, *Social Movements: An Introduction* (Oxford: Blackwell, 2006), p. 202.

[34] Keck and Sikkink, *Activists beyond Borders*, p. 25.

society groups. This opening-up of IOs can be conceptualized as a changed (more open) opportunity structure of transnational movements. Tallberg et al. explain this with several factors: while opening-up is a reaction to public pressure, an overarching norm for participation as well as functional requirements also lead to civil society access; for instance in the area of local implementation, which in the case of the World Bank Group can be outsourced to NGOs.[35] Drawing on a more cognitive approach, Park shows how transnational environmental activist networks 'socialize' the World Bank into making its policies greener over longer periods of time.[36] At first, environmental campaigns are ignored and rejected; only after some time do staff members come to terms with the norms, which are then internalized and result in adapted environmental policies. In IR, these institutional changes are therefore often seen as a selective absorption of ideas and norms from the movement.[37] These processes are not automatic but highly contentious. Therefore, IR has taken up two concepts from social movement studies in order to trace them: contestation and politicization.

Contestation

The clearest overlap of movement research and IR is the concept of contestation, which can be derived from the *contentious politics* paradigm.[38] The turn to contestation in IR can only be described as a stroke of luck. In particular, the prominent constructivist strand of research with a pronounced interest in norms in international politics has benefited from turning to their contested character. Previously, these approaches had often examined the diffusion of norms, that is, an almost natural spread of values and rules across borders. This notion fed on the universalistically charged human rights debate, in which a pronounced belief in progress had concealed virulent actor and power constellations, practices, and conflicts behind a harmonious (sometimes moralistic) veil.[39] Again, a parallel with social movement research

---

[35] Tallberg et al., 'Explaining the transnational design of international organizations'; see also Andrea Liese, 'Explaining varying degrees of openness in the Food and Agricultural Organization of the United Nations (FAO)', in Christer Jönsson and Jonas Tallberg (eds) *Transnational Actors in Global Governance: Patterns, Explanations, and Implications* (Basingtone: Palgrave Macmillan, 2010), pp. 88–109.

[36] Susan Park, *World Bank Group Interactions with Environmentalists: Changing International Organisation Identities* (Manchester: Manchester University Press, 2010).

[37] Jan Aart Scholte, *Building Global Democracy? Civil Society and Accountable Global Governance* (Cambridge University Press, Cambridge, 2012).

[38] O'Brien et al., *Contesting Global Governance* is an early example of this.

[39] Stephan Engelkamp, Katharina Glaab, and Judith Renner, 'Office hours. How (critical) norm research can regain its voice', *World Political Science Review* 10, 1 (2014), pp. 61–89; Naeem Inayatullah and David L Blaney, 'Constructivism and the normative: dangerous

is evident, where the concept of diffusion plays a similarly prominent, and similarly depoliticizing role. But neither norms nor repertoires diffuse per se; they are carried by actors with interests in social, affective, and discursive contexts and clash with other norms and repertoires that are in turn materially, habitually, and discursively embedded. It is not surprising for contestation to occur in that process. Of particular interest, therefore, are those works that not only establish that something (a norm, an institution) *is* contested, but ask which actors engage in contestation, by what means, to what ends, and with what effects.

A flood of works on the topic of contestation has been published in the last twenty years. Wiener was quick to denounce the technocratic focus on compliance in IR norms research and to show that compliance with international law and its norms is always contested, even in the supranationally organized EU and its member states.[40] From this, she developed a research program on contestation as a norm-generating social practice.[41] This practice-theoretical work demonstrates the analytical utility of the concept and the different meanings of contestation both as a social practice of reactive objection to norms (principles, rules, or values) by rejecting or refusing to implement them, and as a proactive mode of critique through participation in a discourse.

The focus on contestation is important because previously the expansion of specific norms was considered desirable and therefore an implicit normative bias regarding the expansion of Western norms and international law (often the two fell into one) was inherent in IR mainstream. Therefore, for decades, the discipline was blind to exploitation, imperialism, and (economic) hierarchy in the international system. It conducted science as if in a laboratory, studying the 'diffusion' of international norms as if the recipients of those norms were children who needed to be taught.[42] This thinking in terms of unilinear diffusion in a clearly defined before and after in processes of change is far too template-like, precisely because the contexts into which the norms are brought are themselves already political fields with contested debates about space and memory.[43] This is why norms

---

liaisons?', in Charlotte Epstein (ed) *Against International Relations Norms: Postcolonial Perspectives* (London: Routledge, 2017), pp. 23–37; Tine Hanrieder, 'Moralische Argumente in den Internationalen Beziehungen: Grenzen einer verständigungstheoretischen "Erklärung" moralischer Debatten', *Zeitschrift Für Internationale Beziehungen* 15, 2 (2008), pp. 161–86.

[40] Antje Wiener, 'Contested compliance: interventions on the normative structure of world politics', *European Journal of International Relations* 10, 2 (2004), pp. 189–234.

[41] Antje Wiener, *A Theory of Contestation* (Heidelberg: Springer, 2014).

[42] See on this Charlotte Epstein, 'Stop telling us how to behave: socialization or infantilization?', *International Studies Perspectives* 13, 2 (2012), pp. 135–45.

[43] Elias Steinhilper, 'From "the rest" to "the West"? Rights of indigenous peoples and the Western bias in norm diffusion research', *International Studies Review* 17, 4

should never be understood as stable objects, but always as contested projects.[44] Contestation as social practice, however, can certainly be read implicitly Habermasian here. Wiener's theory is about the inclusive power of contestation: 'All stakeholders ought to be able to enjoy equal access to norm contestation'.[45] However, she reads this principle of inclusion agonistically.[46] Thus, the conditions are to be created under which robust contestation can take place. Building on this, she asks programmatically: whose contestation practices count?

Deitelhoff, a second prominent representative of the contestation paradigm in the IR, makes the Habermasianism quite explicit: better norms are to be developed in dispute and, in turn, the conditions for this ought to be created.[47] To this end, she was quick to criticize IR's strange fetish of stability, whose constructivist turn had replaced the fiction of stable state interests with supposedly stable norms.[48] Out of this critique, an exciting conceptual toolkit has emerged for international politics that looks at various transnational settings from the perspective of contestation. Zimmermann, Deitelhoff, and Lesch, for instance, argue that practices of contestation can be understood as constitutive of normative action: actors are thus constituted in the process of contestation and do not enter the deliberation arena as fixed entities – an insight similar to movement studies' praxeological perspective on the formation of collective subjects.[49]

As productive as this work is, it also reveals a problem in contestation research. The term can mean just about anything that is somehow

---

(2015), pp. 536–55; Matthias Großklaus, 'Appropriation and the dualism of human rights: understanding the contradictory impact of gender norms in Nigeria', *Third World Quarterly* 36, 5 (2015), pp. 1253–67; Susanne Buckley-Zistel, 'Spatializing memory and justice in transformation processes', in Rachid Ouaissa, Friederike Pannewick, and Alena Strohmaier (eds) *Re-Configurations: Contextualising Transformation Processes and Lasting Crises in the Middle East and North Africa* (Heidelberg: Springer, 2020), pp. 25–35; Amitav Acharya, 'How ideas spread: whose norms matter? Norm localization and institutional change in Asian regionalism', *International Organization* 58, 2 (April 19, 2004), pp. 239–75.

44 Holger Niemann and Henrik Schillinger, 'Contestation "all the way down"? The grammar of contestation in norm research', *Review of International Studies* 43, 1 (2016), pp. 29–49.

45 Antje Wiener, *Contestation and Constitution of Norms in Global International Relations* (Cambridge: Cambridge University Press, 2018), p. 54.

46 Antje Wiener, '*Contestation and Constitution*', p. ix.

47 Nicole Deitelhoff, 'The discursive process of legalization: charting islands of persuasion in the ICC case', *International Organization* 63, 1 (2009), pp. 33–65.

48 Nicole Deitelhoff, *Überzeugung in Der Politik – Grundzüge Einer Diskurstheorie Internationalen Regierens* (Frankfurt am Main: Suhrkamp, 2006), p. 20.

49 Lisbeth Zimmermann, Nicole Deitelhoff, and Max Lesch, 'Unlocking the agency of the governed: contestation and norm dynamics', *Third World Thematics: A TWQ Journal* 2, 5 (2017), pp. 691–708.

resistant: from a critical inquiry in a meeting to a street fight. Contestation as a concept therefore runs the risk of becoming an empty slogan.[50] Wiener as well as Deitelhoff and Zimmermann have reacted to such criticism and elaborated different types of contestation. Deitelhoff and Zimmermann present two ideal types: contestation of norm validity and contestation of norm application.[51] They argue that widespread contestation of a standard's validity is likely to lead to a loss of robustness of the standard. Contestation of norm application, on the other hand, may even strengthen it under certain circumstances. This is an important distinction, but it has its weakness with respect to the content of the contestation. For example, when right-wing and left-wing movements alike mobilize against an international treaty, each contesting the validity of the norms sedimented therein,[52] the distinction between norm validity and norm application may lead to better predictive power regarding the robustness of norms, but it does not help in assessing the political background and multi-layered consequences of the contestation. An even stronger interlocking of the contestation approaches with movement research could remedy this situation.

Politicization

The concept of politicization in international politics has similarly drawn inspiration from social movement studies and adapted it to the study of contentious discourses around IOs. According to Ecker-Ehrhardt and Zürn, an issue, decision, or institution becomes politicized when it is brought from the technical-administrative sphere 'into the political sphere, i.e., transported either into the political subsystem (defined by its own functional logic) or into political space (defined by debates about the appropriate functional logic for a given problem situation)'.[53] This process can have two causes: the legitimacy deficit of an existing IO, or a regulatory deficit in a policy field due to a lack of or too weak IOs.

---

[50] Felix Anderl, Nicole Deitelhoff and Regina Hack, 'Contestation: Introduction to the section', in Felix Anderl et al. (eds) *Rule and Resistance beyond the Nation State: Contestation, Escalation, Exit* (London: Rowman & Littlefield, 2019), pp. 23–6.

[51] Nicole Deitelhoff and Lisbeth Zimmermann, 'Things we lost in the fire: how different types of contestation affect the robustness of international norms', *International Studies Review* 22, 1 (2020), pp. 51–76.

[52] Julia Rone, 'Contested international agreements, contested national politics: how the radical Left and the radical Right opposed TTIP in four European countries', *Review of International Law* 6, 2 (2018), pp. 233–53.

[53] Michael Zürn and Matthias Ecker-Ehrhardt, *Die Politisierung der Weltpolitik: umkämpfte internationale Institutionen* (Berlin: Suhrkamp, 2013), p. 338.

The charm of politicization research lies in the fact that an increase or decrease in politicization can be determined over time.[54] Politicization is particularly linked to the salience of an issue: that is, if a lot is written about an IO, then it is likely to be more politicized than if it were not reported on. Thus, quantitative media analysis can be used to determine the degree of politicization over time – a method close to protest-event analysis in movement research.[55] However, these methods can obviously be combined with others, as Ecker-Ehrhardt and Zürn explicitly lay out in the introduction to their volume. This option, however, has been explored surprisingly little.[56] Yet this insight strongly suggests linking IR politicization research with movement research, that is, based on the observation of an increasingly politicized IO, to investigate its politicization as a practice, for example with ethnographic methods. In this way, an analysis of the extent of politicization could be linked to an examination of its substantive thrust and associated repertoires.

Because politicization research can identify changes over time with relative reliability, it can also take a more articulate stance on sociopolitical issues compared to contestation research. For example, Zürn et al. make a causal link between the increasing authority of IOs and their politicization. The point is not that the organizations in question were less political before, but that more is being debated about them. This reveals another commonality (and weakness) of politicization research and movement studies: they can provide empirical evidence that something is becoming more contentious, but they can hardly take a reasoned position on which arguments are useful in the dispute and which ones are not. Nevertheless, Ecker-Ehrhardt and Zürn find an interesting general change in the discourse on international affairs: 'The instrumental questions of problem-solving and effectiveness have long been interspersed with procedural questions such as legitimacy and normative aspects such as fairness and justice. International institutions can

---

[54] Zürn, Binder and Ecker-Ehrhardt, 'International authority and its politicization'; Edgar Grande and Swen Hutter, 'Beyond authority transfer: explaining the politicisation of Europe', *West European Politics* 39, 1 (2016), pp. 23–43.

[55] Swen Hutter, 'Exploring the full conceptual potential of protest event analysis', *Sociological Methodology* 49, 1 (2019), pp. 58–63.

[56] But see Swen Hutter and Edgar Grande, *Politicising Europe: Integration and Mass Politics* (Cambridge: Cambridge University Press, 2016); Dieter Rucht, 'Globalisierungskritische Proteste als Herausforderung an die internationale Politik', in *Die Politisierung Der Weltpolitik* (Frankfurt am Main: Suhrkamp, 2012), pp. 61–83; Carolina Vestena, 'Rechtliche Institutionen als Vermittlungsort der Politik der Straßen": eine Auseinandersetzung mit der Rechtsprechung der Krise in Portugal', *Forschungsjournal Soziale Bewegungen* 32, 3 (2019), pp. 248–61.

hardly take the road back to a basic functionalist understanding of permissive consensus without suffering damage'.[57]

If we know that procedural questions need to be addressed by IOs in a politicized environment, this still raises the question of differentiation. Who politicizes when, in what form, and for what purpose? Daphi argues for discriminating between internal and external politicization.[58] This provides an excellent bridge for distinguishing between the different possibilities of politicization research, where the 'external' could be researched with approaches from movement studies, and the 'internal' with those from organizational sociology. But this need for more specificity regarding the actors in politicization research also hints at a general blind spot of the concept. From a social movement perspective, IR studies on the issue often fail to distinguish between politicization 'from below' and 'from above', hence only capturing what is in the news and therefore in danger to treat as 'technical' what is in fact highly political. For example, currently the transnational smallholder movement politicizes issues around food production. But they do so because decades ago Western governments and world economic organizations politicized the issue 'from above' in the context of the East–West conflict in order to fight communism with the expansion of a specific agricultural system.[59] These institutions transferred the issue of nutrition from the administrative-technical to the political realm without much newspaper coverage. This reveals a weakness of politicization research, which understands media salience as the basic condition for politicization and thus often overlooks those politicization projects from above.

The lack of media salience despite politicization could be a good indicator of the stability of political rule. For this, however, the understanding of politicization would have to be politicized.[60] Critical theories have long argued that the absence of media criticism is not necessarily an effect of more legitimacy, but that such processes may indicate a strengthening of rule and its means of power, such as repression. From this perspective, I would critically note that – in contrast to the hailing of conflict as a political tool in contestation research – a stability bias can be discerned in some parts of the politicization literature. This implicitly conveys that politicization, understood as controversial discussion of prevailing institutional policies, is

---

[57] Zürn and Ecker-Ehrhardt, *Die Politisierung Der Weltpolitik*, 259.

[58] Priska Daphi, 'Politisierung und Soziale Bewegungen: Zwei Perspektiven', *Leviathan* Sonderband 35 (2020), pp. 97–120.

[59] John Perkins, *Geopolitics and the Green Revolution: Wheat, Genes, and the Cold War* (Oxford: Oxford University Press, 1997).

[60] See also Claudia Wiesner, 'Introduction', in Claudia Wiesner (ed) *Rethinking Politicisation in Politics, Sociology and International Relations* (London: Palgrave, 2021), pp. 1–15.

something problematic that should be reversed.[61] In order to understand politicization strategies from above and below as repertoires in a dynamic, political interaction of conflictual order formation, the definition would need to shift away from salience – and toward political content.[62] This endeavour could be addressed through greater entanglement with movement studies. While this shift would diminish the analytical elegance of the approach, politicization could thereby make an even stronger contribution to understanding a world that is always already politicized, in which ruling institutions and their opponents politicize and de-politicize structures in a dynamic process of interaction.

Dynamics of contention

Based on a similar understanding of vertically stratified politicization dynamics, Daase and Deitelhoff, for instance, have formulated that the international system is characterized by institutionalized relations of superiority and subordination, which they define as rule.[63] They formulate an analytical connection between rule and resistance that is potentially capable of filling the aforementioned voids in an interactionist program, namely the reconstruction of rule from the analysis of resistance.[64] The methodological overlaps with movement research cannot be overlooked here because it is precisely the idea of the 'contentious politics' program to formulate such a theory. Particularly in its later versions, the dynamics of contention approach has learned from the critique of static opportunities and has moved towards analysing contentious episodes in context.[65]

Tilly and Tarrow, probably the most established proponents of this agenda, have formulated a research approach that gravitates around political actors, political identities, contentious performances, and repertoires. They have made clear that theirs is a flexible explanatory framework from which we can select explanatory factors depending on the research question.[66] For making such a selection, theoretical expectations seem paramount. While IR

---

[61] Pieter De Wilde and Michael Zürn, 'Can the politicization of European integration be reversed?', *Journal of Common Market Studies* 50, 1 (2012), pp. 137–53.

[62] Philip Liste, 'In-between juridification and politicisation: zooming in on the everyday politics of law', in Claudia Wiesner (ed) *Rethinking Politicisation in Politics, Sociology and International Relations* (London: Palgrave, 2021), pp. 245–65.

[63] Christopher Daase and Nicole Deitelhoff, 'Jenseits der Anarchie: Widerstand und Herrschaft im internationalen System', *Politische Vierteljahrsschrift* 56, 2 (2015), p. 300.

[64] Daase and Deitelhoff, 'Opposition and dissidence'.

[65] Tilly, McAdam and Tarrow, *Dynamics of Contention*; Tarrow, *Power in Movement*; Charles Tilly and Sidney Tarrow, *Contentious Politics* (New York: Oxford University Press, 2015).

[66] Tilly and Tarrow, *Contentious Politics*, p. 48.

is sometimes too hung up on its theoretical traditions, an overarching social theory helps categorize and utilize various factors even in inductively driven research. A theoretical framework gives a sense of direction. If it is too rigid, we will always end up in the same place, but if we don't have one, the best tools do not lead us anywhere. Therefore, in my view, the context-sensitivity and analytical toolbox of the contentious politics approach is helping IR not to become too abstract and to understand the actors involved on their own terms. A social theoretical grounding, in turn, helps distinguishing those aspects of protest and resistance that are important for international politics and global governance from the ones that are maybe more for a connoisseur of social movements.

But where does such a theory come from? As I will outline in the next chapter, I think that the angle of rule and resistance can provide an overarching framework through which we can do both, mobilize the analytical strengths of social movement studies and match them with a conceptual approach that renders the findings meaningful for international theory. The reconstruction of rule from the analysis of resistance is a powerful approach that needs movement research because it provides the necessary insights into mobilization dynamics beyond institutionalized politics. On the other hand, this advance also provides an opportunity for movement research to embed its findings in a social theory, thus leaving behind its own empiricist touch. In the next chapter, I will sketch the toolkit for such a theory by outlining a concept for rule and resistance in global governance.

2

Transnational Rule and Resistance

In the last chapter, I have argued that IR and social movement studies should work together and fill each other's gaps. I have made the proposal that *rule and resistance* could be a productive framework for analysing the interaction between protests movements and formal political institutions. Social movement studies usually have no problem identifying *resistance* which is embodied by individuals or groups belonging to a social movement (discussed earlier), and articulated through different kinds of critique (by critics) or through physical action (by protesters). It is observable in this context in conscious practices that are directed against the practices of rule, or against the ruling order in general. IR on the other hand has a harder time identifying the counterpart. In the transnational realm, it feels awkward to speak of *rule*. This is because traditionally IR has built its theories on the fundamental distinction that 'domestic systems are centralized and hierarchic', while 'international systems are decentralized and anarchic'.[1] According to that separation, hierarchies can be logically excluded in the international system, for if anarchy and hierarchy are mutually exclusive ordering principles, and if all international systems are anarchic, then international systems cannot be structurally hierarchic.[2] Based on this logic, the absence of an international government has been acknowledged as an objective condition, implying anarchy.[3] At the same time, however, inequality has not only been acknowledged but even characterized as 'the dominant political fact of international life'.[4] For better or worse, this paradox has structured theorizing in IR significantly. Interventions in the 1990s and 2000s signalled a discomfort with this programme, yet only to challenge what anarchy means,

---

[1] Kenneth Waltz, *Theory of International Politics* (Long Grove: Waveland Press, 1979), p. 88.
[2] Waltz, 114.
[3] Jack Donnelly, 'Beyond hierarchy', in Ayşe Zarakol (ed) *Hierarchies in World Politics* (Cambridge: Cambridge University Press, 2016), p. 244.
[4] Waltz, *Theory of International Politics*, p. 144.

not its existence as the ordering principle of the international. Wendt, for instance, has rephrased anarchy from an externally given ordering principle to a socially constructed, changeable, but nevertheless deeply influential one.[5] Lake, moreover, has reconciled the anarchy-inequality problematique by claiming that *relational hierarchies* exist under *structural anarchy*.[6]

This book is not an attempt to disprove the anarchy-assumption; others have done so already.[7] While 'critical approaches never accept the legitimacy of that heuristic in the first place',[8] by now, the claim that hierarchies exist in the international system is a premise also increasingly shared in the wider scholarly community, with even liberal approaches actively building on it.[9] This opens some fertile ground for new forms of inquiry. As Zarakol argues, always having to encounter the anarchy assumption has impeded the productivity of IR.[10] Now that this obstacle is out of the way, theorists can debate the *nature* of hierarchies in international systems: what does it mean that a system is hierarchic? IR can turn to 'inequality, authority, and rule, which have been perversely marginalized in mainstream anarchy-centric IR'.[11]

In a fundamental challenge to this traditional understanding, Donnelly, for instance, argues that 'nearly all international systems are structurally hierarchic'. He notes that the absence of a government 'simply indicates one way in which a system is *not* ordered. ... It does not, however, even begin to tell us *how* an international system is structured/ordered'.[12] Seconding this claim, critical scholars have argued that hierarchy should therefore replace anarchy and become 'the core concept of IR'.[13] While agreeing with

---

[5]   Alexander Wendt, 'Anarchy is what states make of it: the social construction of power politics', *International Organization* 46, 2 (1992), pp. 391–425.

[6]   David A. Lake, *Hierarchies in International Relations* (Ithaca, NY: Cornell University Press, 2009), p. 17.

[7]   See for an overview Janice Bially Mattern and Ayşe Zarakol, 'Hierarchies in world politics', *International Organization* 70, 3 (2016), pp. 623–54; Nicholas G. Onuf, *World of Our Making: Rules and Rule in Social Theory and International Relations* (London: Routledge, 2013); Daase and Deitelhoff, 'Opposition and dissidence'; Ayşe Zarakol, *Hierarchies in World Politics* (Cambridge: Cambridge University Press, 2016).

[8]   Bially Mattern and Zarakol, 'Hierarchies in world politics', p. 630.

[9]   Lake, *Hierarchies in International Relations*; Zürn et al., 'International authority and its politicization'; Michael Zürn, *A Theory of Global Governance: Authority, Legitimacy & Contestation* (Oxford: Oxford University Press, 2018).

[10] Zarakol, *Hierarchies World Politics*, p. 3.

[11] Donnelly, 'Beyond hierarchy', p. 243; see also Caroline Fehl and Katja Freistein, 'Organising global stratification: how international organisations (re)produce inequalities in international society', *Global Society* 34, 3 (2020), pp. 285–303.

[12] Donnelly, 'Beyond hierarchy', p. 245, emphasis in original.

[13] John M. Hobson, 'The twin self-delusions of IR: why "hierarchy" and not "anarchy" is the core concept of IR', *Millennium: Journal of International Studies* 42, 3 (2014), pp. 557–75.

Donnelly that it is hard to think of a non-hierarchical international system, I remain sceptical towards this line of reasoning. Maybe it is precisely the logic of enclosing an entire discipline under one 'core concept' that has led to many pathologies in IR. Furthermore, hierarchy as 'the core concept' is not sufficient either. It 'tells us *that* a system is stratified, not *how*'. Since different social systems have differing structures, forms of stratification and ordering principles, to assume that in 'the international system' there would be just one principle that we simply have to discern 'is an aesthetic prejudice that flies in the face of the historical record'.[14] Therefore, this book, although proposing a specific ordering principle, does not suggest this to become the new 'core concept' that can be applied throughout history wherever there is no central government. Rather, the concept that I do propose is an emergent, historically situated constellation that, I think, best describes the order of transnational politics over the last two decades but is not intended to be a once and for all theorization of international politics. The most basic distinction that should be made here is between inter-*national* relations (relations between states), and other forms of politics beyond the nation state, the institutionalized form of which is often referred to as 'global governance'. Both are part of IR as an academic discipline, and in both cases the relations involve hierarchies, although with the former this may be more obvious. I am, however, concerned with the latter aspect of IR.

Global governance is shaped by a huge number of institutions, some of them more, some less powerful. Scholars have been cautious in bringing up the issue of structural stratification. In the absence of a world government, the question 'who governs the globe?' is a dangerous one, because too straight an answer would likely turn into a conspiracy.[15] Therefore, there is a broad consensus in IR that the institutions currently governing 'the world' are not governments: the 'global governors'[16] govern, but they don't rule.[17]

Legitimate authorities?

So why do actors defer to authorities? In liberal governance theories, this is because they have good reasons for doing so, within a specific knowledge order, a phenomenon that Zürn calls a 'reason-based understanding of

---

[14] Donnelly, 'Beyond hierarchy', p. 245, emphasis in original.
[15] Deborah Avant, Martha Finnemore, and Susan Sell, *Who Governs the Globe?* (Cambridge: Cambridge University Press, 2010).
[16] Karen Mundy, ' "Education for all" and the global governors', in Deborah Avant, Martha Finnemore, and Susan Sell (eds) *Who Governs the Globe?* (Cambridge, 2010), p. 333.
[17] Rhodes, 'The new governance'; James Rosenau and Ernst Otto Czempiel, *Governance without Government: Order and Change in World Politics* (Cambridge: Cambridge University Press, 1992).

international authority'.[18] Therefore, we need to understand the 'special epistemic role of the authority holder', the 'knowing better' which, according to him, is part of every authority. Global governance is thus imagined as a relationship between global governance institutions as authorities that are legitimized by the epistemic community which they serve. This legitimacy hinges on their expert authority rather than on violence – much less the monopoly thereof.[19] David Lake even makes the argument that we can transfer social contract theories, traditionally applied to the state, to governance institutions.[20] Global governance, in this view, is shaped by relational authority, understood as 'a social contract in which a governor provides a political order of value to a community in exchange for compliance by the governed with the rules necessary to produce that order'.[21] This perspective has wide-ranging consequences. In the eyes of these authors, it renders hierarchy *legitimate* and the resulting rules *rightful*. In a nutshell, such a concept of global governance is fuelled by a narrative of a direct and (mostly) conscious relationship between authoritative IOs and reasonable actors who reflect on their authorities and choose to abide by their rules because they value the IO's expertise and hence deem them legitimate. The legitimacy of IOs is the sum total of all agents' beliefs in their expertise or problem-solving capacity. The more powerful such an IO becomes, however, the more will it be exposed to scrutiny by the public.

Zürn argues that, hence, authority relationships are grounded in a social process in which superior knowledge is distinguished from subordinate knowledge. His claim is that global governance institutions such as the World Bank Group are reflexive authorities that send requests instead of commands, and therefore '[t]he internalization of the subordinate role is not a necessary part of [the relationship]'.[22] He can argue in such a way because several context factors are left out of the equation. Consider the argument that institutions send requests (instead of commands) or, even more, deliberate with the 'authority takers' on what requests would be appropriate. This reflexivity is a change of governing practice indeed observable over the last twenty years (discussed later). However, what Zürn's analysis misses is the social structure in which this occurs. Although critics constantly monitor the institution and therefore 'permanent contestation and adjustment' takes

---

[18] Michael Zürn, 'From constitutional rule to loosely coupled spheres of liquid authority: a reflexive approach', *International Theory* 9, 2 (2017), p. 267.

[19] Zürn, *A Theory of Global Governance*, p. 43.

[20] David A. Lake, 'Rightful rules: authority, order, and the foundations of global governance', *International Studies Quarterly* 54, 3 (2010), p. 589.

[21] Lake, 'Rightful rules', p. 587.

[22] Zürn, 'From constitutional rule', p. 267.

place,[23] this very process of contestation and adjustment, under specified and predefined circumstances, re-inscribes relationships of institutionalized super- and subordination, as I will show in this book.

Scholars like Lake and Zürn follow a majoritarian understanding of legitimacy (if people *find it* legitimate, it *is* legitimate). Their theories put a lot of responsibility upon the supposedly reflexive societal actors vis-à-vis the IO. This almost automatically attributes legitimacy to the institution, for if it were not legitimate, people would have abolished it already. This circular logic produces an almost religious edict: if it is an authority, it is therefore also legitimate.

At least in part, this problem can be explained with a selection bias. We do not have the means to actually measure legitimacy on a 'global' scale. Therefore, Lake and Zürn look at those agents who *do* find the IOs in question legitimate, because even those who contest global governance do this largely within its institutional structure. Therefore, even the contestation of global governance, meticulously analysed in Zürn's theory of global governance, is focused on a particular group of mostly Western and moderate NGOs such as Oxfam, World Wide Fund for Nature (WWF), and Amnesty International.[24] To be sure, these NGOs are critics of global governance organizations. However, they belong to a specific strand of critique: their approach is *oppositional* and does not fundamentally challenge the norms and structure of global governance. They are frequently interacting with, and sometimes an indistinguishable component of, the governance process and partly depend on it. Other organizations and movements that fundamentally challenge these institutions (*dissident*) are largely ignored by these liberal accounts of global governance. The problem is therefore not that they ignore contestation but that they couch its occurrence in a theoretical perspective 'so deeply embedded in liberal institutionalism that it limits international rule to the authority of trans- and international institutions and their recognition by their addressees, thereby losing track of more structural forms of rule'.[25]

Since resistance to global governance often does not make the stages in Washington DC or Geneva for material or other reasons, poor peoples' movements, indigenous peoples, and radical NGOs from the Global South, are equally neglected in these approaches. It is these movements, however, who often do conceive of IO policies as violent, and who may not even notice that is was a 'request', not an order, that led to their land being

---

[23] Zürn, 'From constitutional rule', p. 268

[24] See also Scholte, 'Beyond institutionalism', p. 188.

[25] Nicole Deitelhoff and Christopher Daase, 'Rule and resistance in global governance', *International Theory*, 2020, pp. 1–9.

confiscated in the name of development. Zürn reflects on the fact that 'this elite-level segment of the public sphere is … heavily skewed in favour of CSOs [Civil Society Organizations] of Western origin'.[26] But this reflection is not enough, because the omitted movements, who arguably have been exposed to the economic policies of IOs on the receiving end, often have a very different take on the legitimacy of global governance.[27] Excluding their views and practices from the analysis of global governance therefore captures only a specific part of critique, namely the one that is recognized and partly given a stage by the institutions in question (see Chapter 6). By limiting themselves to these institutionalized contestations, liberal IR theories tend to portray the history of global governance as a history of legitimate authorities, while the perspective of the governed is evaded and in effect declared non-IR.[28] Failing to take them systematically into account has the effect of writing a partial, that is a Euro-American, and decidedly affirmative, theory of global governance.

Even when leaving the issue of violence aside, though, the authority-legitimation nexus is not enough to theorize global governance organizations and their opponents. In Zürn's theory, the contestation of a specific knowledge order is part of a broader delegitimating strategy against a specific authority.[29] This is a reductionist view of contentious politics, because, frequently, movements are not primarily directed against specific institutions but rather against the order itself – by which they feel governed.[30] They direct their demands against the institutions because these are symbols of the order, or because specific aspects of the order cumulate within them. Nevertheless, they do not necessarily feel governed by this particular institution but by a bigger structure. Consider the Blockupy protests in Frankfurt 'against' the European Central Bank (ECB). The protest movement made quite clear that the ECB is not their primary target but only a symbol of 'decentralized, global capitalism'.[31] In order to understand 'who governs the globe?', it is therefore not enough to map all authorities in global governance and their

---

[26] Zürn, *A Theory of Global Governance*, p. 165. My insertion.
[27] Scholte, 'Beyond institutionalism'. See also Charlotte Dany, *Global Governance and NGO Participation: Shaping the Information Society in the United Nations* (London: Routledge, 2013), p. 117.
[28] See also Michael Barnett, 'Change in or of global governance?', *International Theory* 13, 1 (2020), pp. 131–43.
[29] Zürn, *A Theory of Global Governance*, p. 47.
[30] Felix Anderl and Philip Wallmeier, '"Institution" als Scharnierkonzept zwischen Herrschaft und Widerstand ', *Forschungsjournal Soziale Bewegungen* 32, 2 (2019), p. 197.
[31] See the mobilizing video available at: {https://www.youtube.com/watch?v=SUVz TTE2M68}.

contestation. One would see a mosaic of institutions, but one would not understand the underlying ordering principle.

The strange case of rule in IR

The subtitle of this book prominently indicates that I see an ordering principle at work in global governance that goes beyond the power of particular authorities. In contrast, I suggest understanding global governance as a fundamentally *ruled* environment. But why make such a fuss about these concepts? A quick excursus into terminology and translation may help to clarify this. Where Zürn imports the US-American term 'authority' into German language (*Autorität*), Klaus Schlichte argues that this is an 'erroneous translation' since the concept was already 'hollowed out' in German where the Weberian tradition would be much more helpful – and induce the term *Herrschaft*.[32] Authority as a concept is either bloated so enormously that everyone can be ascribed to have it, or it is identified with the power to command.[33] Confusingly, if you look up *Befehlsgewalt* (the power to command) in a regular dictionary, it is translated with authority. *Befehlsgewalt*, however, is exactly what Zürn distinguishes from authorities because these send *requests* instead of *commands* in his theory. I therefore follow Morcillo Laiz and Schlichte who argue that 'by resorting to Weber's ideas on rationalization, domination (*Herrschaft*), and organizations (*Verbände*), our ability to penetrate into the reality of internationalized *rule* improves'.[34] They argue that there is more to international institutions than legitimacy and expertise, although only few have the (direct) power to command. It would be a great theoretical impoverishment to only observe 'authorities' because rule and domination are part of the international constellation. Yet, these authors lack an explicit theory of how domination and rule relate, and therefore use them interchangeably.[35] I will in the following distinguish between *domination*, defined as a direct relational hierarchy in which one

---

[32] Klaus Schlichte, 'Warum Zahlen nicht reichen: Plädoyer für eine erweiterte Erfahrung der Internationalen Beziehungen ', *Zeitschrift Für Internationale Beziehungen* 25, 2 (2018), p. 160.

[33] Grit Straßenberger, 'Autorität: Herrschaft ohne Zwang – Anerkennung ohne Deliberation', *Berliner Journal Für Soziologie* 23, 3 (2013), pp. 494–509.

[34] Álvaro Morcillo Laiz and Klaus Schlichte, 'Rationality and international domination: revisiting Max Weber', *International Political Sociology* 10, 2 (2016), p. 170 (my emphasis).

[35] 'We employ here "domination" or, occasionally, "rule" to translate Herrschaft, rather than "authority"'. Álvaro Morcillo Laiz and Klaus Schlichte, 'Another Weber: state, associations and domination in International Relations', *Cambridge Review of International Affairs* 29, 4 (2016), p. 5.

actor forces another actor to do something or is capable of doing so without coercion (*Beherrschung*), and *rule*, which, in contrast, is a constellational concept and can exist even without explicit obedience (*Herrschaft*).

Rule without a government

International politics have become increasingly formalized into a hierarchical structure of super- and subordination. This structure has effects in terms of decision-making and epistemic authority as well as material distribution. Foregrounding rule instead of authority in global governance allows us to analyse international processes 'resulting in a stable pattern of asymmetrically distributed benefits'.[36] But it is often difficult to detect who directly profits from this structure, and the structuring effects of rule typically do not originate from purposive and directional action. In other words: there is no ruler.

This is also the major reason why most liberal accounts do not see rule and domination at work in global governance. Their concept of rule is so strongly tied to a national sovereign that they only recognize it when political authority is not only limited to a specific set of competences but of an overarching quality that can solve collisions between subordinated authorities, and when these authorities are able to ensure compliance by invoking violence.[37] Given such a demanding threshold/indicator for political rule, it is no wonder that they do not observe it in the transnational realm,[38] and that they, instead, find an overwhelming voluntariness of 'compliance' with such authorities, whereas physical compulsion and the constraint generated by the absence of alternatives disappear from view.[39]

How can we then detect structures of rule and how do they work? Instead of reconstructing rule from the compliance it is able to enforce, Daase and Deitelhoff suggest reconstructing rule from the resistance it provokes. This promises an investigation *not* into the capacity of some powerful people or institutions, but rather into the resistance to what is perceived as a ruling order, or rules emanating from this order. This analysis in turn may lead to a reconstruction of what rule *is*.[40] With this proposal, they inscribe their

---

[36] Nicholas G. Onuf and Frank F. Klink, 'Anarchy, authority, rule', *International Studies Quarterly* 33, 2 (1989), p. 169.

[37] Michael Zürn, 'Autorität und Legitimität in der postnationalen Konstellation', in *Der Aufstieg Der Legitimitätspolitik*, 2012, p. 53.

[38] Daase and Deitelhoff, 'Jenseits der Anarchie', p. 302.

[39] Daase and Deitelhoff, 'Reconstructing global rule by analyzing resistance', p. 6.

[40] Daase and Deitelhoff, 'Opposition and dissidence'; Daase and Deitelhoff, 'Reconstructing global rule by analyzing resistance'.

project of transnational rule and resistance in a long history of power analysis, particularly in the wake of Foucault.[41]

One prominent avenue for researching structures of rule not immediately visible is the governmentality approach.[42] Governmentality can be understood as the repertoire of organized practices through which subjects are governed, not only through direct intervention by means of empowered and specialized state apparatuses, but also through the development of indirect techniques for leading and controlling individuals.[43] While governmentality, in principle, can be applied to many forms of governing individuals, Foucault particularly investigated the neoliberal governmentality which is specific in the way it involves individuals in the process of governing. Individuals embody the order by taking the governing on themselves. Institutions are central in this governing structure because in and by them individuals learn how to govern themselves and hence be governed. These 'technologies of the self' are techniques through which individuals work on their own bodies, minds, and lifestyles, in the attempt to transform themselves in line with the requirements of a given order to attain happiness and material saturation.[44]

Transnational governmentality

Neumann and Sending have applied this concept to the international as socially embedded realm of governmentality.[45] They conceptualize it as 'a structure (defined as relations of power) that changes different and changing practices of political *rule* (defined as governmental rationality) and agencies (for example, polities)'.[46] Their concern is with politics as opposed to the administration of subjects, dealing with the question: 'Does the tendency towards "legalization" of ever more global issues ... reduce the level of

---

[41] But also already Peter Bachrach and Morton S. Baratz, 'Two faces of power', *The American Political Science Review* 56, 4 (1962), pp. 947–52; Steven Lukes, *Power: A Radical View* (London: Palgrave Macmillan, 1974).

[42] Michel Foucault, 'Governmentality', in Graham Burchell and Colin Gordon (eds) *The Foucault Effect: Studies in Governmentality* (Chicago: Chicago University Press, 1991), pp. 87–104.

[43] Thomas Lemke, 'Foucault, governmentality, and critique', *Rethinking Marxism: A Journal of Economics, Culture & Society* 14, 3 (2002), pp. 49–64.

[44] Michel Foucault, 'Technologies of the self', in Luther H. Martin, Huck Gutman, and Patrick H. Hutton (eds) *Technologies of the Self: A Seminar with Michel Foucault* (Amherst: University of Massachusetts Press, 1988).

[45] Ole Jacob Sending and Iver B. Neumann, 'Governance to governmentality: analyzing NGOs, states, and power', *International Studies Quarterly* 50, 3 (2006), pp. 651–72; Iver B. Neumann and Ole Jacob Sending, '"The international" as governmentality', *Millennium: Journal of International Studies* 35, 3 (September 24, 2007), pp. 677–701.

[46] Neumann and Sending, '"The international" as governmentality', p. 677, my emphasis.

significance of politics ...?'[47] The institutional apparatus that organizes this perceived shift towards depoliticization has increasingly been in the focus of critical IR scholarship. Ethnographic methods have been proposed to observe these changes.[48] This is because to detect governmentality in the international, and by that reconstruct the being-ruled of subjects, a deep and long-term analysis of their techniques of the self and their interaction with institutions is in order. We have to look deeper than only to conclude from the non-existence of official commands that there *is* no rule.

Tucker and Dean have looked specifically at participation mechanisms in global governance. Dean analyses non-state actors in global governance and shows how 'technologies of agency' seek to deploy new possibilities of participation as governmental tactic.[49] Tucker reconstructs how particular forms of subjectivity are rewarded in the process of participation, thus giving an advantage to moderate and technical NGO behaviour and incentivizing proponents of 'traditional knowledge' to adapt their language and normative frameworks to the governmental order.[50]

In a surprising parallel to Lake's concept of social contract theory for global governance authorities, Burchell's study of civil society already shows how it is brought into the task of governing by virtue of a 'contractual implication' – only that from this perspective, the contract is not understood as 'signed' by free and conscious agents but rather as a signification of a power relation in which the weaker side is subject to forms of deception.[51] Foucault had already shown that concepts of authority drawing on 'civil society' and 'informal arrangements' not controlled by the state, which refer to inclusion and consensus instead of domination, should be seen as a transformation rather than an abolition of rule.[52] Rule, from this perspective, is not challenged but

---

[47] Neumann and Sending, '"The international" as governmentality', p. 691.

[48] Tania Murray Li, *The Will to Improve: Governmentality, Development, and the Practice of Politics* (Durham: Duke University Press, 2007); Sending and Neumann, 'Governance to governmentality: analyzing NGOs, states, and power'; Wanda Vrasti, 'Universal but not truly "global": governmentality, economic liberalism, and the international', *Review of International Studies* 39, 1 (2013), pp. 49–69; Lie, 'Developmentality: indirect governance in the World Bank–Uganda partnership'.

[49] Mitchel Dean, *Governmentality: Power and Rule in Modern Society* (London: Sage, 1999), pp. 167–8.

[50] Tucker, 'Participation and subjectification in global governance: NGOs, acceptable subjectivities and the WTO', p. 377.

[51] Graham Burchell, 'Liberal government and techniques of the self', in Andrew Barry, Thomas Osborne, and Nikolas Rose (eds) *Foucault and Political Reason* (London: University College London, 1996), p. 29.

[52] Michel Foucault, 'Politik und Ethik', *Deutsche Zeitschrift Für Philosophie* 42, 4 (1994), pp. 703–8; Thomas Lemke, 'Max Weber, Norbert Elias und Michel Foucault über Macht und Subjektivierung', *Berliner Journal Für Soziologie* 11, 1 (2001), p. 92.

has rather perfected its means by way of involving and responsibilizing its potential enemies. The 'art of governing' is therefore at the heart of studies in governmentality.[53]

In comparison to repressive strategies of rule which have a long tradition of inquiry in the sociology of social control – participatory regimes oriented at consensual decisions have not received much attention, especially regarding their power mechanisms.[54] Foucault is so central to an analysis of rule beyond the state, because he fundamentally decoupled governing from territorial attachments of the term. He holds that it is not a state or a territory that is being governed; instead governing is directed at people, humans, individuals and collectives.[55] On this basis, Bröckling reconstructs that in a situation where the governed object is detached from territory, governing becomes separated from repression towards participation and consensus.[56] Power takes on a caring role oriented at the welfare of the people, and through that individualizes subjects by being directed at the sum of subjects but also each one of them (omnes et singulatum). For this character of rule, Bröckling argues, the metaphor of the shepherd is most fitting: 'Good shepherds lead gently'. This goes well with recent studies in the 'rule of experts':[57] The experts' paternalism 'consists of interference that is against the will or without the consent of the subordinate party, [and] would seem to be outside any sort of mutual agreement of the sort discussed by David Lake'.[58] Yet it is not directed *against* the subjects, nor is it an (explicit) governing strategy.

From such a view, one could argue that the liberals have simply overlooked the shepherds and their art of governing because the sheep looked so free without a fence. Yet, if the shepherd was not there, the herd would disperse.[59] But this view undermines the potential of governmentality studies for the international arena because, in fact, there *is* a sovereign in this account. The shepherd does not appear to be interventionist, but it is only her who keeps the herd together. The herd would disperse the minute the shepherd walked away. Therefore, this metaphor thwarts the project of investigating

---

[53] Ulrich Bröckling, *Gute Hirten Führen Sanft: Über Menschenregierungskünste* (Berlin: Suhrkamp, 2017), p. 16; Sending and Neumann, 'Governance to governmentality', p. 656.

[54] Bröckling, *Gute Hirten Führen Sanft*, p. 9.

[55] Michel Foucault, *Sicherheit, Territorium, Bevölkerung: Geschichte Der Gouvernementalität I. Vorlesungen Am Collège de France 1977–1978* (Berlin: Suhrkamp, 2006), p. 183.

[56] Bröckling, *Gute Hirten Führen Sanft*, p. 19.

[57] Timothy Mitchell, *Rule of Experts. Egypt, Techno-Politics, Modernity* (Berkeley: University of California Press, 2002); Ole Jacob Sending, *The Politics of Expertise: Competing for Authority in Global Governance*, (Ann Arbor: University of Michigan Press, 2015).

[58] Michael Barnett, 'Hierarchy and paternalism', in Ayşe Zarakol (ed) *Hierarchies in World Politics* (Cambridge: Cambridge University Press, 2017), p. 66.

[59] Bröckling, *Gute Hirten Führen Sanft*, p. 19.

structures of rule because they are not at all complex in the case of the shepherd and the herd. Sheep fear the shepherd and her German Shepherd Dog. No wonder the individuals in the herd use technologies of the self in order not to be bitten. In global governance, however, this metaphor is too simple. It may have value for affected communities where World Bank staff have direct control over the life chances in the project area. In the sphere of institutional contestation of global governance where the major critics are NGOs, mass organizations, think-tanks and other organized subjects, the sheep metaphor quickly reaches its limits. The most interesting question of governmentality studies – Why do these subjects work on themselves with governmental technologies despite the absence of a sovereign? – is rather evaded by it.

The metaphor of the shepherd and the herd does not help to elucidate rule in the international because it leads to a search for the shepherd, an activity prone to fall back into conspiracy theories or versions of 'simple rule' that are not applicable in global governance (discussed further on). But how can we then investigate rule in the international if we assume that there is no shepherd? This brings me back to the proposal by Daase and Deitelhoff who argue that, in contrast to observing rule through its compliance, we can rather observe it in instances of resistance. Rule would hence only become visible where one of the sheep decided to protest or otherwise resist the shepherd's rules. By this, rule and resistance are therefore understood as a relation. Through the latter, we know that the former exists – and can consecutively analyse both through their interaction.[60]

---

[60] This excludes those instances of rule where no resistance takes place. While Daase and Deitelhoff think that this is almost impossible because rule and resistance need each other, particularly postcolonial and feminist interventions have highlighted situations of structural rule under which resistance is not possible or only in a veiled, subtle form. I am not arguing that these are less important, but I focus analytically on those instances where rule *can* be reconstructed from resistance. See for instance Gayatri Spivak, 'Can the subaltern speak?', in Patrick Williams and Laure Chrisman (eds) *Colonial Discourse and Postcolonial Theory: A Reader* (New York: Columbia University Press, 1988), pp. 66–111; Erin Hannah, Holly Ryan, and James Scott, 'Power, knowledge and resistance: between co-optation and revolution in global trade', *Review of International Political Economy* 24, 5 (2017), pp. 741–75; James Scott, *Weapons of the Weak: Everyday Forms of Peasant Resistance* (New Haven: Yale University Press, 1987); Nikita Dhawan, *Impossible Speech: On the Politics of Silence and Violence* (Leeds: Academia, 2007).

3

Complex Rule
in Global Governance

If rule is not immediately observable in direct commands, this does not mean it does not exist. I have made the case that rule can be reconstructed through an analysis of resistance. But where to start such a reconstruction? While I endorse Daase and Deitelhoff's call for reconstructing rule from resistance, they so far have not fully conceptualized how this is to be done. For this purpose, Boltanski's sociology of critique is a promising way of filling this gap. Starting from discontent with a given system, he shows us that the traditional definitions of rule do not suffice to understand how political systems are structured and governed, because in modern capitalist systems, we cannot see structures of rule as easily. They govern in a veiled and indirect ('managerial') fashion. Yet, as much as simple ('traditional') rule, they have the aim and effect of disguising entry points for critique. To rule means to keep critique in fragmentation.[1] Since the starting point of this book is the fragmentation of a social movement, the case lends itself to reconstruct rule from there. By answering the activist's question and reconstructing how the fragmentation of the Global Justice Movement happened, I might produce clues as to how rule has worked its magic.

Institutions and critique

For this purpose, we need to make a quick excursion into Boltanski's understanding of institutions. To him, institutions are beings without a body, to which people delegate the task of 'saying and confirming what matters'.[2] They sort out what is to be respected from what is not. This refers especially to their capacity of differentiation. In a competition, for example, institutions

---

[1]   Boltanski, 'Individualismus ohne Freiheit', p. 142.
[2]   Boltanski, *On Critique*, p. 75.

draw the line between the last one who qualifies for the next round, and the first one who drops out, despite of their performances being almost the same. The importance of this task is obvious when institutions assign possibilities, property or goods to individuals, organizations, or countries. Institutions are a necessary part of human life because they coordinate behaviour and reduce uncertainty. To do so, they make certain actions and ways of thinking possible and exclude others. By defining who and what matters, institutions have an impact on the formation of groups, identities and ways of thinking and acting. Hence, their decisive role in the way rule manifests: it does so not (only) by orders and commands, but also by measurements, definitions, classifications, and guidelines. By saying and confirming the being of what is and its value, institutions decide what is possible, prefiguring and steering human conduct.

With this work of inscribing things into reality, institutions create and affirm social orders.[3] Boltanski has an elegant way to show the different *grammars* that are put in place and actualized within these different orders. These grammars have the function not to supersede, but to circumvent the contradictions of this particular order.[4] Actors learn to position themselves according to these grammars. Without explicit rules, habits are formed, and it is often only from an external standpoint that the regularities thereby produced can be observed. This is even more since within these grammars, a certain tolerance prevails with regard to behavioural differences. The framework of this tolerance is flexible, yet not without limitation. Below a certain 'threshold of tolerance',[5] or what Daase and Deitelhoff call 'within the applicable rules of the game', deviance can be practiced.[6] What follows is a self-limitation to the room within these rules of the game. This serves institutions to 'preserve the appearance of an agreement' which would be at risk of collapse were the contradictions objectified.[7]

Reality, as defined by Boltanski, is always oriented at 'the preservation of order'.[8] It is instantiated and reproduced by qualifications and tests, the former reproducing order through circular effects, the latter reinstituting the institutions of the social by proving their realness. These procedures ('truth tests') are employed by institutions to reaffirm what is already there – they are instances of confirmation. This is achieved by the repetition of specific performances which aim to 'make visible the fact that there is a norm'.[9]

---

[3] Boltanski, *On Critique*, p. 75.
[4] Boltanski, *On Critique*, p. 59.
[5] Boltanski, *On Critique*, p. 65.
[6] Daase and Deitelhoff, 'Reconstructing global rule by analyzing resistance', p. 14.
[7] Boltanski, *On Critique*, p. 65.
[8] Boltanski, *On Critique*, p. 58.
[9] Boltanski, *On Critique*, p. 104.

Empty signifiers dominate the language on these occasions. Rituals and formulae are important in their enactment. These operations for which institutions are responsible, and which have the creation of coherence as a central goal, are termed 'maintenance of reality' in Boltanski's theoretical framework.[10] An example would be grades in school: through the procedure of tests, grades make pupils 'learn' reality, by reproducing the reality of reality. What is more, those who successfully reproduce it and receive good grades will be subsequently more qualified to thrive within, and therefore have an interest in preserving reality. *Common sense* is another feature of retaining reality, established through rituals and tests which delineate what kinds of statements are within, and what kind of statements are outside, or even without, reality. Institutions hence play an enormous role in the preservation of reality, that is of the existing order. Nevertheless, institutions are also the entry points for critique. As the places where reality has been constructed and preserved, they are what is to be resisted, should this reality be identified as pathological.

The possibility of critique derives from a contradiction according to Boltanski – a hermeneutic contradiction to be more precise. This hermeneutic contradiction is situated in institutions. They portray themselves as authorities with purely rational and technocratic proceedings. Yet, when encountering the representatives of these institutions, they are human and therefore subjective and partial – instead of objective and impartial. This is the reason why symbols (robes, uniforms, signs, suits, and so on) play such an important role for the experts in institutions: they have the function of veiling the hermeneutic contradiction, masquerading as epistemic authorities.[11] Therefore, there is always an ambivalence towards institutions, although in daily life most people decide to 'believe' in them, a more or less conscious decision that substantially simplifies and structures their lives. But hermeneutic contradictions also have an empowering aspect because they are entry points of critique, for the critic can utter that *the world* does not accord with what the institutions sold to us *as reality*. 'Something is wrong here' could therefore be an originating thought of critique. It will challenge the *reality of reality*, thereby unmasking its contingent or hypocritical character.[12] This practice of unmasking is the basis for demanding arrangements – orders – of a new kind. Critique can either challenge the institution's reality by confronting it with events from *the world* that do not conform with the institutions' *reality*, or by challenging the 'tests' which have been put into place by institutions in order to prove the reality it wants us to accept.[13]

---

[10] Boltanski, *On Critique*, p. 105.
[11] Boltanski, 'Individualismus ohne Freiheit', p. 136.
[12] Boltanski, *On Critique*, p. 59.
[13] Boltanski, *On Critique*, p. xi.

Since institutions are so central in stabilizing the established order, critique is almost necessarily addressed at them, especially when we assume that 'critique only becomes meaningful with respect to the order that it puts in crisis'.[14]

Ruling by fragmenting critique

Boltanski distinguishes two contemporary forms with the help of which institutions repress contradictions: simple and complex domination. *Simple domination* works through explicit, particularly physical, violence. Slavery is the prime example of this mode, the 'extreme scenario' of simple domination, which he also calls oppression. A specific orthodoxy is maintained through executive power and police violence. Fragmentation of critique is complete and hence the latter is evacuated of the order; justification being no longer relevant.[15] The 'ideological activity directed at the dominated' is therefore no longer oriented at consent. The less extreme case (repression) allows for some critique, which however remains without any effect. Critique can be crushed if necessary, and the official institutions instantiate order through 'a spectacular employment of truth tests' which cover rituals, ceremonies, parades, and decorations.[16]

Complex domination on the other hand, the managerial type of governing others that I will develop further, is 'better adjusted to democratic-capitalist societies'. Critique, in contrast to simple domination, does have effects. Repression is avoided to large extents and there is an imperative of justification for the governing institutions to be perceived as legitimate. In contrast to the truth tests common in oppression or repression, 'reality tests' can be performed within complex domination. 'It is therefore precisely the establishment of a new kind of relationship between institutions and critique and, in a sense, the incorporation of critique into the routines of social life that characterizes these systems'.[17] They do not preclude change, and more challenging types of tests (if not conducted 'excessively') are deemed legitimate. However, and this is Boltanski's core contribution, this incorporation of critique also has the effect of restricting critique by way of fragmenting it. In his view, both types, simple and complex domination, thus have the aim and effect of fragmenting critique.

The ways in which this fragmentation comes about have so far not been theorized adequately. Boltanski's concept of two forms of domination, simple and complex, that both fragment critique through different means

---

[14] Boltanski, *On Critique*, p. 59.
[15] This is where Boltanski departs from Forst who holds that there is no order without justification.
[16] Boltanski, *On Critique*, p. 125.
[17] Boltanski, *On Critique*, p. 127.

(authoritarian and neoliberal) is attractive yet vague in terms of the underlying mechanisms. While they are obvious for the simple form, where critique is crushed, if necessary, the ways of fragmenting critique without oppression remain but suggestions. The remainder of this book will be devoted to theorizing and empirically tracing the *how* of this very link.

Yet, as outlined in the introduction, Boltanski's theoretical apparatus is geared towards the nation state. Lifting it to the transnational level, the locus and direction of domination is even less clear than nationally, and it is only with many preconditions that we can speak of a 'society'. Furthermore, intentionality is overstated in Boltanski's approach. Empirically and also conceptually, I do not find his assumption that domination always has the *aim* and effect of fragmenting critique convincing.[18] The intentionality behind social movement fragmentation is not a given, as Boltanski himself admits: 'the question of knowing who the dominant are ... presents itself as problematic'.[19] What I observe in the empirical chapters are practices of which I can trace the effects, but often the intentionality (and authorship) behind them is veiled or unclear; commands and obedience are rare. In some instances, I am quite certain that the fragmentation of resistance is an unintended effect of a well-intentioned practice of individuals inside institutions. This does not make the effect less devastating. However, it puts into question the assumption that dominant institutions always have the *aim and effect* of fragmenting critique.

My approach is a constellational one and assumes that power is accumulated inside institutions, hence domination being a situational effect rather than a stable pattern with institutions as its conscious authors. If an institution were capable of causing the effects of the constellation studied here, I would speak of domination as a practice. This is, however, not a finding of this study that rather directs readers' focus to the constitution of a specific constellation in global governance. This constellation is, however, hierarchically structured, and will, in many cases, force specific (less powerful) actors into contradictory practices. The constellation itself is hence at the core of what follows. The term constellation goes back to the early critical theorists Adorno and Benjamin. The latter explained that ideas are to objects as constellations are to stars. The constellational concept that I will introduce is as real as constellations are in the heavens, not 'really there', but like star constellations it enables us to perceive relations between objects. 'The stars in the night sky are where they are regardless of how we look at them and there is something

---

[18] Boltanski, 'Individualismus ohne Freiheit', p. 144. In fact, this is the place where Boltanski surprisingly moves back into the language of ideology critique. Simon Susen, 'Towards a critical sociology of dominant ideologies: an unexpected reunion between Pierre Bourdieu and Luc Boltanski', *Cultural Sociology* 10, 2 (2015), pp. 195–246.

[19] Boltanski, *On Critique*, p. 129.

in how they are positioned above us that suggests the image we construct of them'.[20] But the names we use for constellations are embedded in history and cannot be treated as constants. The intention is to refer back to them, and to create theory based on the this 'concrete historical factuality'.[21]

The constellation that I introduce in the following is termed complex rule. I have chosen to stick to 'complex rule' because of the associations of intentionality attached to domination. The way I will be using 'rule' is to denote a constellation, but not only in terms of a positionality of actors but also in terms of what happens between them, that is how it functions. I do this through three dimensions: its governing rationality, its way of communicating, and its organizational structure. These three dimensions will be further developed later. For now, complex rule shall be understood as a constellation in which structures of super- and subordination are institutionalized through incorporation rather than repression.[22]

Although in the arena of global governance, Boltanski's dualistic theory of domination needs to be altered towards a more contingent analysis of rule, his offer of three main facets distinguishing complex from simple ways of fragmenting critique can be utilized for this endeavour.[23] These are:

1. a specific normative logic, namely neoliberalism;
2. a need for public legitimation ('the imperative of justification'); and
3. a specific role for institutions and a corresponding institutionalized form of political organization.[24]

I argue in the following that each of these three dimensions works through specific mechanisms that I operationalize subsequently. As I will then show empirically, these mechanisms collectively present the answer to the activist's question: How has the fragmentation of the movement happened?

The normative dimension: a neoliberal governing rationality

A central dimension to the managerial mode of governing that Boltanski sketches in his theory is neoliberal reason. He traces this from the

---

[20] Ian Buchanan, 'Constellation', in *Oxford Dictionary of Critical Theory* (Oxford: Oxford University Press, 2010), p. 96.

[21] Theodor W. Adorno, *Lectures on Negative Dialectics. Fragments of a Lecture Course 1965/1966* (Cambridge: Polity, 2008), p. xvii.

[22] This is a specification to the definition of rule by Daase and Deitelhof, 'Jenseits der Anarchie', pp. 299–318.

[23] Boltanski, *On Critique*, p. 127–9.

[24] Boltanski, *On Critique*, p. 127.

justifications of the dominating class for why this order is adequate: a reliance on opportunities and 'choice'. This is what he identifies as the 'neoliberal logic' which works by 'shifting onto "individual responsibility" the weight of the constraints that operate at the collective level'. This logic creates allegedly neutral spaces of action in which every subject is formally autonomous and able to access the opportunities provided. Any resultant asymmetries are 'blamed on the victim'.[25] This neoliberal governing rationality has been structuring global economic governance arrangements for decades: a form of political reason that configures all aspects of existence in economic terms.[26] It quantifies issues into indexes and indicators and translates political phenomena into numbers, while presenting this as the only rational mode of governing.[27] I conceptualize 'being governed by neoliberal rationality' as a first dimension of complex rule. It is instantiated by the mechanism of economization (see Chapter 4). In the following, I define the core features of this rationality and elaborate how it relates to complex rule in global governance. Since Boltanski does not theorize the specific ways in which neoliberalism governs, I develop this dimension based on Brown's interpretation, because she explicitly connects neoliberalism with governance by reconstructing how its rationality and concrete institutional governing practices are related.

Brown understands neoliberalism 'as something other than a set of economic policies, [or] an ideology. ... Rather, as a normative order of reason developed over three decades into a widely and deeply disseminated governing rationality'.[28] This understanding of neoliberalism draws heavily on Foucault's lectures at the Collège de France.[29] It fits in with the concept of complex rule because although Foucault and Boltanski derive their insights from different methods, the theoretical claims and even the wording converge when describing *the maintenance of reality*[30] as a core practice of institutionalizing complex rule, and the *acceptance of reality*[31] as a result of neoliberal reason. Rule is perpetuated as a constellation through the

---

[25] Boltanski, *On Critique*, p. 128.

[26] Brown, *Undoing the Demos*, p. 17.

[27] Cris Shore and Susan Wright, 'Audit culture revisited', *Current Anthropology* 56, 3 (2015), pp. 421–44; Cris Shore and Susan Wright, 'Governing by numbers: audit culture, rankings and the new world order', *Social Anthropology* 23, 1 (2015), pp. 22–8; Sally Engle Merry, 'Measuring the world. Indicators, human rights, and global governance', *Current Anthropology* 52, S3 (April 2011), pp. 83–95.

[28] Brown, *Undoing the Demos*, p. 9.

[29] Michel Foucault, *The Birth of Biopolitics: Lectures at the Collège de France, 1978–79* (New York: Picador, 2004).

[30] Boltanski, *On Critique*, p. 117.

[31] Foucault, *The Birth of Biopolitics: Lectures at the Collège de France, 1978–79*, p. 269.

maintenance – or the making acceptable – of this specific (neoliberal) reality, while resistance is fragmented as an effect of it: some act in accordance with this reality and henceforth are included into the ruling order's open doors, while those who don't are subtly excluded; their issues do not have to be taken seriously, because they are voiced from beyond this particular realm and its opportunities which has become the only thinkable reality (their demands being 'unrealistic').

Neoliberalism is hence not a predictor of specific economic policies, although they are governed by the same rationality, nor is it dependent on specific rulers and their intentions.[32] Rather, a governing rationality is a condition for political practice.[33] Thus, the project of identifying and tracing a governing rationality such as neoliberalism supports 'Foucault's effort to harness and develop these precepts for understanding how societies and populations may be ruled intensively, yet indirectly'.[34] Through such an analysis, it becomes possible to understand the economization of institutions and subjects in all aspects and spheres of politics, and social interaction in general, which had been 'noneconomic' beforehand.[35] This emergent conceptualization is able to grasp neoliberalism's non-unified character and still pinpoint identifiable and 'nameable' characteristics, an aspect highly important in times of a certain fatigue with neoliberalism which to some feels like a 'conceptual Swiss Army knife', explaining everything and nothing at the same time.[36] Brown theorizes neoliberalism as a governing rationality which materializes in a specific code of conduct, that is *governance*: 'Contemporary neoliberalism is unthinkable without governance. It is also key to securing accession to the "economization" of all areas of life, the process that Foucault … equates with "accepting reality"'.[37]

Governance is *constituted by* neoliberal reason, and historically traceable to New Public Management schemes in 1980s Britain where the management strategies of private businesses were eagerly transferred to the public sector through public-private-partnerships (PPPs), and generally a shift from public paternalistic welfare and top-down administration towards incentives and entrepreneurial spirit. Governance is also *constitutive for* the further neoliberalization of politics, and paves the way for its institutionalization: a neoliberal form of politics that is

---

[32] William Callison and Zackary Manfredi, 'Theorizing mutant neoliberalism', in William Callison and Zachary Manfredi (eds) *Mutant Neoliberalism: Market Rule and Political Rupture* (New York: Fordham University Press, 2020), pp. 1–38.

[33] See Brown, *Undoing the Demos*, p. 115.

[34] Brown, *Undoing the Demos*, p. 116.

[35] Brown, *Undoing the Demos*, p. 50.

[36] Matthew Eagleton-Pierce, *Neoliberalism. The Key Concepts* (London: Routledge, 2016).

[37] Brown, *Undoing the Demos*, p. 122.

'evacuated of agents' and proceeds in environments less structured by vertical hierarchy than by horizontal, productivity-oriented and network-based organizational forms.[38] It has been broadly established that, by this, the sovereign state has been transformed, if not hollowed out,[39] but, as I want to show, this normativity of governance also changes international institutions and impregnates them with the specific character of complex rule. By that, it secures the accession to economization of politics by way of structuring constraints and incentives alongside the management techniques of complex businesses, thus conducting subjects in accordance with an economized normativity.

The central clue about complex rule as a constellation is that it institutionalizes asymmetries and produces concrete winners and losers, although the hierarchies seem flat. This functions so well, because the actors in and around it are governed by the rationality of neoliberalism, trusting in governance as a sort of post-rule in which all kinds of actors ('stakeholders', see Figure 3.1) can raise their concerns and collectively work towards a better future on rational grounds. Governance thus has a normative connotation and is purported to displace power politics in the interest of teamwork and collaboration.[40] However, as Brown argues, it does not only reconfigure the relations between market, state and citizenry and as such the 'operation of power and rule', it does so in a manner that privileges those who are able to exploit this specific constellation of power effectively.[41] On the surface, it replaces opposition and tension by collaboration and complementarity; it substitutes command and control with negotiation, management and persuasion in all its shapes well established in IR theory: benchmarks, incentives, and indicators instead of top-down, hierarchical enforcement.[42] All this has been occurring in the spirit of

---

[38] Brown, *Undoing the Demos*, p. 124.

[39] Thomas Lemke, 'An indigestible meal? Foucault, governmentality, and state theory', *Distinktion: Scandinavian Journal of Social Theory* 8, 2 (2007), pp. 43–64; Thomas Biebricher and Eric Vance Johnson, 'What's wrong with neoliberalism?', *New Political Science* 34, 2 (2012), pp. 202–11; William Callison, 'Sovereign anxieties and neoliberal transformations: an introduction', *Qui Parle: Critical Humanities and Social Sciences* 23, 1 (2014), pp. 3–34.

[40] See also Dingwerth and Pattberg, 'Global governance as a perspective', p. 193.

[41] Brown, *Undoing the Demos*, p. 126.

[42] Merry, 'Measuring the world'; Richard Rottenburg and Sally E. Merry, 'The world of indicators: the making of governmental knowledge through quantification', in Richard Rottenburg, Sally E. Merry, Sung-Joon Park, and Johanna Mugler (eds) *The World of Indicators: The Making of Governmental Knowledge through Quantification* (Cambridge: Cambridge University Press, 2015), pp. 1–33; Paul Beaumont and Ann E. Towns, 'The rankings game: a relational approach to country performance indicators', *International Studies Review* 23, 4 (2021), pp. 1467–94.

Figure 3.1: Google n-gram analysis of 'stakeholder'

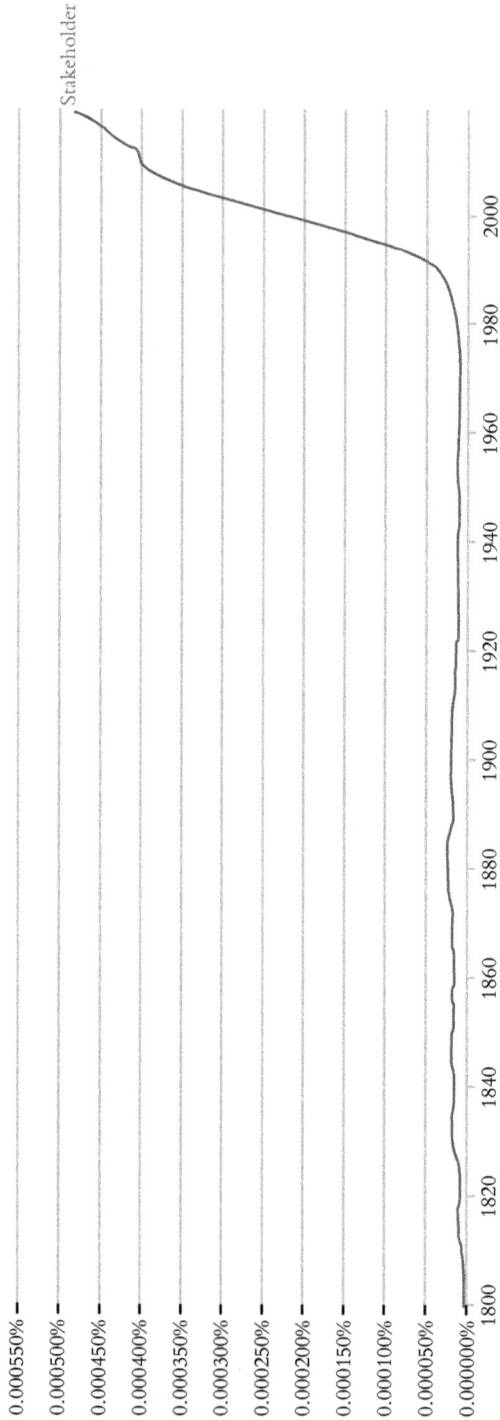

Source: {https://books.google.com/ngrams}

common problem-solving: '[C]onsensus replaces contestation of ... robust expressions of different political positions and desires'.[43]

The incorporation of critique into open institutions is closely entangled with the neoliberal rationality. Inclusion and participation have become indices of democratization,[44] but 'separated off from the powers and the unbounded field of deliberation that would make them meaningful as terms of shared rule'.[45] Governance, as Brown argues, reconceptualizes democracy as distinct from politics and economics by becoming purely procedural. More importantly, its *ends* vanish from the core issue of debate towards *givens*. These givens are of a specific – neoliberal – economic nature. This core feature, the ends as givens, enables governors to set rules by 'benchmarking, consensus building, policy making, and implementation'.[46] Governance becomes an arena of problem-solving in a common enterprise with harmonized, economically measurable, ends. Resistance to these ends is tricky since it involves what Spivak calls 'critiquing the dogmas that we cannot not want'.[47] When the ends are givens, and governance is hollowed-out of politics, economization spreads to all forms of the social which are in a governance institution's jurisdiction. This dialectical quality of inclusion, opening-up towards 'everyone' while putting the burden of politics on the individual, is at the heart of my argument. Therefore, it plays a role in all three dimensions of complex rule.

The discursive dimension: a reflexive order of justification

Every form of rule needs to justify itself. Different social spheres are, however, shaped by different contexts, and different demands for justification.[48] A political order of justification is harder to characterize when we look beyond the nation state. A plethora of media, norms, actors and claims to

---

[43] Brown, *Undoing the Demos*, p. 127.

[44] Klaus Dingwerth, *The New Transnationalism: Transnational Governance and Democratic Legitimacy* (London: Palgrave Macmillan UK, 2007); Allen Buchanan and Robert O. Keohane, 'The legitimacy of global governance institutions', *Ethics & International Affairs* 20, 4 (2006), pp. 405–37.

[45] Brown, *Undoing the Demos*, p. 128.

[46] Brown, *Undoing the Demos*, p. 128. These rules have also captured academic knowledge production, complicating the critique of neoliberalism which itself is necessarily formulated under neoliberal conditions. See Jana Bacevic, 'Knowing neoliberalism', *Social Epistemology* 33, 4 (2019), pp. 380–92.

[47] Gayatri C. Spivak, *Outside the Teaching Machine* (New York: Routledge, 1993), p. 45.

[48] Luc Boltanski and Laurent Thévenot, *On Justification: Economies of Worth* (Princeton: Princeton University Press, 2006); Rainer Forst, *Kritik Der Rechtfertigungsverhältnisse: Perspektiven Einer Kritischen Theorie Der Politik* (Berlin: Suhrkamp, 2011), p. 18.

actorness complement, contradict, and contest each other.[49] To make the argument that open global governance constitutes a specific political order that can be described as 'complex rule', I have to be able to characterize *it* as one specific order of justification and to distinguish it from other constellations that would be better described as simple rule. In this vein, I will now sketch how an order of justification under complex rule should be expected to look.

Justification can be approached analytically or normatively. The bulk of the political theory as well as IR literature on international norm negotiations is strongly driven by the normative idea that (1) the governed, individual or collective, have the right to justification, and (2) governors must justify themselves properly in order to be legitimate.[50] However, one can utilize justification as an analytical category, too. Boltanski and Thévenot have introduced 'six worlds of justification', analysing the specific grammars of justification in each of them, as well as the specific forms of critique arising from these grammars.[51]

The crucial aspect about complex rule is that parts of the critics either actively use or slide into the institutional order of justification, contributing to conflicts with their peers who orient themselves at different justificatory grammars. In contrast to simple rule, which is usually justified with reference to tradition, God or other authoritatively generated principles, complex rule justifies itself reflexively. Enthusiastically theorized by liberal IR scholars with reference to the institutions' dialogical striving for legitimacy, this reflexivity has been named a central feature of global governance in contrast to rule or domination.[52]

I have no idea whether managers at IOs are in fact 'more reflexive' today than they were some decades ago. This is not the point. What we do know is that they have to present themselves as reflexive subjects in public, because

---

[49] Forst therefore promotes a closer cooperation between political theory and IR on this issue. See *Normativität Und Macht: Zur Analyse Sozialer Rechtfertigungsverhältnisse* (Berlin: Suhrkamp, 2015), p. 187.

[50] See also Rainer Forst, *The Right to Justification: Elements of a Constructivist Theory of Justice* (New York: Columbia University Press, 2012); Buchanan and Keohane, 'The legitimacy of global governance institutions'.

[51] Boltanski and Thévenot, 'On justification', pp. 159–211.

[52] R.A.W. Rhodes, *Understanding Governance. Policy Networks, Governance, Reflexivity and Accountability* (Buckingham: Open University Press, 1997); Zürn, *A Theory of Global Governance*. This emphasis on reflexivity is however not mirrored in an increasingly reflexive practice of theory-building. It should not be confused with the 'reflexive turn' in IR. See Inanna Hamati-Ataya, 'Reflectivity, reflexivity, reflexivism: IR's "reflexive turn" – and beyond', *European Journal of International Relations* 19, 4 (2013), pp. 669–94.

'there are no universally shared criteria of legitimacy in global governance'.[53] Although it is by no means certain that there are 'universally shared criteria of legitimacy' in *any* polity, the absence of a constitution or the like objectifies this as a social fact in the international arena. In this environment, it has been shown that particularly those IOs that are contested seek new forms of legitimation and invest heavily into communication, publicly reflecting on their role.[54]

In Boltanski's terms, what makes these institutions reflexive in contrast to those of simple rule is that their representatives (managers) are aware of the hermeneutical contradiction: their institutions representing an impartial whole while they themselves having particular agendas. This process of increasingly reflecting on their own role can be described as resulting in a reflexive order of justification in which the hermeneutic contradiction is recognized by the institutional staff, leading to more complex forms of veiling this contradiction. These, in turn, are access points for critique. Zürn argues that this reflexivity has turned against itself by politicizing institutional practices and hence creating a potential for resistance instead of effectively veiling the contradiction.[55] I will show, however, that while such reflexivity in global governance has indeed created access points for critique, it did so only for oppositional critics who argue within the same order of justification, making it even harder for those critics who reject the very premises on which the 'open' and 'reflexive' discussion is based.

Rather than explaining the rise of reflexivity in evolutionary terms,[56] reflexivity of open global governance shall therefore be understood to emerge and increase as part of a constellation of complex rule. Institutions have to legitimize themselves reflexively in order to remain in a position of power. This need for legitimacy by IOs and their staff is at the core of what makes complex rule's order of justification reflexive. Reflexivity, in this sense, 'means self-transformation through self-confrontation'. The practices that result from this necessity to legitimate the self can be observed empirically. (1) They open-up their policy-making by inviting stakeholders, 'affected people', and generally civil society. (2) They legitimate themselves by making transparent the hermeneutic contradiction and explaining their own actions, not as self-evident, but as the result of rational political discourse.

---

[53] Steven Bernstein, 'Legitimacy in intergovernmental and non-state global governance', *Review of International Political Economy* 18, 1 (2011), p. 22.

[54] Ecker-Ehrhardt, 'Self-legitimation in the face of politicization'; Gronau and Schmidtke, 'The quest for legitimacy in world politics'.

[55] Michael Zürn, 'Global governance and legitimacy problems', *Government and Opposition* 39, 2 (2004), p. 276.

[56] See for this Zürn, 'Global governance and legitimacy problems'.

The opening-up of IOs and the proactive way of legitimating themselves in public discourse shall be understood as two interrelated characteristics of the reflexive order of justification operationalized by the mechanisms of incorporation and legitimation (see Chapter 4).

The organizational dimension: a managerial bureaucracy

The third dimension of complex rule is its bureaucratic form of organization. In an attempt to understand the under-theorized field of international bureaucracy, many have recently re-read Max Weber.[57] Weber has been drawn upon heavily in constructivist IR in order to explain the power and pathologies of IOs.[58] While Weber, however, studied bureaucracy in order to complete a theory of domination, conceptualizing it as the everyday face of state power, such a critical twist has so far barely been part of mainstream IR utilizing Weber.[59] As Steffek argues, this is due to an imagined duality between hegemonic power politics versus supranational governance institutions.[60] Preferring the latter over the former, constructivists like Barnett and Finnemore hide their disenchantment with bureaucracy while remaining 'normatively committed to the project of rationalization', therefore defending the process of international bureaucracy's expansion. As enshrined in Weber's concept of bureaucracy, its normative implications are ambivalent: on the one hand, it has probably led to more peaceful means of settling disputes in the international, on the other hand it has been contributing to the depersonalizing, technocratic order we are living in. What I will add to this relatively obvious ambivalence is that this process of international 'rationalization' which IOs have contributed to,

---

[57] Álvaro Morcillo Laiz and Klaus Schlichte, 'Special section: international organizations, their staff and their legitimacy: Max Weber for IR', *Cambridge Review of International Affairs* 29, 4 (2016), pp. 1441–1519; Michael Barnett and Martha Finnemore, *Rules for the World: International Organizations in Global Politics* (Ithaca: Cornell University Press, 2004).

[58] Jens Steffek, 'International organizations and bureaucratic modernity', in Richard Ned Lebow (ed) *Max Weber and International Relations* (Cambridge: Cambridge University Press, 2017), pp. 119–42; Michael Barnett and Martha Finnemore, 'The politics, power, and pathologies of international organizations', *International Organization* 53, 4 (1999), pp. 699–732.

[59] But see Morcillo Laiz and Schlichte, 'Rationality and international domination'; Morcillo Laiz and Schlichte, 'Another Weber'; Klaus Schlichte, 'Max Weber in Mosambik: Bürokratische Herrschaft in der Weltgesellschaft', in Christopher Daase et al. (eds) *Herrschaft in den Internationalen Beziehungen* (Wiesbaden: Springer, 2017), pp. 73–93.

[60] Steffek 'International organizations and bureaucratic modernity', p. 121.

is based on an understanding of the *rational* closely coupled with Western concepts of the Enlightenment. Weber's theory, originally developed in Wilheminian Germany, to have such an explanatory power for IOs is a good indication for the fact that a particular historical understanding of efficient administration has fused into normative conceptions of global governance more generally. Beyond the dominating aspects of bureaucracy as a general form, I will therefore highlight the specific effects of this Western project of rationalization on the diverse critics of the order.

The analysis of IOs in IR has developed significantly through sociological perspectives, especially regarding their inner lifeworld. Building on Weber,[61] Barnett and Finnemore showed that IOs exhibit the traits of bureaucracies as a cultural form. The implications of this are twofold. On the one hand, these organizations have a productive side, which is supported by their inherent rational-legal authority. This gives them a great deal of power. We should therefore look at them as actors, not only as arenas. On the other hand, however, the cultural form of a bureaucracy can mean that they are obsessed with their own rules, making them inefficient and potentially self-defeating. With these 'pathologies' vis-à-vis the power of IOs, Barnett and Finnemore suggest that 'the very features that make bureaucracies powerful can also be their weakness'.[62] Yet, what is seldomly reflected in the studies on bureaucracy is, first, the hierarchical constellations that these organizations produce, shape and re-inscribe;[63] and second, the embedding of bureaucratization in a broader framework of 'modernization'.[64]

Bureaucracy is a system of governing in which decisions are taken through administrative, rather than openly political, procedures. It is associated with a body (institution) of governing officials who qualified for these positions by means other than public elections. They are experts rather than politicians.[65] Their expert status and the high degree of formality of their institutions gives them a 'rationalized' aura. Moreover, the particular subset of bureaucratic institutions dealt with here (IOs) are not only rationalizations themselves but have been working towards the rationalization of international politics and hence can be seen as agents of rationalization. The most obvious examples of this are their attempts to codify international disputes through

---

[61] Max Weber, *Economy and Society: Vol. 1, Part 2* (Los Angeles: University of California Press, 1978), pp. 956–1005.

[62] Barnett and Finnemore, 'The politics, power, and pathologies of international organizations', p. 701.

[63] Fehl and Freistein, 'Organising global stratification'.

[64] Nicholas G. Onuf, *The Mightie Frame: Epochal Change and the Modern World* (Oxford: Oxford University Press, 2018), p. 155.

[65] Marieke Louis and Lucile Maertens, *Why International Organizations Hate Politics: Depoliticizing the World* (London: Routledge, 2021), p. 10.

international law, but also through other means such as measurements, indicators, and lists.[66]

Different forms of 'rationality' can be found in different areas of the world but also in different sectors. For the sphere of global governance, Weber's approach to *legal-rational* domination by way of rationalizing the political sphere stands in the centre of analysis. Drawing on Morcillo Laiz and Schlichte, rationalization can be defined as:

> the intellectual and practical systematization of a life sphere in a 'theory', that is, a body of general principles and operations that are arranged in logics of hierarchy, departments, or sequences. Rationalization, by design, minimizes mere coincidences and seeks regularities; it aims at rules, procedures, and categories by which a sphere of life becomes first intelligible and then apt to be systematized.[67]

My argument here is that through these processes of rationalization, hierarchical constellations are produced, shaped and re-inscribed. The regularities, rules, procedures, and categories can be summarized as a political knowledge order in which experts are trained and well-versed and therefore enable their institutions to govern more effectively. Other actors need to train themselves in the ways that political issues are discussed and justified within that order. Nobody forces them to succumb to this order, but actors' *lifeworlds* – to use that pompous academic term – are increasingly colonized by it if they actively engage with these institutions. I will operationalize this process later as the mechanism of professionalization.

IR has long only analysed such bureaucratic institutions in functional terms.[68] Morcillo Laiz and Schlichte make the argument that this might be due to IR overemphasizing the differences between forms of organization, attributing too much singularity to the state because of a limited understanding of 'rule as coercion'. They state that 'relations of domination are at play whenever organizations advance a rationalization'. Quoting Weber, they emphasize that 'in daily life domination means primarily: *administration*'.[69] This understanding has two major implications for a conception of bureaucracy in the international. First, whether state, IO or international NGO, 'they all resort to money and expert knowledge

---

[66] Marieke de Goede, Anna Leander and Gavin Sullivan, 'Introduction: the politics of the list', *Environment and Planning D: Society and Space* 34, 1 (2016), pp. 3–13.

[67] Morcillo Laiz and Schlichte, 'Rationality and international domination', p. xx.

[68] Jens Steffek, 'Max Weber, modernity and the project of international organization', *Cambridge Review of International Affairs* 29, 4 (2016), pp. 1502–19.

[69] Morcillo Laiz and Schlichte, 'Rationality and international domination: revisiting Max Weber', p. 171, emphasis in original.

to wield more or less rational dominations'.[70] The takeaway message from this is that there are actors other than states that have successfully engaged in activities of bureaucratization, covering the political with their particular rationalities – and selling these as rationality per se. Second, the 'pathologies' that have been analysed in IOs on the basis of Barnett and Finnemore are no exceptions but should be understood as indicators for a social struggle, or in Weber's terms 'paradoxes of rationalization'.

How is this connected to social movement fragmentation in complex rule? The depoliticizing character inherent to the increasingly bureaucratic form of institutions are a trend that Weber depicted as 'a world inhabited by specialists without spirit and sensualists without heart'.[71] This is because when bureaucracies are outward-facing in the process of rationalizing not only themselves but others, the immanent contradictions, analysed as pathologies by Barnett and Finnemore, will turn into tools of bureaucratic rule. This is most apparent if this rationalization is part of their mission such as in development aid, where rationalization is an external prescript that will be measured sequentially.[72] It is, however, also part and parcel of bureaucratic rule in more subtle ways when a supra- and subordination is institutionalized by absolutizing a particular organizational form 'as rational'. Others henceforth have to play the rules of the game introduced by its administrative structure. 'The emergence of IOs as an organizational form is associated with the expansion and professionalization of public administration that has taken place in the Occident'.[73] The globalization of bureaucracy therefore holds in itself a story of expansion.[74]

This bureaucratic expansion 'presented the[ir] categories and arrangements as a general standard, for both scientific knowledge and social practice. Every country in the world was now to be measured and understood in relation to this universal model'.[75] The hierarchized perception of the world based on these rationalizations was then institutionalized into IOs. Nowhere is this more obvious than in the World Bank Group and the IMF where the American and European shareholders are formalized as decision-makers in a paternalist-internationalist project that governs the world economy.

---

[70] Morcillo Laiz and Schlichte, 'Rationality and international domination', p. 171. See also the section 'expert rule' in Onuf, *The Mightie Frame*, chapter 11.

[71] Max Weber, *The Protestant Ethic and the Spirit of Capitalism* (T. Parsons, trans.) (New York: The Citadel Press, 1930), p. 182.

[72] Merry, 'Measuring the world', p. 83.

[73] Steffek, 'International organizations and bureaucratic modernity', p. 119.

[74] Klaus Schlichte, 'Cubicle land – Bürokratie und Demokratie in der Regierung der Welt', in *Ordnungsbildung und Entgrenzung* (Wiesbaden: Springer, 2015), pp. 175–97; Aram Ziai, *Development Discourse and Global History: From Colonialism to the Sustainable Development Goals* (London: Routledge, 2015).

[75] Mitchell, *Rule of Experts*, p. 7.

There is a close connection between the Weberian understanding of the bureaucratization of the world with the Western project of enlightening others by way of permeating their (irrational) lifeworlds with (rational) institutions.[76] Those, in turn, emanate from western civilization and have to be transported to places other than the West in order to rationalize these others.[77] Only then will their equal potential be realized. This intellectual line of reasoning is at the heart of the depoliticizing praise of technical expertise and the real-world consequences of these ideas in the 20th century: more and more domains of action being transferred from traditional modes of coordination to formally organized modes, particularly markets and bureaucracy.[78]

IOs stand out in this regard: their structure as expertise-based governing bodies represents the turning-away from the political and can hence be read as instances of technocratic utopia.[79] The critique of bureaucratization and its depoliticizing effects is especially obvious when applied to 'development' organizations.[80] My argument here is not so much focused on the World Bank Group's specific promise of emancipation *through* development and the ambivalent effects of this promise, though.[81] Rather, I will show how open global governance is situated in a bureaucratic structure that is built on the premise that a formalized regulation will lead to fair procedures and hence the rationalization of politics.[82] This line of reasoning is underlying the last mechanism through which the critique of global governance organizations is being fragmented (regulation).

In this chapter, I have introduced the concept of complex rule on the basis of Boltanski's theoretical insight that simple as well as complex rule can be detected from their fragmenting effects on critique. I reconstructed three dimensions of complex rule in global governance in an attempt to

---

[76] Thomas McCarthy, *Race, Empire, and the Idea of Human Development* (Cambridge: Cambridge University Press, 2009), p. 143.

[77] Epstein, 'Stop telling us how to behave'; Charlotte Epstein et al., 'Forum: interrogating the use of norms in international relations: postcolonial perspectives', *International Theory* 6, 2 (2014), p. 293.

[78] See also Habermas, *The Philosophical Discourse of Modernity* (Cambridge, MA: MIT Press, 1979).

[79] Jens Steffek, *International Organization as Technocratic Utopia* (Oxford: Oxford University Press, 2021).

[80] James Ferguson, *The Anti-Politics Machine: 'Development', Depoliticization, and Bureaucratic Power in Lesotho* (Minneapolis: University of Minnesota Press, 1994); Aram Ziai, 'The discourse of "development" and why the concept should be abandoned', *Development in Practice* 23, 1 (2013), pp. 123–36.

[81] But see Aram Ziai, 'Development: projects, power, and a poststructuralist perspective', *Alternatives: Global, Local, Political* 34, 2 (2009), pp. 183–201.

[82] Sending, *The Politics of Expertise.*

operationalize Boltanski's abstract theoretical model. Complex rule in global governance is guided by a neoliberal governing rationality, legitimizes itself according to a reflexive order of justification, and is organized as a managerial bureaucracy. These three dimensions are aspects of an increasing institutionalization of super- and subordination that is instantiated not by repression but, to the contrary, by its openness towards, responsibilization and incorporation of critique. As argued by Boltanski, critique will struggle with this managerial mode of rule because it 'can avoid the accusation of deriving from a will to domination'.[83] Critique therefore becomes disoriented and fragments as a result. In the next chapter, I will operationalize this process for the subsequent empirical study that investigates the question: *how* does complex rule fragment critique?

---

[83] Boltanski, *On Critique*, p. 129.

4

Mechanisms of Fragmentation

Rule keeps critique in fragmentation. In the specific case of open global governance, a constellation in which critique is endorsed and invited in, instead of crushed, I have argued that this happens in a complex way, critique fragmenting without being exposed to repression. Yet how exactly does that work, given that global governance is not a sovereign state but a conglomerate of heterogeneous institutions? For examining such a *how*-question, *process tracing* offers itself as an adequate technique of inquiry.

Process tracing is rather a framework for inquiry than a method itself. It usually has the aim of detecting the mechanisms which connect a given independent variable (X) with a given dependent variable (Y). Beach and Pedersen distinguish three types of process tracing: theory-testing, theory-building and outcome-explaining.[1] Theory-testing process-tracing evaluates whether a hypothesized causal mechanism linking X and Y was indeed present in a given case. Theory-building process tracing constructs a theory about the causal link between X and Y with the aim of generalizing it. In contrast to the theory-testing version, the researcher starts from a situation in which she is 'in the dark regarding the mechanism'. The third version aims at explaining a particularly puzzling historical outcome. While the first two approaches are theory-centric, the third version is case-centric.[2] In theory-centric designs, causal mechanisms can be understood as 'parsimonious pathways whereby X contributes to producing Y'. In case-centric approaches, theories must be used more pragmatically, for the mechanisms discovered during the process-tracing are highly context-specific. In all three variants, it is the aim of process tracing not to remain with observing series of empirical events, 'but instead the underlying theorized causal mechanism itself'.[3]

---

[1] Derek Beach and Rasmus Brun Pedersen, *Process Tracing Methods: Foundations and Guidelines* (Ann Arbor: University of Michigan Press, 2013), p. 11.
[2] Beach and Pedersen, *Process Tracing Methods*, p. 12.
[3] Beach and Pedersen, *Process Tracing Methods*, p. 15.

The three variants of process tracing face common challenges, the main one being the clarification of concepts. In contrast to King, Keohane and Verba, for whom mechanisms are 'simply chains of intervening variables that connect the original posited cause and the effect',[4] Beach and Pederson highlight that such a 'regularity understanding of causality' leads to a 'grey-boxing' of mechanisms. They remain underdetermined and, maybe, unobservable.[5] The latter view has been made explicit by George and Bennett who hold that mechanisms are 'ultimately unobservable [processes] through which agents with causal capacities operate'.[6] When we understand mechanisms as intervening variables, they remain at the level of abstract concepts and may often expose new problems for operationalization. By unpacking them, Beach and Pedersen imagine each component as a single wheel in a series of treadmills which transmits energy to the next part of the mechanism.[7]

Referring the three variants of process tracing to the design of this study, 'theory-building process-tracing' is the closest match. This can be performed yet again in two versions. First, in an X–Y-centric theory-building, we know about the correlation/causation of X and Y but are in the dark about the ways that X influences Y. The second variant is when the scholar knows an outcome (Y) but is unsure about what caused it to happen.[8] This second version is roughly the situation encountered in this study. As I outlined in the introduction, I start from the observation that a social movement has fragmented considerably after the millennium until today despite increasing opportunities and despite a continuing disaffection with its enemies. This outcome can be understood as Y.

Messy mechanisms

My study is designed as a Y-centric theory-building process tracing that has, however, a theoretically informed idea about the causal path leading to Y. As elaborated in Chapter 3, I start out with the concept of 'complex rule' (X) producing fragmentation (Y). Yet, the character of X as defined based on Boltanski is too fuzzy to operationalize a causal mechanism from

---

[4] Gary King, Robert O. Keohane, and Sidney Verba, *Designing Social Inquiry: Scientific Inference in Qualitative Research* (Princeton: Princeton University Press, 1994), p. 37.

[5] Beach and Pedersen, *Process Tracing Methods*, p. 46.

[6] Alexander L. George and Andrew Bennett, *Case Studies and Theory Development in the Social Sciences* (Cambridge, MA: MIT Press, 2005), p. 137.

[7] Beach and Pedersen, *Process Tracing Methods*, p. 39; see also Roy Bhaskar, *A Realist Theory of Science* (Brighton: Harvester, 1978).

[8] Beach and Pedersen, *Process Tracing Methods*, p. 60.

it. Therefore, by drawing on other theories of rule, I theorized three dimensions of the concept that can be identified in Boltanski's writing. From these dimensions, I develop mechanisms which, taken together, lead to Y. All this looks like an, albeit clumsy, deductive design.[9] Yet, my interest is in showing that processes can be meaningful and traceable even if they are not linear and spurred by one clear-cut object. In other words, the real world is messier than a series of treadmills in which one wheel transmits energy to the next. This picks up on what Guzzini calls 'process tracing not in terms of a linear scheme, but as the intermeshing of several parallel processes'.[10] The way in which I will conceptualize mechanisms, they do not kick in one after the other, but they are interrelated processes that cannot be separated entirely from each other. This is because they are constituted by a constellation that I call complex rule, but they also constitute this very constellation. Formally put, what I claim is that these mechanisms collectively produce the fragmentation of social movements, and that this fragmentation stabilizes the constellation of complex rule which had originally triggered the mechanisms to begin with. Of course, a critical reader will see a danger in tautological theorizing. But I agree with Guzzini that process factors do not need to be 'variables' that cumulatively explain a linear causal chain. 'The input itself needs to be explained, and such explanation is partly provided by factors that the input generates during the process'.[11] Complex rule is both effect and cause of the fragmentation of critique.

Thus, there are two major differences distinguishing this study from a textbook approach. First, the causal arrow in this study is not one-directional. This becomes especially clear when examining the observable implications of the mechanisms, they are both on the side of the institution as well as on the side of critics – collectively their practices produce the outcome under investigation. Building on that, second, the metaphor of the different wheels that systematically drive each other from X to Y in a step-by-step logic does not apply either. Therefore, a chronology of mechanisms is not suggested. Rather, the five mechanisms that I trace play into each other in the form of a constellation: together they constitute X and Y. While X is the structure in which Y happens, X is re-instantiated through Y: the institutionalization of complex rule is reinforced through the fragmentation of critique. Hence Y happens under the condition of X, while X is reinforced through Y.

---

[9]   Beach and Pedersen, *Process Tracing Methods*, p. 15.
[10] Guzzini, 'Social mechanisms as micro-dynamics in constructivist analysis', p. 251.
[11] Guzzini, 'Social mechanisms as micro-dynamics in constructivist analysis', p. 254.

From causation to constitution

Boltanski is very clear on the causal connection: rule leads to the fragmentation of critique. But he is unclear about exactly how this works. When following Daase and Deitelhoff's proposal to reconstruct rule in the international (X) from the study of resistance (Y), the causal arrow is studied in reverse at least in research practice:[12] They propose to study resistance to learn something about the process in which rule is institutionalized. Furthermore, rule and resistance depend on each other. As they outline, the relationship is one of mutual dependence, making it difficult to establish clear causal paths: 'Although rule and resistance may constitute a reciprocal referential context, this says nothing about what is cause and what effect'.[13]

To answer my question, I trace the processes that lead to the fragmentation of critique (Y), hypothesizing that this fragmentation is the effect of a constellation that I call complex rule (X). Hence, I inquire the de-mobilization of resistance rather than its rise as suggested by Daase and Deitelhoff. The results will not illuminate the relationship between rule and resistance in general, but the relationship of a specific form of rule with a particular effect on resistance. However, there is no ready-made theory on that particular form of rule. Hence, I trace the processes through which Y is fragmented, building on theoretically derived, modelled processes (mechanisms) that I arrive at in iteration of theories of rule and my empirical material. Only through understanding these processes can I define complex rule as their 'cause' (X).

More generally, the understanding of a 'systematic and relatively simple mechanism' in the theory-building approach of Beach and Pedersen is at odds with the emergent theorization of complex rule as a historical constellation that I utilize here.[14] In this book, the research interest is hence slightly different. This is because the mechanisms themselves are observed in practices on the institutional side as well as on the side of their critics. They are therefore not only derived from X (while their main effect is on Y). Although there are X and Y, and they are connected through $M_{1,2,3,4,5}$ I will argue that – X being a historically emergent constellation – we can understand it only *through* $M_{1,2,3,4,5}$. The process is thereby given a more significant place in social theory. It is not only the transmission belt between two variables but itself necessary to understand what X *is*.

On an epistemological level, when taking seriously the idea of 'conditions' as historically grounded concepts, there is not a way they can be analytically

---

[12] Daase and Deitelhoff, 'Opposition and dissidence'.
[13] Daase and Deitelhoff, 'Reconstructing global rule by analyzing resistance', p. 13.
[14] Beach and Pedersen, *Process Tracing Methods*, p. 60.

distinguished from the mechanisms through which they produce an outcome. This is because first, if they produce an outcome, this outcome will have an effect on them, too, for there are no social phenomena which stand outside history and produce other objects without being affected by them.[15] Second, concepts are only well-described if the description entails what those concepts do. A sharp distinction between a concept and the mechanisms that arise from it is therefore not only artificial but leads to an impoverished concept-formation. The already stylized conceptualization of X → Y in positivist social science becomes therefore even more implausible when really diving into the mechanisms that connect them.

Nevertheless, it is important to theorize explicitly about the time-dimension involved in the workings of the process.[16] Depending on the nature of the process, however, it need not be the best option to draw a temporal graph from X to Y in which the mechanisms kick in one after the other. In a study on 'groupthink' that is used as an example by Beach and Pedersen,[17] for instance, Janis explains: 'I do not present the case studies in chronological order. The sequence I use was chosen to convey step-by-step the implications of group dynamics hypotheses'.[18] Step-by-step can hence mean a sequential logic but also a permeation of the empirical material with the theorized mechanisms, one after the other. By using a mix of these approaches in the empirical chapters, I hope to deliver both a plausible and entertaining sequential 'story' (Chapter 5), and an analytical reading of the material (Chapters 6–9) that is aimed at complementing the chronological process.

Mechanism 1: Economization

Based on the first dimension of complex rule developed in Chapter 3, I will now specify the mechanism of economization, and operationalize it for empirical observation. Economization renders appropriate the neoliberal governing rationality. Based on a rationality that normatively favours to 'regulate society by the market',[19] it instantiates this rationality as 'reality', and

---

[15] Alexander Wendt, 'On constitution and causation in international relations', *Review of International Studies* 24 (1998), pp. 101–17.

[16] Beach and Pedersen, *Process Tracing Methods*, p. 59; Andrew Bennett and Jeffrey T. Checkel, *Process Tracing. From Metaphor to Analytic Tool* (Cambridge: Cambridge University Press, 2015), p. 26.

[17] Beach and Pedersen, *Process Tracing Methods*, p. 61.

[18] Irving L. Janis, *Groupthink: Psychological Studies of Policy Decisions and Fiascoes* (Boston: Houghton Mifflin, 1983), pp. viii–ix.

[19] Michel Foucault, *Discipline and Punish: The Birth of the Prison* (New York: Vintage Books, 1978), p. 145.

the only reality that is of worth.[20] This is observable in the practice of dividing real knowledge vs particular knowledge, and hence the division of reasonable (as in economically useful) from irresponsible critique. Economization is not a top-down process, however. Critics also transform their agenda in such a way. Continuously, the terms of debate are economized, and the subjects concerned with governing assume this economized logic: Economization thereby contributes to an overall commensuration in that it 'changes the terms of what can be talked about, how we value, and how we treat what we value'.[21] This works slowly by 'establishing an order of truth by which conduct is both governed and measured'.[22] But what is economization exactly and how do we recognize it when we see it?

I define economization as the adoption of a neoliberal governing rationality and its utilitarian, cost-benefit maximizing and quantifying logic of social progress and its individualizing effects. This co-construction of a particular reality functions through the practice of rituals and repetition in the quest to confirm '*the being of what is* and its *value*'.[23] As one of the mechanisms of complex rule, economization is the process in which some significant parts of the critics assume this normative form of reason. While they may initially do this for instrumental purposes, they are increasingly governed by this rationality in further action. Combined with the other four mechanisms of complex rule, this contributes to the fragmentation of critique, since radical parts of the movement try to avoid this governing rationality, and resent its neoliberal language, rituals, instruments, and values. They can no longer be sure to be 'on the same side' with those parts of the movement that have already been – or are suspected to be – subsumed under neoliberal rationality. Economization as a mechanism can be observed on two sides, the institutional and critical actors when it constructs and confirms the neoliberal governing rationality through subjects who engage in its repetition or assume its logic over time. This is observable in two classes of implications (observables), one institutional, one on the side of critique (see Table 4.1).

---

[20] Boltanski, *On Critique*, p. 75.

[21] Wendy N. Espeland and Mitchell L. Stevens, 'Commensuration as a social process', *Annual Review of Sociology* 24, 1 (1998), p. 315. It can well be argued that measurements undertaken in the context of economization (quantifying the world) are a property of positivism which would then be the overarching concept. Yet it also matters what is being measured. In global governance, particularly the governance of development, quantification is strongly geared towards economic, not just any, measurements. Therefore, I focus on this aspect because it guides practice more specifically than the overall reliance on positive measures in general. Thanks to Nicholas Onuf for this criticism.

[22] Brown, *Undoing the Demos*, p. 118.

[23] Boltanski, *On Critique*, p. 73, emphasis in original; see also Katja Freistein, 'Quantification as bureaucratic ritual' (Paper written for the ECPR General Conference, 2018).

Table 4.1: Economization and its observable implications

Mechanism 1: Economization	Observable in ...	
	Institutional practices	**Practices of critique**
	Dividing global vs particular knowledge	**Accepting neoliberal governing rationality:**
		• move from 'existential tests' to 'reality tests'
	Quantification	• usage of economic and technical language
		• adoption of ends
		vs delineation from economized logic
		→ **fights over basic values underlying the critique of the institution**

Institutional observations

Dividing global vs particular knowledge is the first institutional set of practices that serve as an indicator for economization. The division of global from particular knowledge renders ends as (economic) givens.[24] Since the ends of governance are presumed to be the only reality, they are excluded from conversation. This can be observed when the goals of specific operations are either left out, veiled, or alleged as givens. Neoliberal rationality is constructed as 'the' reality and the only reality through a division of real knowledge from particular forms of knowledge, the latter being subordinated to a less relevant status. This also refers to how critique is received and commented upon, critics being divided into reasonable and irresponsible forms. Since the ends are givens, dissent is likely to be called 'ideological'. Based on flat hierarchies, the opportunity to voice concerns, and the spirit of teamwork towards a better future for all (that is, economic progress), radical critique is ridiculed or presented as counter-productive and out of touch with reality. The realness of this reality is continuously confirmed through rituals that showcase the reality of the economized ends.

How exactly can this mechanism be observed in practice? The economization of a political debate may typically happen by making it about a time investment of the involved individuals, hence framing the conversation in an 'efficient' fashion. Questions that go beyond problem-solving within the given logic will consecutively be framed as unreasonable.

---

[24] Boltanski, *On Critique*, p. 105.

By a technical, seemingly non-political, agreement ('we all want to be constructive/forward-looking'), hard questions are shut out and the overarching goal of projects is beyond what can possibly be discussed. By this work of shifting the possible terms of debate towards a moderate and consensus-oriented approach within the framework of the given economic structure, radical interventions are rendered inappropriate. Matters of principle cannot be part of the discussion and will be excluded, reminding everyone involved to focus on 'implementation', expecting that everyone accepts the same economized principles. These principles will likely be kept vague ('development'/'progress'/'welfare') and to dispute them will seem absurd to many participants.[25]

The presupposition of ends as givens also grants the institution a special place. The institution, being conversant with the 'global' knowledge of the matters in question, represents the knowledge that is good for everyone. Therefore, the underlying goals of the goal-oriented debate are not up for debate themselves. The ends are already clear, because they must be oriented at the global knowledge that the institution possesses or produces. When 'development' for instance is set up as an uncontested goal, the World Bank Group is credited with expertise and, in turn, the principle itself becomes a representation of the institution, being bearer of this goal. If criticizing this knowledge, the critic is portrayed as driven by a particular agenda, even more so when her critique is delivered in a non-efficient way. This excludes other ways of looking at the issue in question. The confirmation of what already is may then be expressed through an openly communicated disbelief towards its critique. The critics' unwillingness to confirm with the terms of debate and its pragmatic, goal-oriented character can be portrayed as overly radical and ideological, as well as impolite, for it wastes the precious time of others who are ready to work 'efficiently'. Critics are, therefore, morally accused of making 'unrealistic' suggestions and hence disturbing a process which, despite their unawareness of it, is better for everyone. The economization of issues can hence be observed when ends are presumed as (economic) givens and thereby excluded from the discussion. Debates are rendered so abstract that 'everyone' agrees regarding these ends. Consecutively, the means are elaborated in a highly technical and financial language which potentially intimidates non-economists and neutralizes the approach of the institution so far that deviation must be 'ideological'. 'Reasonable' critique, on the other hand, remains within the means proposed by the institution.

Related to this, *quantification* is another observable for the mechanism of economization. The sociology of quantification has shown how numbers are

---

[25] See Ziai's analyses of 'development' as an empty signifier Ziai, 'Development: projects, power, and a poststructuralist perspective'.

increasingly guiding how we make sense of events, attributing significance to some and not others.[26] Quantification allows the valuation or measuring of different objects within a common metric.[27] This is practical and allows for better planning, but it also creates specific types of relationships by transforming all kinds of difference into quantity. By that, objects are encompassed under a shared cognitive system that incorporates every irritation into its logic. 'Difference or similarity is expressed as magnitude, as an interval on a metric, a precise matter of more or less'. Quantitative measures are therefore 'a key mechanism for the simplifying, classifying, comparing, and evaluating that is at the heart of disciplinary power'.[28] Two key effects of quantification are hence that (a) it attributes authority to those institutions that create or embody the statistics, and that (b) it disciplines others to think within the same logic. Through 'accountability' and 'transparency', metrics become ever more all-encompassing, making it easier for authorities to monitor and discipline subjects.[29] Quantification permits scrutiny of complex or disparate phenomena in ways that enable judgment.[30] This component of rule does not have to be legitimated, because 'reality' often is invoked by the producers and consumers of statistics, and the facts are regarded as 'self-evident'. A sociology of quantification must therefore interrogate this self-evidence, examining how it is established, implemented, and upheld as 'the reality'.[31]

In concrete political practice, quantification is observable when the progress in reaching the predefined ends must be measured in (economic) benchmarks. This is expressed in a utilitarian language as opposed to, for instance, subjective and embodied experience. Quantifiable 'facts' trump other forms of experience or documentation. Concrete stories from the life-worlds of individuals are disqualified from the debate. They do not confirm the reasonable and aggregated style of debate which is interested in the general good. Such 'stories' will then likely be ridiculed or ignored

---

[26] Wendy N. Espeland and Mitchell L. Stevens, 'A sociology of quantification', *Archives Europeennes de Sociologie* 49, 3 (2008), p. 405; see also Theodore Porter, *Trust in Numbers: The Pursuit of Objectivity in Science and Human Life* (Princeton: Princeton University Press, 1995).

[27] Espeland and Stevens, 'Commensuration as a social process'.

[28] Espeland and Stevens, 'A sociology of quantification', pp. 408–14.

[29] Wendy N. Espeland and Berit Vannebo, 'Accountability, quantification, and law', *Annual Review of Law and Social Science* 3 (2008), pp. 21–43.

[30] Sung-Joon Park, ' "Nobody is going to die": an ethnography of hope, indicators and improvizations in HIV treatment programmes in Uganda', in Richard Rottenburg et al. (eds) *The World of Indicators: The Making of Governmental Knowledge through Quantification* (Cambridge: Cambridge University Press, 2015), pp. 188–219.

[31] Alain Desrosieres, 'How "real" are statistics? Four possible attitudes', *Social Research* 68, 2 (2001), pp. 339–55.

by shifting back to a technical register that is more 'reasonable' than the particular values and knowledges transported in single stories. If this technical register is put into question or contrasted with a specific local grievance or morality, the critic must be irrational.

Practices of critique

Economization is not only reserved for institutions, it changes the methods and subjectivities of resistance movements as well. Quantification is, for instance, not only a change of descriptive categories; it influences how people see and interpret the world and plan to act upon it. Observing economization on the side of resistance is possible when the subject position of critics changes and moves towards an overt or covert acceptance of the neoliberal governing rationality. This process of economization contributes to the fragmentation of critique because parts of the critics accept the neoliberal governing rationality while others delineate themselves from it. This leads to fights within social movements over basic values underlying the critique of the institution.

Accepting the neoliberal governing rationality is the first of these observables. Since it is not directly visible how individuals and groups of individuals conceive their worlds, I further break this down into three indicators. First, we can observe the acceptance of a neoliberal governing rationality in a moving-away from what Boltanski calls 'existential tests' to 'reality tests'. For Boltanski, reality tests are reformist, while existential tests are radical.[32] Reality tests question the reality of reality, hence 'the validity of the forms of organization' with which agreed-upon norms shall be implemented. Existential tests, on the other hand, go beyond the agreed-upon. They are 'based on experiences, like those of injustice or humiliation, sometimes with the shame that accompanies them, but also, in other cases, the joy created by transgression'.[33] They hence fundamentally challenge the logic of the institution, or the 'rules of the game'. Together reality and existential tests make up the sphere of critique.[34] However, when critics move from existential tests to reality tests, they will be issuing increasingly 'realistic' forms of critique, oriented at the institution's governing rationality and with more 'rational' arguments instead of rage or joy.

Second, the adoption of economic and technical language by the critics is an important indicator. When critics take on the economized logic of

---

[32] Boltanski, *On Critique*, p. 103.
[33] Boltanski, *On Critique*, p. 107.
[34] 'Truth tests', in contrast, are the repertoire employed by institutions. Only symbolically questioning reality, they are 'instances of confirmation'.

the institution and try to argue in favour of their own goals in the terms of the institution, this is a strong sign for economization. Critics utilize the language of their adversary rhetorically to convince her of a line of action the outcome of which they would support, although they might have different reasons to the ones they give. Finally, an even stronger indication of the economization of critique is when not only the adoption of language but an adoption of ends can be observed. If critics increasingly take up arguments from the institutional governing rationality and start to adopt a non-controversial goal at the expense of more radical ones, for instance when they orient themselves at transparency and efficiency instead of justice, this is an indicator for economization.

Vs Delineation from economized logic: Not all critics are willing to adopt such an economized approach. When parts of the critique, instrumentally or not, economize in the previously described fashion, it is likely that other parts of their movement criticize this process. This is visible in internal debates on the terms of how far one should rhetorically approximate the economized logic of institutions to reach certain goals. This may be discussed as a tactical question, but these discussions can easily escalate and hold mutual accusations where the economized parts call the others illusionary or naïve, while the latter accuse the economized parts of serving the interests of the institution (or capital) because they have been subjugated to the neoliberal logic of their former opponents.

Fights over basic values underlying the critique of the institution: This creates debates on the question of who still represents the original cause of the movement. The accusations towards the economized groups, coupled with their tactical choice to side with institutions on some issues (for instance transparency), and hence toning down their language, creates economized subjects versus those ones who criticize such behaviour. The latter reacting with disbelief and frustration about the economization of the former, these processes are breaking the solidarity of the movement. The critics are then occupied with internal quarrels on what the original intention of the movement was, with the economized parts claiming reforms as their victories, and the radical groups ridiculing those as cheap handouts that reinforce the neoliberal logic. These fights touch such fundamental normative questions that they considerably fragment the critics with mutual accusations rampant on the two sides.

Mechanism 2: Incorporation

I outlined in Chapter 2 that complex rule in global governance is shaped by a specific order of justification. I argued that IOs such as the World Bank Group are reflexive, hence justifying themselves to their critics. Some of the critics, in turn, enter this order of justification while others remain outside of it, justifying themselves vis-à-vis other actors and in different grammars of justification. This contributes to the fragmentation of resistance. There are two mechanisms through which this dimension becomes instantiated: incorporation and legitimation. In the following, I outline what I mean by incorporation and how it is observable.

IOs increasingly must legitimize themselves reflexively to remain in a position of power. They must change constantly in order to survive, 'continually altering the contours of reality as if to inscribe the world in it, as a site of constant change'.[35] Reflexivity, in this sense, 'means self-transformation through self-confrontation'.[36] The opening-up of IOs is a proactive way of achieving such self-confrontation.

Several social movement scholars have highlighted the possible danger of inclusion for critics, hinting at the cooptation of social movement actors.[37] However, to be precise, we should not equate all forms of institutional access with cooptation.[38] It is conceptually possible to attend meetings inside an IO and not to change one's substantial position. Also, inside-outside tactics have been highlighted by many scholars.[39] If such an advocacy strategy is consciously drawn upon by activists, the concept of cooptation seems misleading, for it attributes a passive, almost naïve role to the social movement actors in question. For these reasons, the mechanism of incorporation is split in two observable parts (see Table 4.2). First, institutional opening-up itself is the practice of institutions to create fora for dialogue and policy exchange with CSOs.[40] On the side of the critics,

---

[35] Boltanski, *On Critique*, p. 123.

[36] Zürn, 'Global governance and legitimacy problems', p. 276.

[37] Patrick G. Coy and Timothy Hedeen, 'A stage model of social movement co-optation: community mediation in the United States', *Sociological Quarterly* 46, 3 (2005), pp. 405–35; Karen Nakamura, 'Resistance and co-optation: the Japanese Federation of the Deaf and its relations with state power', *Social Science Japan Journal* 5, 1 (2002), pp. 17–35; Tana Johnson, 'Cooperation, co-optation, competition, conflict: international bureaucracies and non-governmental organizations in an interdependent world', *Review of International Political Economy* 23, 5 (2016), pp. 737–67; Catherine Eschle and Bice Maiguashca, 'Reclaiming feminist futures: co-opted and progressive politics in a neo-liberal age', *Political Studies* 62, 3 (2014), pp. 634–51.

[38] Anderl, Daphi, and Deitelhoff, 'Keeping your enemies close?'; Jessica Duncan, *Food Security Governance: Civil Society Participation in the Committee on World Food Security* (Abingdon: Routledge, 2015).

[39] Piper and Uhlin, 'New perspectives on transnational activism'; María Elena Martínez-Torres and Peter M. Rosset, 'La Vía Campesina: the birth and evolution of a transnational social movement', *Journal of Peasant Studies* 37, 1 (2010), pp. 149–75; Lisa Maria Dellmuth and Jonas Tallberg, 'Advocacy strategies in global governance: inside versus outside lobbying', *Political Studies* 65, 3 (2017), pp. 705–23.

[40] Nele Kortendiek and Jens Steffek, 'Participatory governance in international organizations', in Hubert Heinelt (ed) *Edward Elgar Handbook on Participatory Governance* (Cheltenham: Edward Elgar, 2018), pp. 203–24.

Table 4.2: Incorporation and its observable implications

Mechanism 2: Incorporation	Observable in ...	
	Institutional practices	**Practices of critique**
	Procedural opening-up: access for CSOs	**Participation:** practices shift from protest (outside) to lobbying (inside) **vs non-participation** → **fights about participation or non-participation**
	Active cooptation: • hiring individuals from the movement • creating material incentives for moderate organizations	**Elevation of individuals:** individuals from movement raised as 'representatives'; accumulation of offices by professional civil society individuals → **irritation about the 'coopted' individuals and organizations**

the opening-up can lead to fragmentation, because some parts might decide to join these fora while others decline the offers of participation. Entangled but not equivalent with opening-up, second, institutions may actively try to coopt parts of their critics. My point is that both processes take place and, although they sometimes overlap, they can be analytically separated: the procedural opening-up towards civil society by international institutions is not yet a cooptation, although it may result in coopted activists. Active cooptation on the other hand exceeds opening-up. I will speak of active cooptation when critics are hired by institutions, when specific individuals from among the critics are elevated into prestigious positions, or when material incentives are created for politically moderate organizations or for organizations to become more moderate. This produces individuals or organizations among critics who receive more rights and an elevated status. These individuals, however, may be antagonized by other critics who call them 'coopted'. This antagonization fuels the fragmentation of a movement.

Institutional observations

In complex rule, repression is avoided to a large extent and there is an imperative for the governing institutions to be perceived as legitimate. In contrast to the truth tests common in oppression or repression, reality tests can be performed within complex domination. 'It is therefore precisely the establishment of a new kind of relationship between institutions and critique and, in a sense, the incorporation of critique into the routines of social life that characterizes these systems'.[41] They do not preclude change, and particular cases of tests (if not conducted 'excessively') are deemed legitimate. This changes the behaviour of both institutions and their critics, a development that can be empirically observed.

Procedural opening-up can be observed when institutions change their rules and grant access to the public, to specific CSOs or to affected people. Promising or granting institutional access is equally indicative of such opening-up, for the latter also hints at a greater appreciation of the target audience in the IO's legitimation efforts. Opening-up can be observed when an institution creates new fora for dialogue, invites civil society to existing fora, or when structural or ad-hoc consultation processes are introduced. Beyond the introduction of opportunities for dialogue, access can go further than that when IOs also include civil society into the planning of events and involve them in the drafting of programmes or let them make suggestions regarding the location and moderators of these fora. On a day-to-day basis, opening-up can be observed when institutions create regular channels through which critics can voice their issues, such as in open phone calls with NGOs, regular updates on mailing lists, or possibilities to share knowledge and co-produce content on open websites or servers. Opening-up refers to formal access. It does not signify a change in policy of the institution, nor does it guarantee that the points made by critics are taken seriously.

Active cooptation is indicated when an instrumental purpose behind such an opening-up can be proven. This is hence the much more presuppositional indicator which requires either a 'smoking gun'[42] or a very convincing case for the interpretation as intentional behaviour on the side of the institution. If all parties dealing with a process (institutional and oppositional actors for instance) agree with such an interpretation in interviews, this would be sufficient proof for an active cooptation, even without a 'smoking gun'. Further observable practices that indicate active cooptation are when an institution hires individuals from the ranks of critics that had been pressuring the institution beforehand. This is especially so when these individuals are put in positions where they must deal with their former peers and hence function as 'buffer zones' for the institution. It is also an observable for active cooptation when there are material incentives for specific moderate organizations or individuals to attend meetings, or when participating individuals are rewarded with jobs or other merits.

---

[41] Boltanski, *On Critique*, p. 127.
[42] Stephen Van Evera, *Guide to Methods for Students of Political Science* (Ithaca, NY: Cornell University Press, 1997), p. 32.

Practices of critique

On the side of the critics, the first indicator for incorporation is *participation*. The shifting from protest (outside) to lobbying (inside), can be seen as the other side of the coin of opening-up. It is observable when (parts of) the critics join the previously-mentioned fora for dialogue and consultation processes. This is not necessarily connected to a change in policy, nor does it necessarily mean that other repertoires of protest are abandoned. If other critics decline offers to access institutional meetings, this is an indicator for *non-participation*. Yet, it is not helpful to count every absence into this category. Otherwise, most humans would have to be counted here. Therefore, only the principled rejection of institutional offers for access shall be understood as non-participation. This can be observed when (a) advocacy networks assemble for strategy meetings and parts of them openly contest the plan of others to join institutional fora; (b) when critics make public statements against joining such consultation processes; or (c) when individuals retrospectively report in interviews that they did not seize these opportunities on principled grounds.

If both these indicators can be observed in response to a process of institutional opening-up, this is likely to lead to movement-internal *fights about participation or non-participation*. These can be observed in debates between those who decided to join institutional fora and those who did not. They can also happen during consultation processes when sections of the participants decide to leave the process on principled grounds. The more hostile these movement-internal debates are, the more strongly one can expect a rift within the critics which contributes to the overall fragmentation of the movement. If such processes happened in the past, one would need testimonies from both discursive positions to arrive at a solid indication that the observable processes indeed took place. If such debates cannot be observed, this indicates either a general trend for one of the two options (participation or non-participation) among critics, or a concerted inside-outside strategy. This can be reconstructed through interviews.

Second, the flipside of 'active cooptation' is observable in the *elevation of individuals* among the critics. This is visible when specific critics are put into positions where they earn more or have additional access, but also when they are staged as 'civil society representatives' and hence receive the possibility to speak 'for the movement' in public events of the institution. These processes will typically have the effect that the elevated individual will be handled equivalent to 'the critique' and allowed to say critical things inside the institution, yet within the 'rules of the game' of the institution and within a consensus that the institution itself is not to be attacked on radical terms.

If these processes take place, they lead to *irritation about the coopted* among the non-elevated critics. This can be observed when they (a) attend the meeting and talk negatively about the elevated individuals; (b) when they publicly distance themselves from these individuals; or (c) when they criticize the individual or gossip about them in interviews. Opportunities for some will hence provoke a division on the question of what effective advocacy looks like. The elevated status of a few critics will likely mobilize others to deny these individuals the right to even be conceived as 'critics': we can observe the breaking ties of solidarity between different factions.

Mechanism 3: Legitimation

With reference to theories of justification, I have outlined that a reflexive order of justification underlies complex rule in global governance. Beyond the incorporation of critics, institutions of open global governance are interested in establishing a particular reality as *common sense*. This is established through rituals and tests which delineate what kinds of statements are within, and what kind of statements are outside reality. Institutions hence play an enormous role in the preservation of reality, rendering imaginaries and specific ways of order-making possible, and others impossible. For this work of preserving the current order, institutions typically portray themselves as authorities with purely rational and technocratic proceedings. Yet, in a reflexive order of justification, the individuals working for the institutions are aware of the hermeneutic contradiction attached to this 'objective' work and need to legitimate their position vis-à-vis reflexive opponents. For this reason, and short of means to govern top-down, they need to explain themselves better in public discourse. They actively engage in 'learning' exercises and endorse critique (see also 'professionalization' further on). Nevertheless, they need to establish themselves as the experts in the field. This works through *legitimation*. This mechanism is observable on the institutional side in a specific way of arguing which refers to an objectified 'complexity' which is beyond the understanding of critics. It, furthermore, disarms critics by engaging with their arguments eulogistically without necessarily following up. On the side of the critics, the mechanism of legitimation is observable in their increasing willingness to engage pragmatically with the institutional arguments: The institution and its logic is increasingly taken for granted by parts of the movement. Yet, others reject granting legitimacy to the institution, which leads to an estrangement between the two groups, bolstering the overall fragmentation of critique (see Table 4.3).

Institutional observations

Legitimation works through the application of discourses which put institutional policies in a good light by way of normalizing practices and

Table 4.3: Legitimation and its observable implications

Mechanism 3: Legitimation	Observable in ...	
	Institutional practices	**Practices of critique**
	Arguing with complexity **Rhetorical disarming:** • schmoozing civil society actors • constructing a common goal • anticipating and diluting criticism	**Legitimating the self in accordance with the institutional order of justification:** • maximum demands lose traction • demands already framed as compromise • 'taken for grantedness' of institution **vs rejecting legitimation vis-à-vis institution** → **estrangement between 'weak' opposition and 'irresponsible' dissidents**

justifying reflexively their underlying imaginaries. They address member state governments, international institutions' staff, and the wider public.[43] Regarding the wider public, the legitimation strategies of IOs 'have to target very general and broad norms. Thus, they often aim at widely shared norms such as the promotion of the global common good and democratic governance'.[44] When directly faced with critics, these legitimation strategies are not enough, however.[45] For this particular arena of legitimation, two observable practices serve as indicators for institutional legitimation: arguing with complexity; and rhetorical disarming.

Arguing with complexity is a rhetorical tactic that can be observed in the 'quest for legitimacy' of IOs. These rhetorical practices highlight a particular factual constraint due to a complex situation, either internal or external to the institution. One such aspect of complexity is the multi-layered process of decision-making in the institution; legitimacy is portrayed with reference to democracy.[46] Since staff members of international institutions are reflecting on their own position vis-à-vis their critics, they consider the

---

[43] Ecker-Ehrhardt, 'Self-legitimation in the face of politicization', p. 527.

[44] Gronau and Schmidtke, 'The quest for legitimacy in world politics', p. 545.

[45] Klaus Dingwerth et al., *International Organizations under Pressure: Legitimating Global Governance in Challenging Times* (Oxford: Oxford University Press, 2019).

[46] Dingwerth, Schmidtke, and Weise, 'The rise of democratic legitimation'; see also Hans Agné, Lisa Maria Dellmuth, and Jonas Tallberg, 'Does stakeholder involvement foster democratic legitimacy in international organizations? An empirical assessment of a normative theory', *The Review of International Organizations* 10, 4 (2015), pp. 465–88.

latter's preferences and attribute problems to institutional patterns that these would perceive as legitimate.[47]

Knowing that many critics are in favour of deepening democracy as well as global justice, they highlight the complexities that arise from just those principles. The 'internal' democracy of the institution may be invoked.[48] In the case of the World Bank Group this is the Board of Directors where all member states are represented. Furthermore, external complexities such as geographical representation and heterogenous ideas about governance may be drawn upon. In the eyes of critics, both examples are likely perceived as 'legitimate'. Therefore, critique can be encountered by giving these complexities as reasons for failure or contested policy decisions, be they in fact influenced by these complexities or not. Sharp criticism can be portrayed as not complex enough. The argument of institutional complexity hence works as a legitimation tool for institutional staff in contested fields, positioning themselves as progressive allies without, however, any means for critics to hold them accountable, because tracing the institutional pathways would be 'too complex'.

Rhetorical disarming is the second set of practices indicating of institutional legitimation in complex rule. This includes the anticipation and dilution of criticism, the construction of a common goal, as well as the outright schmoozing of critical actors. *The anticipation and dilution of criticism* can be observed in rhetorical practice when critique is taken up and rhetorically accepted. The institution portrays itself as open and accepting in the face of criticism or assures critics that they are already aware of problems raised and will take care of them. Such a rhetoric makes it hard for critics to press a certain issue, because the institution does not contest it, hence it would seem ridiculous to fight the institution on this point.[49] This act of legitimation may or may not be followed by a real political change. If the issue remains only rhetorical, this is a strong indicator for legitimation.

Another such indicator is the *schmoozing of civil society actors*. It is observable when a specific actor from among the critics (an individual or an organization) is picked by the institution and presented as 'reasonable', or more aware of the complex issues than others. They are selected for prestigious positions and get a seat at the table. Furthermore, they are mentioned in public by the institution as 'partners' or positive examples.[50] This can be a double-edged sword for critics who may feel flattered but also endangered to lose their critical image in favour of

---

[47] See Tobias Lenz and Lora Anne Viola, 'Legitimacy and institutional change in international organisations: a cognitive approach', *Review of International Studies* 43, 5 (2017), pp. 1–23.

[48] Catherine Weaver and Stephen C. Nelson, 'Organizational culture', in Jacob Katz Cogan, Ian Hurd, and Ian Johnstone (eds) *The Oxford Handbook of International Organizations* (Oxford: Oxford University Press, 2017), p. 920.

[49] Catherine Weaver, *Hypocrisy Trap: The World Bank and the Poverty of Reform* (Princeton: Princeton University Press, 2009), p. 7.

[50] Uhlin and Kalm, *Civil Society and the Governance of Development*, p. 112.

a conventional one. We can expect the schmoozing of specific critics particularly in moments of crisis, when institutional staff try to create new alliances with critical actors, or to break the unity of actors assembled in opposition to them.

Constructing a common goal is the final observable for rhetorical disarming, signalling the mechanism of legitimation. Besides the rhetorical schmoozing of specific, moderate critics, institutions also try to rhetorically disarm their critics by constructing a common goal and highlighting the great pains to which they themselves went because this goal was important to them. This can be observed when institutional representatives emphasize agreement with their critics or when they highlight the parts of their own plans which they expect to converge with the major concerns of critics. In all the aforementioned indicators, the openness for critique and the ability to criticize the self is expected to have a disarming effect on (parts of) the critique. They are not necessarily tactical in kind, however. These practices can also be a form of honest appreciation of critics.

Practices of critique

On the side of the critics, legitimation can be observed when they legitimate the self in accordance with the institutional order of justification. This practice is observable when maximum demands of the movement lose traction and their claims are, instead, increasingly framed as compromises already. Furthermore, when activists take for granted what the institution offers to them as possible tableaux of options, this indicates high levels of the legitimation of complex rule. This is, however, unlikely to happen in an uncontested fashion. Other parts of the movement can be expected to reject this legitimation vis-à-vis the institution and feel accountable to other actors and discourses. They reject the rules of the game and the legitimizing requirements of the institution. This leads to the estrangement between those who have internalized the institutional order of justification and therefore perceive the maximalists who remain outside as irresponsible. The latter, on the contrary, are likely to feel that they stick to their roots and legitimate themselves to other radical actors, not granting legitimacy to the institution, while they think about their peers that these have become weak or mainstream, hence diminishing their solidarity with their former comrades.

Legitimating the self in accordance with the institutional order of justification can be observed when critics argue within the rules of the game. Maximum demands lose traction because the logic of the institution is either endorsed or thought to be impossible to circumvent.[51] In both cases, one can assume

---

[51] Magdalena Bexell, Jonas Tallberg, and Anders Uhlin, 'Democray in global governance: the promises and pitfalls of transnational actors', *Global Governance* 16, 1 (2010), p. 54.

a high degree of normalization and internalization. As Steffek argues, 'taken for grantedness is the best indicator for a successful legitimation process'.[52] The reference to 'rules of the game' already signifies that this indicator is close to 'participation' through which I observe the mechanism of incorporation. Arguing with the institutions on their terms may even seem self-evident when one decides to attend an institutional forum. Yet, the style of participating can vary strongly from interrupting meetings to critically intervening into the rules to simply accepting them as they are. If critics, furthermore, legitimate their own approach with reference to the institutional order, this strongly indicates that the institutional order of justification is taken for granted. Radical demands must lose traction in such conditions because they seem 'unrealistic' in the institutional order of justification. The more critics will adapt to this logic, the clearer the debate will be pragmatic and friendly instead of antagonistic and hostile. Actors are more understanding towards the issues of the respective other because they legitimize themselves according to the same order of justification.

This development is not uncontested. The legitimation of critics in accordance with the institutional order of justification is likely encountered by *a case for remaining radical*: I expect to observe such deviation in criticisms of the deliberative approach within a given institutional logic. The move to approximate the institution rhetorically is criticized and the increased understanding which may result in compromises based on an institutional logic is sharply attacked as false. These more radical actors highlight the issue of cooptation by questioning the logic of the institutions in general, contemplating more radical approaches and denigrating their peers who have internalized the institutional order of justification.

These rival approaches refer to two different audiences of legitimation.[53] Not only do IOs have different audiences to which they have to legitimate themselves, the critics feel similarly accountable to different, more or less radical, audiences. This leads to a split in their legitimacy communication, producing a general estrangement between 'weak' oppositionists and 'irresponsible' dissidents. In internal discussions, this is observable when one faction advertises for more acceptance and compromise, while the other faction makes the case for more aggression, denigrating the approach of the former as 'coopted'. This divide is strongly connected to the question what it would mean to 'win'. For the dissidents, the abolishing of the institution

---

[52] Jens Steffek, 'The power of rational discourse and the legitimacy of international governance', Florence, EUI Working Papers No. 2000/46, 2000, 22.

[53] Magdalena Bexell, Kristina Jönsson, and Nora Stappert, 'Whose legitimacy beliefs count? Targeted audiences in global governance legitimation processes', *Journal of International Relations and Development* 24, 2 (2020), pp. 483–508; Dingwerth et al., *International Organizations under Pressure*, p. 8.

and its core norms and practices remains the goal. The reformists, on the other hand, have internalized the institutional logic over the course of events. In principle, they believe in the legitimacy of the institution and are interested in making its practices less harmful. They measure success at the baseline of what is already there and think that the maximalist approach – to measure the institution against utopia – is irresponsible. This estrangement is so fundamental that it contributes to the fragmentation of the movement.

Mechanism 4: Professionalization

Complex rule, as opposed to simple rule, is set up as a managerial bureaucracy. Boltanski therefore uses the term 'managerial' interchangeably with 'complex'. I outlined earlier that this way of bureaucratization contributes to a depoliticized institutional environment in which conflicts are solved professionally and with reference to universal rules. The organization of complex rule is a rationalized one. This rationalization holds 'paradoxes' that make it hard to study.[54] As I discussed previously, this process is not 'good' or 'bad': it holds the promise of a less arbitrary rule, but it also swallows non-rational arguments, 'rationality' being defined by powerful institutions.

How can we study bureaucratic rule? Schlichte and Morcillo Laiz connect it to formal rationalization and offer two empirical indicators: the numeric calculation of means and the codification of rules as statutes.[55] Rationalization is an overarching concept which I also alluded to in the mechanism of economization where the numeric calculation of means (quantification) serves as an indicator. The second mechanism for bureaucratic rule, the codification of rules as statutes, will be discussed in the last mechanism (regulation). This should not gloss over Weber's equally important sociology of professions. Boltanski's emphasis on the managers highlights that complex rule is rationalized not despite of them but through them. Yet, in contrast to simple rule with slightly inert civil servants, complex rule is heavily dependent on dynamic expertise. This is in line with other analyses of global governance that find a strong trend in the 'rule of experts'.[56] The process underlying this trend is what I call professionalization.[57]

---

[54] Morcillo Laiz and Schlichte, 'Rationality and international domination', p. 190.

[55] Morcillo Laiz and Schlichte, 'Rationality and international domination'.

[56] Sending, *The Politics of Expertise*; Mitchell, *Rule of Experts*; Niilo Kauppi and Mikael R. Madsen, 'Fields of global governance: how transnational power elites can make global governance intelligible', *International Political Sociology* 8, 3 (2014), p. 327; Nele Kortendiek, 'How to govern mixed migration in Europe: transnational expert networks and knowledge creation in international organizations', *Global Networks* 21, 2 (2021), pp. 320–38.

[57] See also Maïka Sondarjee, 'Change and stability at the World Bank: inclusive practices and neoliberal technocratic rationality', *Third World Quarterly* 42, 2 (2020), pp. 348–65.

Table 4.4: Professionalization and its observable implications

Mechanism 4: Professionalization	Observable in ...	
	Institutional practices	Practices of critique
	New management style: external protest as productive irritation	**Sharing responsibility:** self-organization as 'civil society' within institutional frame **NGOization:** project logic and competition for funding; acceptance of 'civil society' label **vs stressing spontaneity and direct action** **→ decreasing trust levels between professionals and activists**

Professionalization can be observed on both sides (see Table 4.4): the institution adopts a neoliberal management style that embraces protest as a productive external irritation. It operates based on networks and projects and therefore reaches out to all sorts of communities, partners, and audiences. Furthermore, Management learns how to calm down complainants by applying their language instead of earlier confrontational modes. On the side of the movement, an *NGOization* can be observed.[58] These NGOs adopt roles within the institutions, for example they self-organize the civil society outreach of the World Bank Group. This makes them refrain from radical demands and it creates hierarchies within 'civil society' – between the professional ones and the old-school ('poorly informed') ones.

Institutional observations

The professionalization of institutions in complex rule can be observed in their taking-up of a new management style in line with New Public Management. The formerly inflexible and hierarchically organized structures of public institutions shift towards incentive-based and outcome-oriented management structures open to public dialogue and change. This development also applies to IOs. Their professionalization can be observed when 'managers' of the institution react to external protest in a pragmatic manner and frame it as a productive irritation that perfects their own operations rather than as a hostile

---

[58] Aziz Choudry and Dip Kapoor, *NGOization: Complicity, Contradictions and Prospects* (London: Zed Books, 2013).

attack. They will likely speak of 'learning' and organize platforms for mutual exchange. Part of this professionalization is, however, that the critique is expected to be brought forward in a particular way. The institution is ready to learn, yet only from critics who adopt the positive and forward-looking terms of debate. Managers try and move discussions in a less radical direction by appealing to the critics' sense of reality, competence, and eagerness to influence the proceedings. Influence is promised to those critics who behave professionally. They bureaucratize the exchange with critics, drawing less on emotions and more on formalities. Official institutional channels for handling external critique are implemented.

Institutional professionalization is visible when gatekeepers *formalize* the relations with critics and decide which critics are already professional enough to be involved in a pragmatic debate. Such a professionalization can be observed when managers react to contentious issues by highlighting how important these are for them, and by channelling them into institutional departments responsible for such questions. Instead of fighting the external challenge, it is professionally handled and dispatched, almost in a seller–customer relationship. The critics are exposed to the choice of either being reasonable – that is, to professionalize and to play their role alongside the offered channels – or to be 'unprofessional' and, by that, to spoil the process which was there to help the principles they stood for.

Practices of critique

Professionalization is also observable on the side of the critics who co-constitute this mechanism of complex rule. It is visible in an NGOization of critics, and hence a move from spontaneous direct-action movements to formalized advocacy groups, and the sharing of responsibility of these NGOs and their representatives who take over roles in the official interaction with the institutions. Other parts of the critique are dissatisfied with this professionalization and stress the qualities of non-formalized street-action. The disagreement among critics on the more effective or 'real' way of activism contributes to the overall fragmentation of critique.

NGOization is observable when critics increasingly accept the 'civil society' label attributed to them. They identify with or work for one organization which professionally lobbies the institution instead of protesting against it. This goes alongside the necessary project logic and competition for funding in such organizations. The logic of action shifts from disruption to productive influence and reform because these are measurable and can be presented as a tangible success of influencing politics. Critics become part of the 'indicator industrial complex'.[59]

---

[59] Beaumont and Towns, 'The rankings game', p. 5.

This change in organization is also mirrored in different, more professional advocacy strategies. Conscious empathizing with the opponent and trying to understand their position to find common ground is a sign of 'professionalized' advocacy in contrast to earlier, more radical, approaches drawing on scandalization and stressing the irreconcilable differences between the (bad) institution and (good) advocacy network. Professionalized NGOs see the value in consultation: they endorse the formalized bureaucratic culture and enjoy the grown opportunities for participation and exchange. Furthermore, closer relations between NGO staff and institutional staff and even staff swaps occur in a professionalized environment because these are simply jobs in a shared issue area, not hostile fronts in an irreconcilable conflict. When individuals among the critics switch jobs to the 'other side' after an exchange with the institution, this is a strong indicator for professionalization.

Sharing responsibility is another, even more far-reaching, indicator for professionalization based on the previously-described change of organizational culture in both the institution and the critics. Cherishing the fora that have been granted to critics, the latter would self-organize as 'civil society' within an institutional frame. This is observable when critics take over organizational burdens of the institution to guarantee a smooth running of events and watch over their peers so that these stick to the professionalized style of debate. This can be observed when they defend the norms and style of the institution and urge their colleagues to only make 'realistic' suggestions. They explain the process to newcomers and keep order. Professionalization is observable, furthermore, when critics formally designate representatives or speakers who make it easier for the institutions to communicate with their critics. These will then function as contact points for the institutions and in turn must justify their decisions in front of their colleagues, thus taking over organizational and policy-oriented responsibility of the institutions.

Other parts of the advocacy network distance themselves from this form of professionalization, instead *stressing spontaneity and direct-action.* These other critics reject the collaboration with institutions and the formal setup of NGOs, their hierarchies and market logic. They are likely to stress the advantages of less formalized – more direct – forms of action. The professionalization of some critics is therefore likely to provoke conflict inside social movements, the more radical parts lacking understanding for the professionalized ones who seem to care more about the institutional logic than for a resistant one. They can be expected to think that the 'professionalized' approach is a diluted one. In turn, the professionalized parts of the critics, organized in foundations, NGOs and other formalized organizations, may well look down upon those who have not yet understood how to *really* influence the institution. Condescending statements and lectures about how to play and use the rules of the game can follow.

Such a mutual estrangement between 'professionals' and 'activists' can lead to a relative strengthening of identities in the respective factions and be voiced in contempt for the approach of the other side of critics. It contributes to the breaking of solidarity between them. This can be observed in verbalized or non-verbalized form. Either it is observable in negative statements about the 'unprofessional' behaviour, or 'business-like', 'corporate' attitude of the other respectively. Or it is observable in non-verbalized statements, when professional critics roll their eyes at the esoteric practices of their peers; or when the radicals shake their heads, grin, or imitate sarcastically the overly assimilated behaviour of the self-acclaimed professionals. This mutual estrangement co-produces the overall fragmentation of critique and hence plays into the decline of social movements under complex rule.

Mechanism 5: Regulation

Subjective rights grant power to subjects which they would otherwise not have. If we understand subjects as holders of power, rights *subjectify* them in the sense of making them real subjects before the law. But rights are not only empowering, because the obligation of using them in a specific form is imposed on the subject at the same time.[60] Subjects are empowered by rights at the cost of bringing their thinking, acting, and feeling into a regulated form.

There are many studies on the 'legal' character of global governance, regarding specific legal cultures in IOs and how they affect advocacy,[61] a suspected 'global constitutionalism',[62] or a general 'legalization' of international politics.[63] There is a rough consensus that global governance is becoming increasingly legalized. For liberals, this is a normatively desirable process since it promises to overcome anarchy and strengthen peace. I am not inquiring whether there is more or less (enforceable) law and whether we are approaching global constitutionalism. Interested in the forms of subjectivation that critical actors are adopting in open global governance, I focus on rule-following, law being but one source of such rules.

Following Onuf, there are three types of rules: directive-rules (commands), commitment-rules (formal rights, contracts), and instruction rules

---

[60] Christoph Menke, *Kritik Der Rechte* (Berlin: Suhrkamp, 2015).
[61] Galit Sarfaty, *Values in Translation: Human Rights and the Culture of the World Bank* (Stanford: Stanford University Press, 2012).
[62] Nico Krisch, 'Global governance as public authority: an introduction', *International Journal of Constitutional Law* 10, 4 (2012), pp. 976–87; Jan Klabbers, Anne Peters, and Geir Ulfstein, *The Constitutionalization of International Law* (Oxford: Oxford University Press, 2009).
[63] Deitelhoff, 'The discursive process of legalization'.

(guidelines).[64] Although the infrastructure of global governance is provided by hard law (treaties creating institutions and granting formal powers, and so on), the interaction of institutions with their critics draws heavily on the latter type of rules. Onuf explains that all speech acts producing rules have regulative effects because all rules are regulative. If all rules are 'regulations', those rules produced by directive speech acts (commands) are one type of such regulation ('directive rules').[65] Therefore, to capture all kinds of rule-creation and rule-following – not only those captured by commands and obedience – I use the broader term regulation instead of legalization.

There is a debate whether instructions and conventions are rules at all. Some scholars insist on the distinction between constitutive and regulative rules. Habermas, for instance, acknowledges their normativity but not their regulative character.[66] I agree with Onuf that this distinction is arbitrary and unhelpful because 'all social rules, and not just instruction-rules, are necessarily and simultaneously constitutive and regulative'.[67] Whether requiring compliance or offering guidance, they regulate behaviour in a specific way. Even these instruction rules which are communicated and formalized in progress measurements, definitions, classifications, and guidelines are underpinned by a proto-legal reasoning which shapes the action of subjects who increasingly act in accordance with these rules and regulate their behaviour alongside them (they become *regulated*).

In practice, this can be observed as a formalization of rules underpinned by legal reasoning, or simply by 'rights-talk' of institutions.[68] Such 'legal reasoning' constitutes an increasing depth of a regulated logic (that is a rule-based framing of problems) being applied to potentially all aspects of institutionalized interaction, even if they are not technically regulated by a law. This works through the introduction of rules or through the rule-based framing of situations.[69] These rules (be they legally binding or not) instantiate rule, or to paraphrase Onuf: rule rules through rules.[70]

In complex rule, instruction rules in particular regulate behaviour through offering guidance, formalizing procedures, and structuring interaction in a regulated way. I define regulation as the successive

---

[64] Onuf, *World of Our Making*, pp. 85–8.

[65] Onuf, *World of Our Making*, p. 87.

[66] Jürgen Habermas, *Communication and the Evolution of Society* (Boston: Beacon Press, 1979), pp. 54–5.

[67] Onuf, *World of Our Making*, p. 86.

[68] Thanks to Nicholas Onuf for his critical comments on my previous attempt at conceptualizing rule formation and rule compliance.

[69] Lars C. Blichner and Anders Molander, 'Mapping juridification', *European Law Journal* 14, 1 (2008), p. 47.

[70] Onuf, *World of Our Making*.

Table 4.5: Regulation and its observable implications

Mechanism 5: Regulation	Observable in ...	
	Institutional practices	**Practices of critique**
	Creating rules. Ordering and disciplining of critique: • formalization of proceedings • introducing rules for participants **Justification based on rules**	**Endorsement of institutional rules and self-policing** **vs critique of regulated logic** → **forced or self-induced exclusion of groups and their claims 'external' to rules of the game**

creation, deepening, and formalization of rules with a disciplining effect on subjects. Regulation is observable on the institutional side when rules are created, and ordering/disciplinary techniques are developed or executed. On the side of the critics, I observe regulation when they endorse these rules and/or self-police to remain within the rules of the game (see Table 4.5). This will likely be contested by other critics which can lead to their dissociation from the regulated subjects and a forced or self-induced exclusion from the formalized interaction with institutions. This contributes to the overall fragmentation of critique and the erosion of solidarity-ties in the movement.

Institutional observations

On the side of the institution, regulation is observable in the creation of rules, the ordering and disciplining of critique and in the justification of political decisions with reference to rules. In political practice, the *creation of new rules* and the stricter application of existing rules can be seen when meetings or fora become formalized through accreditation procedures, when the format of an exchange is transformed into that of a formal conference, and when the actors eligible to speak, as well as the possible topics, are pre-selected by the institution. These processes are especially indicative for regulation when they enclose the possibilities of critique by the creation of rules and standardization procedures which limit the possibilities to disrupt for those critics who choose to (or are made to) abide by them. The steering effect of pre-selection can be observed when, over time, it preconfigures the possible subjectivities present at the encounters with institutions. If, for instance, the composition of critics changes over time and there is reason to believe that the non-attending parts of the critics were not able to meet the official criteria for registration, this would indicate a regulation. Inside these meetings, regulation can be observed when the forms of contention are pre-defined to rhetorical interventions in a technical debate of which the character has been imposed by rules of the institution.

In the context of such processes, *the ordering and disciplining of critique* can be observed when critics are reminded of specific rules, directly or indirectly limited or censored, or when they are positively induced to communicate in a specific, rule-based, way. Critics are responsibilized for outcomes of deliberations: a moral weight is put on institutional rules, which are said to not only support order itself but also lead to better outcomes. Legal comparisons from jurisdictions more legalized than global governance may serve as allegories to managers who couch their regulated reasoning therein. This can be observed when a critic's point is evaded by shifting the debate away from the substantial issue to the question of rights: who has the right to speak? Who has the right to decide? What are the right procedures for this issue? Concrete proposals or criticism are encountered by highly abstract and technical institutional arrangements. It is especially indicative of regulation when institutional actors demand from critics to subscribe to such abstract logic or otherwise not to make the argument at all; hence not to make invalid arguments from the lifeworld as opposed to the institutional world which is valid and can be encountered with regulated arguments alone.

Justification based on rules: regulation can also be observed when institutions react to criticism by retreating to a rule-based logic. They evade the political by putting forward a legal or quasi-legal reasoning which de-legitimizes critique by naming existing rules as an argument. The institution is then said to be right (in a legal sense). This may hold even though quite possibly in violation of the human rights of affected people, because the rules are that way – irrespective of whether the rules being externally-given or made by the institution itself. This can also be observed when institutions try to evade critique by framing the debate with technical terms from the regulatory realm. If critics bring up a contested issue and institutions re-brand the topic with less contested, more technical terms, this may therefore also be seen as an indicator for regulation. The critics' issues may be endorsed morally, but the institution's action will then be justified on legal grounds, or with reference to the rules of the game.

Practices of critique

The mechanism of regulation is not only instantiated by the institution but also by its critics. It can be observed when critics endorse specific institutional rules and engage in acts of self-policing. By that, they co-produce the increasing grip of institutional rules and the consecutive limitations arising from them. Other parts of the movement, however, reject this regulated approach and would rather have the system fall than to subsume themselves under its rules; they want to play a different *game* altogether.

Endorsement of institutional rules can be observed when activists take up the logic and habitual consequences of institutional rules and defend them vis-à-vis their fellow critics. This may be driven by an instrumental logic in which activists perceive these rules as an opportunity to put forward their agenda, by careerist goals, or by internalization. Activists may see a specific procedure as an opportunity for their cause and agree to the rules underlying its process. If the rules start to restrict substantial contributions, they may purport that once a specific game was joined, one shouldn't leave in the middle of the process or contest the rules one has agreed to. This leads to a rules-based, formalized advocacy rather than disruptive interventions.

Self-policing: building on the conviction that once you have agreed to rules, you should not discard them; or on the idea that – instrumentally – these rules may serve a specific purpose, individuals, or organizations remind their fellow critics to stick to the rules of the game. They publicly endorse these rules and thereby put pressure on fellow critics not to disturb the institutional logic and its formalized tools for interaction. It is a strong indication of this when critics self-police to the extent that they restrict themselves to specific advocacy goals and consciously omit others that do not accord with existing rules. It is also observable when interventions by critics will be followed by others who criticize that this kind of intervention is not viable (or allowed) in this institutional setting.

Vs opposing the regulated approach: this regulation of critique can be expected to provoke opposition from other critics. They will likely remind their peers of the values and methods of social movements and call for a different approach to resistance, drawing on street protests and direct action. They can be expected to express irritation about those who do defend the institutional rules. They may criticize an especially soft advocacy style in which grievances are left out in the spirit of pleasing the institution or playing along with a regulated organizational culture. They complain about a corset of rules and especially about their colleagues who endorse this form of interaction. Publicly, or among the critics, they complain about this increase in regulation and its effects on other critics. The limiting structure of 'open' fora is then highlighted. The inclusion into institutions may be perceived as restricting and authoritarian. Ensuing discussions about the validity of these rules and the expected annoyance of those who oppose them in the face of their peers, who endorse them, can be expected to cause trouble within the group of critics. If the rules of interaction get ever more self-evident to parts of critics, this regulation can lead to a forced or self-induced exclusion of groups and their claims 'external' to rules of the game: either they will be excluded by the institution, or they will increasingly dissociate from the institution and their regulated peers for they feel estranged by the whole setup of the interaction and its formalistic culture and proto-legal reasoning (see Table 4.6 for an overview).

Table 4.6: Dimensions and mechanisms of complex rule

Dimensions of complex rule	Mechanisms of complex rule	Observable in ...	
		Institutional practices	Practices of critique
Dimension 1 (ideological): a neoliberal governing rationality	Mechanism 1: Economization	Dividing global vs particular knowledge; quantification	Accepting neoliberal governing rationality vs delineation from economized logic → fights over basic values underlying the critique of institution
Dimension 2 (discursive): a reflexive order of justification	Mechanism 2: Incorporation	Procedural opening-up	Participation vs non-participation → fights about participation or non-participation
		Active cooptation	Elevation of individuals: → irritation about the 'coopted' individuals and NGOs
	Mechanism 3: Legitimation	Arguing with complexity; rhetorical disarming	Legitimating the self in accordance with the institutional order of justification vs rejecting legitimation vis-à-vis institution → estrangement between 'weak' opposition and 'irresponsible' dissidents
Dimension 3 (organizational): a managerial bureaucracy	Mechanism 4: Professionalization	New management style: external protest as productive irritation	Sharing responsibility, NGOization vs stressing spontaneity and direct action → decreasing trust between professionals and activists
	Mechanism 5: Regulation	Creating rules; ordering and disciplining critique; justification based on rules	Endorsement of institutional rules and self-policing vs critique of regulated logic → forced or self-induced exclusion of groups and their claims 'external' to rules of the game

5

A History of Interaction:
The World Bank Group and its
Early Critics

Although this is not a study of *the* Global Justice Movement, an analysis of the interaction between resistance groups and the World Bank Group must start from there. Not all groups of the Global Justice Movement are relevant to this study, but all groups that *are* did at one point in time associate with it. As I will outline, the big push for mass protests against the World Bank Group arose with the issue of Structural Adjustment Programs, a theme also foundational to the Global Justice Movement of which the 'origins lie in an earlier cycle of protests that took place in the Third World against structural adjustment policies'.[1] While this study is hence not *about* the overall movement, the latter is closely connected to – if not constituted by – the critique of the World Bank Group.

The Global Justice Movement was a loose assembly of various groups and individuals. Since it had varying ends and means, it also received various labels. While in the German and French context the labels *anti*, or *alter-*globalization movement were popular, in the Anglophone world the terms 'globalization from below', and the 'Global Justice Movement (GJM)' were widely used.[2] Daphi defines the GJM as a network of left groups active mostly between the mid-1990s and the late 2000s.[3] It was diverse in terms of geographical, socio-cultural and ideological backgrounds, and forms of organization, including both reformist and radical approaches, ranging from

---

[1] Valentine M. Moghadam, *Globalization and Social Movements: Islamism, Feminism, and the Global Justice Movement* (Lanham, MD: Rowman & Littlefield, 2009), p. 92.

[2] Catherine Eschle and Bice Maiguashca, *Making Feminist Sense of the Global Justice Movement* (Lanham: Rowman & Littlefield, 2010), p. 2.

[3] Priska Daphi, 'International solidarity in the global justice movement: coping with national and sectoral affinities', *Interface: A Journal for and about Social Movements* 6, 2 (2014), p. 164.

institutionalized organizations, such as trade unions, religious associations, and NGOs to grassroots groups, citizens' initiatives and direct action networks.[4] The GJM had a wide range of claims and mobilized around many different issues and was therefore dubbed the 'movement of movements'.[5] McMichael argues that three main frames coalesced in the GJM: environmentalism, feminism, and food sovereignty.[6] These overarching goals were sought by mobilizing 'around issues relating to the redistribution of resources as well as notions of justice, solidarity and democracy on a global scale'.[7] Although it included several issues, grievances and guiding principles, the common denominator was the fight against neoliberal globalization and the poverty, displacement and cultural domination it was alleged to cause.

The form of neoliberal globalization that the movement attacked was strongly associated with powerful transnational companies; therefore the movement regarded itself 'united in opposition to corporate tyranny',[8] which, in the eyes of the activists, was enabled by global governance organizations, particularly the World Bank Group, the World Trade Organization (WTO) and the IMF.[9] Resistance against policies of these IOs became visible particularly early in the context of Southern countries' debt, which was interpreted as both a symbol and a cause of unfair global distribution. Della Porta and colleagues show with their frame analysis what an important role the World Bank Group played as a symbolic antagonist for integrating the GJM.[10] The identity of the 'movement of movements' drew on a shared master frame which brought together the groups' different diagnostic and prognostic framing. Within this master frame, the various groups' differing interpretations (for example, international solidarity, communism, anti-capitalism) were merged into a shared definition of the problem (neoliberal

---

[4] Priska Daphi, 'International solidarity in the global justice movement', p. 164.

[5] Helen Hintjens, 'Appreciating the movement of the movements', *Development in Practice* 16, 6 (2006), pp. 628–43; Eschle and Maiguashca, *Critical Theories, International Relations and 'the Anti-Globalisation Movement'*, p. 6.

[6] Philip McMichael, *Development and Social Change: A Global Perspective* (London: Sage, 2017), pp. 179–211.

[7] Marco Giugni, Marko Bandler, and Nina Eggert, 'The global justice movement: how far does the classic social movement agenda go in explaining transnational contention?', Civil Society and Social Movements, UNRISD Working Papers, Geneva, 2006, 7, available at: {http://www.unrisd.org/unrisd/website/document.nsf/(httpPublications)/8647C 951DCB7E800C12571D1002D7BE4?OpenDocument}.

[8] Sarah Peart, 'What is the GJM', on the blog of the Scottish Socialist Party. Available at: {https://scottishsocialistparty.org/what-is-the-global-justice-movement/}.

[9] Ulrich Brand, 'Order and regulation: global governance as a hegemonic discourse of international politics?', *Review of International Political Economy* 12, 1 (2005), pp. 155–76.

[10] Donatella della Porta et al., *Globalization from Below: Transnational Activists and Protest Networks* (Minneapolis: University of Minnesota Press, 2007).

globalization), of culprits (IOs, particularly the World Bank) and of countermeasures, for instance the globalization of social rights.[11] The goal-dimension was characterized by a concrete will to stop exploitative practices, but also included utopian aspects.[12]

I am interested in the critique that was embodied by an activist network in the practice of actively contesting the World Bank Group. The Global Justice Movement played an exceptional part in this mobilization and, therefore, the history of this critique strongly overlaps with the histories of the movement which enabled and magnified the critique of the World Bank Group but was also created on its basis. To that effect, Daphi argues that:

> [a]cross all sectors, activists … identify the protests against the meeting of the IMF and World Bank in 1988 in Berlin as … important precursors of the Global Justice Movement, while not [yet] forming part of [it]. Activists describe how these protests brought together for the first time different groups around the issue of global finance such as environmental organizations, international solidarity groups and trade unions'.[13]

In what follows, I thus refer to the transnational network of activists that laid the grounds for the Global Justice Movement by starting to resist World Bank Group policies and organizing protests in the early 1980s. These activist groups were strongly influential in shaping the movement structures starting in the 1980s and succeeded to become a fully-fledged transnational social movement in the 1990s. After its peak around the millennium, many parts of the movement went into different directions, leaving behind an active and well-connected transnational activist network which has been continuing to draw on the GJM but can no longer itself be called a movement after the mid-2000s because they lack mass mobilization.

The strength of the GJM was its capacity to organize and uphold solidarity across a large variety of groups, ideologies and repertoires over a comparably long time-frame. The stamina also made the movement dangerous to its enemies, or in the words of one protester: 'If you go to a demonstration and then go home, that's something. But the people in power can live with that. What they can't live with is sustained pressure that keeps on building, groups that keep on doing things, people that learn from the last time and do it better next time …'[14]

---

[11] See also Daphi, *Becoming a Movement*, p. 21.
[12] Eschle and Maiguashca, *Critical Theories, International Relations and 'the Anti-Globalisation Movement'*, p. 105.
[13] *Daphi*, p. 44.
[14] Anonymous protester quoted in David Harvie et al., *Shut Them Down! The G8, Gleneagles 2005 and the Movement of Movements* (West Yorkshire: Dissent! and Autonomedia, 2005), p. 3.

The observed fragmentation of the movement that I outline in this book is therefore of political importance and the question *how it happened* is significant in light of this idea. This fragmentation did not only just occur because of the end of a movement cycle but stands in direct connection to specific measures by the World Bank Group and a number of mechanisms with different origins as I show in the following sections. I will now describe the beginning of the protests in the early 1980s until the millennium, highlighting their capacity to organize solidarity across a plurality of actors from a broad political spectrum, from outspokenly radical direct–action groups to reformist and institutionalized organizations. In the subsequent section, I will set out the reactions to these protests by the World Bank Group and describe how this changed the mode of interaction. This mode can be observed in several changes: the discussion is economized in its political horizon; moderate parts of the movement are drawn into the institution; the institution legitimizes itself and explains issues to the activists; a considerable part of the movement professionalizes its approach in NGOs, and the interaction is put under the roof of a rule-based procedure. All this contributes to the fragmentation of the movement and to its overall decline.

Radical resistance against the World Bank Group in the 1980s and 1990s

In the beginning of the 1980s, only a small number of (mostly US American) activists was concerned with the World Bank Group. They demanded environmental and social safeguards for its projects and publicized information about development schemes and their negative externalities for affected people. Their advocacy was strongly shaped by and heavily dependent on the leaking of documents from inside the World Bank Group (Interview, US-NGO). They built strategic alliances with individuals from the institutional management who gave them information on projects. Equipped with this knowledge, the activists were able to connect the World Bank Group's projects with outcomes and 'repeatedly focused on vivid cases of "development disasters" that revealed the bank's persistent difficulty in meeting its own promises of reform'.[15] They also delivered information to affected people at project sites and social movement actors in the respective countries, which would then organize decentralized protests. These activities brought environmental problems on the agenda of development policy. The World Bank Group had five employees responsible for the environment in

---

[15]   Jonathan A. Fox, 'Introduction: framing the inspection panel', in Dana Clark, Jonathan Fox, and Kay Treakle (eds) *Demanding Accountability. Civil-Society Claims and the World Bank Inspection Panel* (Lanham: Rowman & Littlefield, 2003), p. xiii.

1985, a number that increased to 270 in 1990.[16] It was made responsible and 'caught in the hot reflective glare of burning rain forests and dam-displaced villages'.[17] Environmental problems hence constituted the primary entrance point for public protest during the early 1980s.

During this time, a limited number of advocacy NGOs coordinated the campaign against the World Bank Group, among them the Environmental Defense Fund (EDF) as a driving force. In the mid-1980s, a number of Direct-Action Groups had also started protesting against the World Bank Group, particularly the Rainforest Action Groups (RAGs). One of their founders told me that his group heard about the neoliberal agenda of the IOs and the destructive nature of their extractive projects, and "so we kind of added that to our demonstration list, [practicing] civil disobedience and organizing, and we would bring in indigenous peoples and then let them speak on their own behalf around their own concerns" (Interview, US activist). In 1985, the RAG Network had 150 local RAGs in the US and Europe, and a Rainforest Information Centre in Australia. "That was at least a bit of a movement in addition to the civil society energy" (Interview, US activist). The network concerned with the World Bank Group hence grew bigger and more diverse in terms of tactics.

The big push came as a reaction to the structural adjustment policies. Pre-empting the Washington Consensus, in the early 1980s the World Bank Group reacted to the scarcity of capital in its borrowing countries by creating a

> propitious environment for the counterrevolution in development thought. ... Taking advantage of the financial straits of many low- and middle-income countries, [they] foisted on them measures of 'structural adjustment' that did nothing to improve their position in the global hierarchy of wealth but greatly facilitated the redirection of capital flows toward sustaining the revival of US wealth and power.[18]

In a situation of several states defaulting (such as Mexico in 1982), this austerity policy received furious criticism. Protests grew rapidly in size and aggressiveness in the indebted countries, predominantly in Latin America and Southeast Asia. The issue was suitable for organizing Third World Solidarity Groups in the North, but particularly for self-organized

---

[16] Bruce Rich, *Foreclosing the Future: The World Bank and the Politics of Environmental Destruction* (New York: Island Press, 2013), p. 17.

[17] Fox, 'Introduction: framing the inspection panel', p. xiii.

[18] Giovanni Arrighi, 'The world economy and the cold war, 1970–1985', in Melvyn P. Leffler and Odd Arne Westad (eds) *The Cambridge History of the Cold War, Volume 3* (Cambridge: Cambridge University Press, 2010), p. 35.

anti-imperialist protests in the Global South. These 'localized' anti-debt riots were culminating in the mid-1980s.[19] This is also reflected in increased levels of organization. One of the most influential national advocacy groups of the 1990s, the Freedom from Debt Coalition (FDC) was founded in 1988 in the Philippines.[20] From the perspective of labour unions, too, the World Bank Group and IMF started to be adversaries in the mid-1980s because of Structural Adjustment Programs (Interview, US labour union). Coordinated by the International Trade Union Confederation (ITUC), unions suddenly observed closely the work of international financial institutions (IFIs), and these unions became paramount for the mass demonstrations within the next two decades.

Thus, in the mid-1980s, momentum was created, bringing anti-debt activists and environmentalists together to mobilize a first big demonstration at the World Bank Group's Annual Meeting in 1986. Not only was the network able to cohere various issue-based groups, but it also accommodated varying protest repertoires. The Rainforest Action Network, together with other groups, convened a Citizen's Conference followed by an international day of demonstrations at the World Bank Group's headquarters. At the end of the conference, a first act of civil disobedience was executed: RAGs chained themselves to the World Bank building and put up a huge poster at the headquarters. In terms of issues, these environmentalists, highlighting the World Bank Group's role in tropical rainforest destruction, actively constructed bridging narratives towards the anti-debt groups in their rhetoric: 'By bankrolling mega-projects in the world's most sensitive ecosystems, the World Bank was paving the way for irresponsible development and imposing mountains of debt on the world's poorest countries'.[21]

1986 can hence be seen as the first coalition-building across sectors and protest repertoires that led to the disruption of a World Bank Group Summit. This was a big success for the organizers in Washington DC. However, the activists understood the main harm was done not to them but to people living in poor countries far away from the World Bank Group headquarters. These were suffering from resettlement, environmental destruction, and high national debt rates – without necessarily knowing that the IO was responsible for, or at least connected to, their grievances. Therefore, protests in countries of the Global South, although they already occurred on a massive scale in the 1980s, were hard to bind together. Furthermore, some local protests

---

[19] Ruth Reitan, *Global Activism* (New York: Routledge, 2007), p. 69.
[20] Uhlin and Kalm, *Civil Society and the Governance of Development*, p. 104.
[21] See the history on 'catalyzing a movement' online, available at: {https://www.ran.org/catalyzing-movement}.

against projects came too late because local organizers were not aware of the World Bank Group's plans and could only react once it was too late for an intervention.

Because of these problems, in 1987, Washington DC-based activists founded the Bank Information Center (BIC). Its original mandate was to get access to planning and policy documents. These documents were sometimes even public.

> 'But it was so esoteric, if you didn't know how to find them and get them, and certainly if you lived in Argentina where the dam was gonna be build or, you know, in Ivory Coast, or on the Island of Borneo, you certainly couldn't get access to the stuff or understand how that worked. And some of the main groups, like EDF ... they're international people, they knew how to get those things, but they didn't have the ability to systematically get those documents around the world to the environmental, the civil society groups in those countries early in the process when you may be able to stop a project. So, the original mission of the Bank Information Center was: Get those documents and ... get them out to those countries, systematically.' (Interview, US activist)

An early warning network was created. Fed with information from Washington DC, activists knew how to approach groups from affected communities: "We knew the international network, the main groups around the world, whether it was Friends of the Earth Nigeria, Friends of the Earth Malaysia, precursors to the Third World Network and the Global South groups" (Interview, US activist).

1988 in Berlin: the beginning of a movement?

In 1985, the IMF and the World Bank Group officially announced they would be holding their Annual Meeting of 1988 in Berlin. Providing fertile grounds for large-scale protests, Berlin's left-wing subcultures immediately started to plan the events around that summit. The 'Alternative List' (a local election collective close to the German Green Party), as well as peace activists and labour unions started preparing a counterprogram that built on the 1986 experiences at the counter-summit in the US. Furthermore, groups from the autonomous and anarchist radical left prepared the summit on their respective terms.[22] The extraordinary feature of the eventual protests was the capacity of these various groups to coalesce under one protest framework,

---

[22] See for the following the report 'We will disrupt this conference' by 'Dissent', available at: {https://web.archive.org/web/20051219063747/http://www.daysofdissent.org.uk/berlin.htm}.

although preferring different tactics and orienting themselves at strongly different political trajectories.

From the early planning phase on, there were two factions – even within the autonomous block: one wanted to physically undermine the Annual Meeting by blocking the proceedings, and the other 'regarded this as "illusionary action-ism" and placed more importance upon the development of theoretical discussions'. Furthermore, there was wide disagreement on whether one should cooperate with the other groups sceptical of the IFIs or whether a 'pure' action-centred disruption would be preferable. A central role in coalition-building fell to the Bundeskoordination Internationalismus (BUKO) which hosted Third World solidarity campaigns, fair-trade groups, church groups and direct-action networks. Within BUKO, two factions quarrelled whether this was *the* chance to go mainstream with specific issues by adopting a moderate position, or whether to signal strong dissidence to the World Bank Group and IMF by focusing on street action. In the end, the network decided on a common agenda: debt relief for the poorest nations, and reform of the institutions through stronger involvement of poor countries as the main policy goals; and the organization of one big and peaceful rally and counter-conference to the summit. More importantly, it decided to support both, one big demonstration and counter-conference, as well as the autonomist 'days of action' that were being planned simultaneously.[23]

Similarly, the autonomous scene was divided on the cooperation with BUKO. While the agenda discussed there seemed very moderate to the radical left, they saw the need for a big rally. Of course, there were very different ideas about the form such a rally should take; yet the involved groups managed to cohere because the autonomous scene temporarily overcame its differences and announced a vague common campaign slogan: 'We will prevent this Conference!' It was signed, 'Autonomous Groups of West Berlin'.[24] This symbolic openness was meant to enable a new anti-imperialist wave,[25] which allowed many other groups to join in and finally led to a counter-summit that prefigured the Global Justice Movement 'while not forming part of [it]'.[26] A large coalition of groups such as 'hippies' and 'punks' – otherwise rather hostile towards each other – coalesced alongside a common frame.

---

[23] See a report by the German newspaper 'Taz', available at: {http://www.taz.de/!1865 378/}.

[24] Jan Schwarzmeier, *Die Autonomen: Zwischen Subkultur Und Sozialer Bewegung* (Göttingen: Dissertation: Universität Göttingen, 2001), p. 134.

[25] Thomas Klein, *'Frieden Und Gerechtigkeit!' Die Politisierung der Unabhängigen Friedensbewegung in Ost-Berlin während der 80er Jahre*, (Köln: Böhlau, 2007), p. 419.

[26] Daphi, *Becoming a Movement*, p. 44.

Seen from today, when it has become common practice of moderate left groups to dissociate from radical protests around the Annual Meetings (discussed later), it is telling to look at 1988 through the eyes of an autonomous activist:

> One sign of 'unity' within the campaign appeared when the Rote Zora, a women's guerrilla group, carried out arson attacks at the HQ of Adler and eight of its other buildings. Adler were targeted as an act of solidarity with striking workers in their South Korean factories. The communiqué referred directly to the IMF/World Bank campaign. The autonomists saw the action as an example of an action form worth repeating, and, surprisingly, there were none of the usual condemnations by the reformists![27]

The ensuing militant campaign against the IFIs kicked off in April 1988 with arson attacks on six banks. In even stronger contrast to what I describe about the later interactions of activists and the World Bank Group after the latter's opening-up, the left-leaning newspaper 'Taz', had to cancel its plan to organize its own conference in the forerun to the Annual Meeting, because its idea to invite critics as well as representatives of the institution was not acceptable to large parts of the resistance in 1988.

1990s: the movement is growing

From that point onwards, there were mobilizations around every Annual Meeting, the only exception being 1991, when the transnational activist network decided not to protest at the meeting in Bangkok out of respect for the Thai progressive movement whose organizers were in danger from the repressive regime (Interview, US activist). There were many reasons why the movement attracted an increasing number of activists from various sectors. An issue that structurally favoured NGOs and other organizers over the World Bank Group in the 1990s was the Internet. One activist reflected that "we were used to working together completely informally, while in the administrations, there is the chain of command. The information goes up and over and then down again. Not at all how the Internet works" (Interview, US NGO). Other reasons for the increasing size and reception of the mobilizations were two very effective campaigns: the activism around the Narmada dam, as well as the "50 years is enough" campaign.

While infrastructure projects in the Global South financed by the World Bank Group had been subject to criticism before, the Narmada Valley

---

[27] 'We will disrupt this conference'.

Development Project in India was probably the most globally contested one.[28] The project was in fact a conglomerate of 3,200 dam projects threatening to leave 800,000 indigenous people without their lands.[29] The biggest of the many dams was 'Sardar Sarovar' in Gujarat. The government of India promised that this multi-purpose dam would irrigate more than 1.8 m hectares and bring drinking water to drought-prone areas. Opponents claimed that these benefits were vastly exaggerated, and that more than 300,000 people (60 per cent of them indigenous) had to be displaced for this dam alone. A grassroots movement, the Narmada Bachao Andolan (NBA) resisted the project, building on Gandhian principles of nonviolence, and criticized its social impact as well as the lack of an environmental assessment. They were increasingly able to gain international support and media attention. Late in 1990, thousands of people began a 'long march' across three Indian states that would be affected by the project. They wanted international publicity but were also ready to halt construction through peaceful occupation of the dam site. A standoff with the police ensued, leading to a hunger strike whose participants demanded a comprehensive review of the project.[30] Twenty-six days later, the fasters succeeded: because of the huge outrage, particularly in the US, an external commission to review the project in India was put in place.

The World Bank Group was forced to react to the international outrage created in solidarity with the Indian activists. A review was published in 1992 around the Rio Earth Conference of the United Nations, leading to the introduction of the Inspection Panel in 1993 (explained later). Furthermore, the discussion led to the introduction of the World Commission on Dams (WCD), an international multi-stakeholder initiative introduced commonly by the World Bank and the International Union for the Conservation of Nature (IUCN) in 1997 as a response to the never-ending protests, even after the World Bank Group had withdrawn from the Narmada Project.[31] The Commission had the mandate to review the development effectiveness of large dams and develop guidelines for

---

28 Aram Ziai, 'Can the subaltern file claims? The World Bank Inspection Panel and subaltern articulation', *Momentum Quarterly: Journal for Societal Progress* 5, 4 (2017), p. 258; Bruce Rich, *Mortgaging the Earth: The World Bank, Environmental Impoverishment, and the Crisis of Development* (London: Earthscan, 1994).

29 Praadeep S. Mehta, 'Fury over a river', in Kevin Danaher (ed) *50 Years Is Enough: The Case Against The World Bank and the International Monetary Fund* (Boston: South End Press, 1994), p. 117.

30 Dana Clark, 'Understanding the World Bank Inspection Panel', in Dana Clark, Jonathan Fox, and Kay Treakle (eds) *Demanding Accountability. Civil-Society Claims and the World Bank Inspection Panel* (Lanham, MD: Rowman & Littlefield, 2003), pp. 3–4.

31 See the documentation page by International Rivers, available at: {https://www.internationalrivers.org/campaigns/the-world-commission-on-dams}.

the planning, construction and operation of dams. The WCD found that 'in too many cases an unacceptable and often unnecessary price has been paid to secure those benefits, especially in social and environmental terms, by people displaced, by communities downstream, by taxpayers and by the natural environment'.[32] The report, launched under Nelson Mandela's patronage, agreed with many of the critics' concerns. The World Bank Group pledged to stick to stricter safeguards and to install a new resettlement policy. Yet, if the World Bank Group had reasoned that this externally forced reaction would cool down the protests, these hopes were in vain. On the contrary, in 1994, the biggest international campaign so far was staged: '50 years is enough!'

50 Years Is Enough developed into an effective network, counting over 205 associations as their members in 1999.[33] The aim was to show the world that the World Bank's 50th birthday was no reason for celebration; that those who should be profiting from the institution's development aid were in fact sick of the neoliberal austerity regime, the destruction of nature and the forced resettlements. Staging the campaign, the Annual Meeting in Madrid developed into a mass protest, scaring World Bank Group management with 'vigorous protests'.[34] The institution hired a 'public-relations troubleshooter' to counter the negative impact in the media, yet the protesters were already at the top of their game, blending in several generations of protest. One of the more senior protesters remembered his cooperation with European student organizations who had joined in:

> 'They all were spike-headed, you know, wonderful students with purple hair and often smart as hell on the issues, but they were pretty identifiable in the crowd. I've got about 19 civil disobedience arrests [laughs] on my belt. And anyway, I almost always try to wear a suit and tie when I get arrested, so that I don't look like an ageing Hippie – which I am [laughs]. But I had a suit and tie on and ... just sat down in the middle of a four-lane highway when the limousines full of finance ministers were coming up the road to go to the meeting. They created a break and then, as the police ran over to get me, you know, 60, 80, other activists were there waiting, waiting just to rush through, to breaking the line and then join me in the middle street, which they did.' (Interview, US activist)

---

[32] The World Commission on Dams, *Dams and Development: A New Framework for Decision-Making. The Report of the World Commission on Dams* (London: Earthscan, 2000).

[33] O'Brien et al., *Contesting Global Governance*, p. 172.

[34] James D. Wolfensohn, *A Global Life: My Journey among Rich and Poor, from Sydney to Wall Street to the World Bank* (New York: Public Affairs, 2010), p. 261.

Newly developed, creative repertoires of contention were probed; a winning spirit proliferated and major groups such as Greenpeace joined the protests: while the Spanish King Juan Carlos was addressing the participants in the meeting's huge exhibition hall, two of their activists climbed to the top and showered the attendants with fake dollar bills carrying the slogan 'No $s for Ozone Layer Destruction'.[35] Unsurprisingly, in the course of the campaign, the diversity of the movement also led to internal irritations. When many church groups actively joined the protests in 1994, the more radical ones were annoyed by their apologetic attitude: "50 Years is Enough was a bunch of religious groups, and … religious people by nature tend to be naive people, they wanna give you a chance. They're not go-for-the-throat activists, they're not hard-nosed Rainforest-Action-Network-civil-disobedience types" (Interview, US activist).

Retrospectively, this activist even thought that 50 Years is Enough was a strategic mistake, because "there is a way in which the Bank manipulates pressure in opposition and referring to it as 'set the clock back to zero'" (Interview, US activist). He remembered that already in the mid- and late 1980s, when campaigns on the World Bank's tropical rainforest and indigenous peoples' policies were rampant, the institutional staff had answered by saying: "Okay, you're right, over the last ten, 20 years we've made a lot of mistakes but now, you've pointed it out, so we will set the clock back to zero, and don't criticize us anymore, and give us a chance to do it correctly and judge us on our future work". Looking back at the campaigns in the 1990s, he added: "you can see two, three, four cycles of this 'set the clock back to zero'. And then you look over 40 years and you don't see very substantial change in the portfolio, what actually gets funded and the destruction that it does to the natural system" (Interview, US activist).

Approaching the millennium: peak turmoil

These slight tensions between groups were strategically bridged and the different strands of social movements strongly coalesced. The network grew enormously, fed into the Global Justice Movement, and was fed by it in return, to a degree that, by then, it had become synonymous with the movement. In order to understand how and why this happened, Daphi's account of the movement's shared narrative is helpful.[36] Using Germany as an example, she shows that '[w]hile a first critique of international institutions developed as early as in the late 1980s … it was not until the late 1990s

---

[35] See World Heritage Encyclopedia, available at: {http://self.gutenberg.org/articles/eng/anti-globalization_movement}.

[36] Daphi, *Becoming a Movement*, pp. 63–86.

that mobilisations for global justice took off at a larger scale'.[37] The Annual Meeting in 2000 mobilized new activist groups in Europe, particularly its Eastern countries, against the World Bank Group. These groups had not been active on international issues before but remained a part of the movement afterwards.[38] This shows the enormous importance of the mobilizations against international summits, especially those of the World Bank Group and the IMF for 'becoming' the GJM.

The merging of different strands of the movement can be seen in the integration of organizational structures. For instance, the Ruckus Society, a direct-action network which had been largely responsible for the planning and execution of the WTO summit protests of Seattle in 1999, was repeating its practice in a leading role one year later at the World Bank Group.[39] Huge protests followed. With respect to the World Bank Group, the Annual Meeting 2000 in Prague marked the peak of these activities. In 2001, shortly after the 9/11 terrorist attacks, no Annual Meeting was convened.[40] Another major asset in building up the movement was the integration of trade unions. Although large parts of their base were not very interested in international issues, the organizers were able to mobilize them during the formation of the Global Justice Movement, which led to a significant increase in the numbers of anti-summit demonstrations (Interview, labour union). One activist estimated "that probably 85 per cent of the people in the streets in Seattle against the WTO were labour union people. And yeah, there were the save the turtle people (laughs) and the rainforest people and environmental people, but the bulk of the number were labour unions" (Interview, US activist).

In the euphoria of movement success in Seattle, the Prague Annual Meetings in 2000 met this overall spirit (see Chapter 6). 'Anti-capitalist activists describe the early end of the IMF and World Bank summit in Prague in 2000 as "the validity of a new way of finding ourselves side by side in the world's streets, confronting global problems"'.[41] As Graeber has argued with reference to direct-action groups, 'Prague was in many ways just extraordinary'.[42] He describes how activists had attended trainings on consensus building in the preparatory phase and had managed to facilitate a council. Quoting one activist, he illustrates that many had expected the

---

[37] Daphi, *Becoming a Movement*, p. 6.

[38] Daphi, *Becoming a Movement*, p. 11.

[39] John D. Clark, 'The World Bank and civil society: an evolving experience', in Jan Aart Scholte and Albrecht Schnabel (eds) *Civil Society and Global Finance* (London: Routledge, 2002), pp. 111–27.

[40] See the IMF history page, available at: {https://www.imf.org/external/am/2001/index.htm}.

[41] Daphi, *Becoming a Movement*, pp. 91–2.

[42] David Graeber, *Direct Action: An Ethnography* (Oakland: AK Press, 2009), p. 46.

differences between the various groups to be too large: European protest tactics were viewed sceptically by Americans. Furthermore, feminist activists were shocked by the machoism in parts of the Southern European activist groups. Referring to 'Ya Basta!', one activist remembered: "To be honest, at first they rather gave me pause. In part, it was the blatant sexism. For three days of meetings, there was one guy, Luca, who did all the talking. He spoke a little English, but mainly he spoke in Italian. Then there was a woman who did all the translation work. ... Both women spoke perfect English, too, but they didn't venture an opinion once the whole time."[43]

The achievement of the Global Justice Movement was to bridge those strongly diverging trajectories towards a broad left-wing transnational solidarity. The mobilizations against the World Bank Group and IMF, especially in Prague, were milestones in this regard. They were decidedly radical, but also very diverse. Trade unions, local direct-action groups, NGOs, church groups, advocacy specialists, development organizations and student activists all joined together into a de-centralized network of people with diverse repertoires and levels of grievances, in other words: they formed a fully-fledged transnational social movement.

Institutionalizing interaction: from ignorance to incorporation

These increasingly successful mobilizations had institutional effects. The World Bank Group reacted to this external challenge by opening-up its procedures, becoming more transparent and accountable. Whether deliberately or because of a limited understanding of the protest movement's diversity, the World Bank Group, however, used NGOs and 'civil society' synonymously and directed its reactions to institutionalized advocacy organizations which spoke a language it could refer to.

> Confusing NGOs with 'civil society' is convenient for the Bank; development NGOs are much more appealing interlocuters than trade unions or social movements, which tend to be more overtly political and with whom it is much more difficult to establish common institutional procedures and norms on which to base interactions.[44]

This explains its reactions being almost exclusively limited to the procedural level. We can distinguish three forms of opening-up in the World Bank Group: information disclosure, citizenship engagement, and access to

---

[43] Graeber, *Direct Action*, p. 47.
[44] O'Brien et al., *Contesting Global Governance*, p. 58.

policymaking. First, the World Bank Group, under pressure from groups who criticized the 'secretive' nature of its decision-making, has introduced more disclosure of documents in the 'Access to Information' framework.[45] In the early 1980s, most information that leaked out of the World Bank Group was slipped to individual activists by World Bank staff members anonymously (Interview, US activist). Some was spectacularly stolen.[46] In 1985, with the 'Directive on disclosure of information', the World Bank for the first time allowed its staff members to disclose specific project-related knowledge, dividing information into three categories: published, available to specific audiences, or restricted.[47] Regulated as a positive list, it specified the kind of information that was accessible to the public. In 1993, the Board revised this policy, expanding the number of document types that were to be publicly disclosed. Furthermore, it introduced the Project Information Document which gives advocates the chance to connect to local communities that might be affected by specific projects and to protest before the implementation starts. The disclosure policy was updated in 2001,[48] including more types of documents, and in 2009 when the Board approved new access for stakeholders.[49] Information has increasingly turned into a right of civil society. This right has empowering effects for the affected communities and critics, for it allows them to make more informed arguments. It also puts the burden on them to make arguments based on data provided by the institution and in accordance with institutional channels of communication. These are, in effect, reducing the means of advocacy to a specific type of institutional complaint procedure, a pattern that I call *regulation.*

Second, the World Bank Group has increasingly enabled affected communities at the project site to enter dialogue with the country offices. The 'Citizen Engagement' framework mainly applies to CSOs from the countries in which projects are implemented, and it is often executed by the country offices.[50] When I asked World Bank staff about their civil

---

[45] See for the following dates: {http://www.worldbank.org/en/access-to-information/overview#3}.

[46] Walden Bello, *Development Debacle: The World Bank in the Philippines* (Manila: Institute for Food and Development Policy, 1982).

[47] World Bank, 'Directive on disclosure of information' (Washington DC, 1985).

[48] World Bank, *The Wold Bank Policy on Disclosure of Information*, 2002, available at: {http://www1.worldbank.org/operations/disclosure/documents/disclosurepolicy.pdf}.

[49] World Bank Group, 'The World Bank Access to Information Policy' (Washington DC, 2010).

[50] World Bank Group, 'Strategic framework for mainstreaming citizen engagement in World Bank Group' (Washington DC, 2014), available at: {https://consultations.worldbank.org/Data/hub/files/consultation-template/engaging-citizens-improved-resultsopenconsultationtemplate/materials/finalstrategicframeworkforce_4.pdf}.

society policies, they referred to the 'Citizen Engagement' framework, while activist interviewees would rather think of the access to policymaking (discussed later). While this study is, in effect, mostly focused on the latter form of interaction, because it follows the transnational activist network that has figured as the critics' integrative centre, it is important to note that these two forms of interaction are interlinked in many ways: without local protests at project sites, advocacy in the IO's headquarter would be less potent and without advocacy for more civil society access, the citizen engagement at project sites would not have developed to the same extent. According to the World Bank Group, citizen engagement, understood as multi-stakeholder consultations, 'began in the 1970s, was formalized in the 1980s, and deepened throughout the 1990s through participatory approaches in operations'.[51] In 2004, the World Development Report was dedicated to the topic 'making services work for poor people', and stressed the importance of consulting citizens.[52] Accordingly, the 2007 GAC strategy made it mandatory to engage with on-site population and 'explore the views of stakeholders'.[53] In 2012, the Global Partnership for Social Accountability (GPSA) was created. It provides direct funding to some CSOs in countries that 'have agreed to these approaches'.[54] This has ambivalent effects. On the one hand, it is an outstanding opportunity for organizations from poor countries to travel to Washington DC. On the other hand, the national governments have a say in the decision which organizations benefit from this money, making it difficult for critical CSOs to compete. This funding may exacerbate the imbalance between well-equipped, moderate CSOs close to governments and marginalized critical ones. GPSA is a good example for an instrument that contributes to the fragmentation of critique, supporting a specific kind of 'civil society', thereby creating an image of a moderate and professional civil society on the world stage. A process that I call *professionalization*.

Thirdly, the World Bank Group's involvement of civil society on the terms of policy-making – and policy itself – has considerably evolved during the last three decades. Under pressure from the social movement activities described here, the World Bank Group increasingly granted institutional access to organized advocacy groups. I call this process *incorporation* and describe it in more detail in the following.

---

51   World Bank Group, 'Strategic framework', p. 1.
52   World Bank, 'World Development Report 2004: making services work for poor people' (Washington DC, 2004), available at: {https://doi.org/10.1093/jae/ejh019}.
53   World Bank, 'Strengthening World Bank Group engagement on governance and anticorruption' (Washington DC, 2007), p. i.
54   World Bank Group, 'Strategic framework for mainstreaming citizen engagement in World Bank Group', p. 1.

Regular meetings with civil society

A forum for institutionalized interaction was created as early as 1982, the 'NGO-World Bank Committee'. It assembled on an annual basis and was composed of large international NGOs and some institutional staff. These first meetings had a rather informal character and were not documented well. Based on narratives of World Bank staff at the CSPF (discussed later), these were still rather exceptional circumstances, which did not have a profound impact on the generally hostile relationship between the IO management and its opponents, the former being 'afraid' of the latter.[55] Over the years, the critics achieved that civil society membership in the group became self-regulating. One of my interviewees recalled: "Those who were originally members got to nominate the other members that would follow them. So, you know, nepotism, cronyism" (Interview, US activist). Since some funds for civil society were made available during these meetings, fights for the distribution followed suit. One of the participants who started attending in 1989 recalled sarcastically: "The first thing that the members would do – especially from the South – was, well, how can we get money from the World Bank. Oh, that's a really critical stance to have when you want to criticize them over, you know, reforms".

Apart from the meetings in the 'NGO World Bank Committee', participation in these early years "almost completely revolved around the IDA replenishments" (Interview, US NGO). Much more central to the World Bank Group's overall portfolio at that time, member states meet every three years to replenish funds of the International Development Association (IDA) and review its policies. They evaluate the work of this most classic part of World Bank development financing. They reassess the need for money and discuss the shares of each member state. For critics, these meetings were a rare opportunity: "Every three years the World Bank staff would come out of hiding to talk with civil society" (Interview, US NGO). Because of this triannual scheme and the still rather limited scope of potential influence on the World Bank Group in direct interaction, many pressure groups rather used the 'state channel'[56] in the late 1980s, particularly via US Congress.[57] Activists used the power of the purse before and during these meetings by indirectly lobbying via the US House of Representatives, their goal being "to really shake up

[55] So said the manager Hartwig Schäfer at the CSPF 2016.
[56] Pallas and Uhlin, 'Civil society influence on international organizations'.
[57] Susan Park, 'Changing the international rule of development to include citizen driven accountability – a successful case of contestation', in Felix Anderl et al. *Rule and Resistance beyond the Nation State: Contestation, Escalation, Exit* (London: Rowman & Littlefield International, 2019), pp. 27–49.

funding and condition US-funding on things like information disclosure, an inspection panel and the safe-guards. Then, the bank was really forced to pay lots of attention to any US-NGO that was talking to the Congress" (Interview, US NGO). In the view of US activists, the newly won access to IDA replenishment "was a real thing and it did have structure and it was a dialogue, it was considered a big deal by people who participated" (Interview, US NGO). But despite the success of receiving attention by the World Bank Group Board and Management as well as the mainstream media during these events, there was no consensus within the critics whether to utilize this opportunity. Radical groups already then warned that these dialogues were a form of cooptation (Interview, US activist). Furthermore, there were "big confrontations with African NGOs, who said: US-NGOs, European-NGOs get your hands off our money, this is our money! You're actually stopping or threatening to stop money to our countries. Like, that's wrong" (Interview, US NGO).

With the major political interaction taking place at the IDA-replenishments, critics were rather successful in focusing their advocacy on the US contribution to IDA. Consider the 1989 'Pelosi Amendment' for information disclosure within MDBs. Presented by Congressional member Nancy Pelosi and authored largely by the Sierra Club, an important NGO in the early campaigns against the World Bank Group, the amendment placed conditions on the US Financial Institutions Act.[58] The US Treasury was now required to instruct US Executive Directors (EDs) of the World Bank and other MDBs to oppose any environmentally significant project that had no environmental assessment.[59] Activists managed to get shareholder countries on their side temporarily, and 'material pressure led to instrumental reactions'.[60] These experiences were the start of a process that I call *economization*: the debate remains in a narrow aisle of what can consensually be accepted as economic knowledge and arguments are (instrumentally or not) based on a given economic logic.

Narmada and the inspection panel: opening-up by force

One important campaign executed by activists around these IDA replenishments was the scandalization of the Narmada dam project. Among the world's most controversial infrastructure projects, the World

---

58 Park, 'Accountability as justice for the multilateral development banks?'; Keck and Sikkink, *Activists beyond Borders*, p. 149.
59 Paul J. Nelson, 'Transparency mechanisms at the multilateral development banks', *World Development* 29, 11 (2001), p. 1839.
60 Park, *World Bank Group Interactions with Environmentalists*, p. 27.

Bank financed it through IBRD and IDA.[61] Under pressure of protests, the World Bank President Barber Conacle established an independent review commission in 1991, led by the former head of UNDP, retired Republican US Congressman Bradford Morse.[62] Many were caught by surprise when the final report agreed with the critics. The authors highlighted the institution's failure to comply with its own rules on involuntary resettlement, environmental assessment, and indigenous peoples.[63] Furthermore, India had violated its loan agreements, yet was not punished by the World Bank in return. Shockingly to World Bank Management, the report did not recommend improving measures but asked the institution to withdraw from the project.[64] The World Bank was, however, not ready to do so and instead continued the project with modest changes to the original plan. This created another major setback: in 1992, US-based NGOs in collaboration with international partners, published a full-page ad in the *Financial Times*, openly threatening to lobby US Congress on cutting the World Bank's funding for the next IDA replenishment (Interviews, US activists). The year after that, the Board could not decide on a coherent policy regarding the matter and the problems continued, leading the government of India to announce the end of the World Bank's engagement in the project.

Despite the end of Narmada, activists used the publicity in 1993 and continued lobbying before US Congress to achieve institutional reforms in the World Bank. Consequently, the US government threatened to withhold the World Bank's IDA-10 replenishments, depending on the creation of a World Bank accountability mechanism. Although the negotiations for IDA funds from 1993 to 1996 had already been concluded in December 1992, the US contribution still had to be passed into law by Congress.[65] Activists testified to the House of Representatives before the Subcommittee on International Development which was chaired by Congressman Barney Frank.[66] Chairman Frank was considered a strong ally by many activists (Interview, US NGO). He made clear that the US would not authorize IDA funds unless the Bank established such a mechanism, raising the prospect of withholding IDA-10's third year of funding. Under pressure from the

---

[61] Ibrahim F. Shihata, *The World Bank Inspection Panel: In Practice* (Oxford and Washington DC: Oxford University Press/The World Bank, 2000), p. 5.

[62] Ziai, 'Can the subaltern file claims?', p. 258.

[63] Bradford Morse and Thomas R Berger, 'Sardar Sarovar – Report of the Independent Review', *Report of the Independent Review* (Washington DC, 1992), available at: {http://www.ielrc.org/content/c9202.pdf}.

[64] Ziai, 'Can the subaltern file claims?', p. 258.

[65] Kathryn C. Lavelle, *Legislating International Organisation: The US Congress, the IMF and the World Bank* (Oxford: Oxford University Press, 2011), p. 24.

[66] Park, 'Accountability as justice for the multilateral development banks?'

transnational activist network, US Congress reached the compromise to authorize funds for the first two years of IDA, while withholding funds for the third year until evidence of significant progress in terms of accountability was presented.[67] This had a considerable impact on the Board: Several Executive Directors proposed a new accountability mechanism. Succumbing to these external and internal pressures, the Board of Directors issued a resolution on the creation of the Inspection Panel in September 1993.[68] Narmada was hence the 'singularly defining reason for the necessity for the inspection mechanism within the Bank'.[69] This mechanism is the start of a henceforth increasing trend within the World Bank Group to justify its own action publicly, vis-à-vis affected people and other audiences. The institution has by now several accountability-mechanisms and puts great efforts into explaining its policies. This trend, which accelerated during the 1990s, can be understood as *legitimation*.[70]

1996: Wolfensohn's Tenure

The creation of open global governance had already started in the mid-1990s, but Wolfensohn's appointment intensified these changes enormously. Chosen by President Bill Clinton, he came with the promise to 'revolutionize the Bank' by shifting from a lazy loan-approval culture to 'effectiveness', 'accountability', and 'results'.[71] This conviction was inspired by external protest, particularly the contested Annual Meeting in Madrid in 1994. James Wolfensohn approached these protests in a different style from his predecessors. Referring to the example of one activist who was particularly well-known and had published a widely-read book on the World Bank Group's destructive projects,[72] one interviewee portrayed Wolfensohn's approach vividly:

> 'He was invited to Wolfensohn's house for dinner! Because Wolfensohn wanted to shut [him] up. He came out with that book in 1994 ... . And Wolfensohn invites him over for dinner. And, the next thing you know, the World Bank opens and starts encouraging staff to talk to civil society. So, I'd say, the mid-90s was a turning point.' (Interview, US NGO)

---

[67] Clark, 'Understanding the World Bank Inspection Panel', p. 9.
[68] Ziai, 'Can the subaltern file claims?', p. 258.
[69] Park, 'Accountability as justice for the multilateral development banks?'
[70] See also Heupel, Hirschmann, and Zürn, 'International organisations and human rights'.
[71] Rich, *Foreclosing the Future*, p. 34.
[72] Rich, *Mortgaging the Earth*.

During these years, the anti-structural-adjustment movement as well as the environmental movement targeted Wolfensohn directly and aggressively. In his memoirs, Wolfensohn recounts his approach as follows:

> To get a measure of the antagonism towards the Bank, I read the material prepared by our major critics among the NGOs. Typically, they were arguing that the Bank's projects were doing more harm than good. ... Oxfam claimed that the Bank was not paying enough attention to poverty. ... This NGO was particularly aggressive in its criticism, clashing with the World Bank ... over the reluctance of the financial establishment to consider debt forgiveness. ... Friends of the Earth complained that many of the Bank's major projects – for example, financing the building of dams and roads ... were hurting the environment. Transparency International asserted that the Bank turned a blind eye on corruption and graft.[73]

Looking back at how his predecessor and the institutional staff had reacted to criticism, Wolfensohn saw that they 'tended to ignore all such critiques'. While he could understand the impatience with which the professionals reacted to shrill and overly moralizing external criticism, he thought that it was important 'to distinguish between serious organizations with knowledgeable people in the field and well-intentioned but ignorant and naïve dreamers'. He realized that NGOs were mainly seen as trouble-makers in the institution, yet 'the widespread criticism was indeed having an impact. Inside the organization, it hurt morale, to the point where a senior management retreats, veteran World Bankers would debate whether the Bank was indeed becoming a "sunset institution"'.[74]

Wolfensohn was hence ready to listen to what particular (*professional*) critics had to say. Being ridiculed as a 'Renaissance banker' before the start of his tenure, he felt that 'you have to decide whether you'll be a figurehead or a real boss. If you don't impose yourself on the institution starting the minute you arrive, you never will'.[75] He made the decision to be 'a real boss'. Opening the institution and creating a culture of dialogue with critics hence served at least two goals: it was – in Wolfensohn's opinion – making the World Bank Group's work better, and it paved the way for him as a strong leader with an agenda of change. These thoughts stemming from Wolfensohn's autobiography, we must be careful not to take them at face value. Yet, in their function as indicating a major rupture in organizational

---

[73] Wolfensohn, *A Global Life*, p. 259.
[74] Wolfensohn, *A Global Life*, p. 260.
[75] Wolfensohn, *A Global Life*, p. 262.

culture, they can be granted high validity because even Wolfensohn's opponents agree to the role he played in opening towards critics. Although many of the activists from that time are disappointed because they perceived policy changes as merely rhetorical (discussed later), many still told me that Wolfensohn was 'the best' President so far. He tried to introduce a new way of thinking into the World Bank Group. Beyond the opening-up, this also meant to 'change the approval culture to an effectiveness culture'.[76] Speaking to critics and becoming more economical were two sides of the same coin for Wolfensohn: he wanted to use the NGOs' knowledge and prevent crises, both in the attempt to make the institution more effective at what it did. Hence, from that point onwards, *incorporation* and *economization* were institutional policy.

"A brilliant choice": hiring individuals from the movement

During these years, participation action plans were adopted at the regional level and civil society specialists were hired to work in over 80 World Bank Group offices.[77] Many of these specialists were recruited from outside the institution, some of them explicit critics of the World Bank Group. The personal decisions by critics to take on a lucrative job in the institution were widely criticized at that time, or to quote one of my interview partners speaking about one such individual: "the fact that he would sell out in that manner is just breath-taking" (Interview, US NGO).

Selecting this individual and making him responsible for civil society relations followed the pattern described previously: to distinguish 'serious' voices with knowledge and expertise from 'unreasonable' troublemakers. My interlocuter who had collaborated with the "sell-out" activist before he moved into the World Bank Group, explained to me that Latin American voices had been more influential than African or Asian voices in the campaigns of the early 1990s, going back mainly to their advocacy against the debt regime. The individual who crossed the line from advocacy to working for the World Bank Group had been active in Latin America as an advocate and knew the activist structure there.

> 'So, the choice meant that [he] could communicate with people in their own language and with a really deep and profound … understanding of their nature and culture. And then he could sharply distinguish between

---

[76] Rich, *Mortgaging the Earth*, p. 34.
[77] See the history page of its outreach activities, available at: {http://www.worldbank.org/en/about/partners/brief/history}.

advocacy voices and civil society voices, and bring the voices that he wanted into the discussion, and marginalize the others ... I mean it was a brilliant choice.' (Interview, US NGO)

This story is not exceptional. Many activists told me about 'losing' friends and colleagues to the institutions they had previously fought together. Notably, John Clark, one of the earliest activists to 'switch sides' did so as early as 1992 to become the World Bank's social scientist (Interview, US NGO). Under Wolfensohn, however, a particular trend of putting former activists in operational positions was established. They subsequently figured as entry points for some activists and gatekeepers for others. Another quite prominent figure in the NGO scene told me that when he changed to the World Bank Group in 1998, "I was heavily criticized by some people in my ... community, for good reasons, you know: another sell-out, another trade, another naive person who thinks you can do something which is impossible." (Interview, World Bank Group manager & NGO).

Analysing CVs of civil society officers, this pattern has been kept alive until today with the IMF Head of Civil Society Team hailing from Oxfam, and the World Bank Head of External Relations from the 'One Campaign'. What has significantly changed though, is the reception of these career choices in the NGO community. While early cases were heavily criticized or ridiculed, today such a career choice seems to be widely accepted. The case of the current IMF head of Civil Society Team is strikingly similar to the aforementioned cases. He, however, got exclusively positive feedback from his former colleagues at Oxfam and other critics of the World Bank Group (Interview, IMF manager). Many were even happy to have such a "good guy" as their contact point in the IMF. When I told one of those who had been heavily attacked for the same move 20 years earlier, he laughingly referred to the IMF and said: "Well, that's ... even more of a sell-out than me!" (Interview, World Bank Group manager & NGO). Telling him that none of the former colleagues had criticized the younger "sell-out" for the move, he replied: "Interesting. ... Well, it makes sense, doesn't it? If it has become a highly professionalized process, you need people like that, to give you that and try to ... share documents, so it's actually great, it's actually essential to a professional advocacy strategy to have those internal contact points".

It is one of the significant changes of the Wolfensohn era that critics are hired from oppositional NGOs, putting them into positions where they regulate the interaction with their former colleagues. While these staff exchanges were scandalized as "sell-out" in the beginning, over time they have become normalized and individuals who make such career decisions are not condemned any more. This change in civil society goes back to the elevation of individuals in circles of critics and a general *professionalization* of 'civil society' that changed the kinds of practices that were considered acceptable within the transnational activist network.

Open towards some, ignorant towards others

Wolfensohn did not only hire 'civil society specialists', but he also listened to what the critics had to say and forced Management to do the same. The openness of the Wolfensohn years had consequences for institutional relations with critics and instigated changes, both policy-based and procedural. In terms of the former, the introduction of the Compliance Advisor Ombudsman (CAO), an accountability mechanism particularly for IFC which was founded in 1999, stands out here.[78] Regarding the institutionalized exchange of critics and World Bank Group staff that transcends the complaints on single projects, the following two case studies capture the major developments created during the Wolfensohn era. On the one hand, two unparalleled, far-reaching consultation efforts were started, the World Commission on Dams (WCD) and the Extractive Industries Review (EIR, see details in Chapters 6 and 7). On the other hand, the World Bank Group introduced the Civil Society Policy Forum (CSPF) which institutionalized the interaction with civil society groups and included it in the Annual Meeting (Chapters 8 and 9).

Many of my informants conceded that this 'friendly' approach to civil society had tangible effects – but that it was important to distinguish what effects it had on what kinds of organizations:

> 'What I would say, in terms of civil society groups doing advocacy on the World Bank, there is a spectrum, you know, from let's call it left to right. And, I'd like to call the ones on the left the ones that have the least interaction with the World Bank, and on the right, that have the most. And they're like ... they practically live in the World Bank. And there are some other ones who lived there and which I respect in some ways. Like Oxfam. And, I've seen a very interesting movement of staff, between the World Bank and Oxfam in both directions.' (Interview, US activist)

This statement makes an important distinction between different kinds of critics. While Wolfensohn denominated Oxfam as the most aggressive of the

---

[78] Park, 'Changing the international rule of development to include citizen driven accountability'; Park, 'Accountability as justice for the multilateral development banks?'; Samantha Balaton-Chrimes and Fiona Haines, 'The depoliticisation of accountability processes for land-based grievances, and the IFC CAO', *Global Policy* 6, 4 (2015), pp. 446–54.

critical organizations, more radical ones are not even named or recognized. But as I have shown previously, protests against the World Bank Group were much more diverse than the selection of NGOs that Wolfensohn named in his memoirs. Considering the RAGs, for instance, they were not at all interested in joining the World Bank's meetings or working on its transparency. Rather, they wanted the World Bank Group's destructive projects, or better the whole institution, to end (Interview, US activist). This was by no means a marginal position, particularly in the Global South. Oxfam was therefore not at all among the most radical critics. What Wolfensohn described as 'particularly aggressive' was in fact a moderate form of critique if compared to the breadth of the movement at the time.[79] Wolfensohn wanted to distinguish between reasonable and well-informed NGOs and 'naïve dreamers'. Oxfam, thus, figures as the most radical outpost of the still acceptable critics in his view. Based on this categorization, it is interesting that staff members of Oxfam have been particularly in demand for filling in civil society related jobs in the World Bank Group. Building on these observations, the practices of critics can be divided alongside each mechanism (see Table 4.6). For every mechanism, like incorporation here, there are some individuals and organizations that support the introduction of, and then play along, the institution's newly created opportunities. Others are irritated by this behaviour, creating fights within the rows of critics.

Early 2000s: let the fragmentation begin!

The institutional division of critics – the reasonable ones and the 'naïve radicals' – contributed to the long-term fragmentation of the social movement attacking the World Bank Group. This process is observable in three aspects:

1. Moderate groups that had been granted access during the Wolfensohn era began to distance themselves from the radical character of the protests against the World Bank Group around the millennium, something they had not done in the years before. These NGOs did not want to risk their prestige and accompanying access to the institution.
2. Northern and Southern groups became estranged from each other over questions of substance and representation.
3. The World Bank Group created its own 'civil society groups', which subsequently took over the moderate messaging, thereby supporting Wolfensohn's framing of Oxfam and the like as 'aggressive' ones. This left no acceptable space for those that were seen as radical before.

---

[79] Wolfensohn, *A Global Life*, p. 259.

1. NGOs publicly discredit radical peers

In 2000, thousands of people gathered in Washington DC for the World Bank Group and IMF Spring meetings. Inspired by the events at the WTO Ministerial Meeting in Seattle the year before, some groups took up the chants and partly violent tactics of the protests there. Clark describes the position of the NGO community:

> The veteran civil society campaigners had mixed feelings. The street events put the right issues onto the public agenda, but did they single out the right institution? In recent years the Bank has added its voice to NGO pressure on G7 governments for debt relief. It … gives civil society a role in formulating development strategy. … It has pioneered Participatory Poverty Assessments to listen to poor people's priorities for fighting poverty. In many other ways, too, the Bank talks the language of NGOs. Veteran campaigners still see much in the Bank to criticize, but they want to reform, not abolish, the institution, and they prefer argument to abuse. Hence the main US operational NGOs wrote the Bank to distance themselves from the protest.[80]

Despite the evolving rupture in the movement against the World Bank Group, agreements between moderate and radical activists were still in place. The former had asked the latter to respect the protests and not to meet with World Bank Group staff during the demonstrations. Most of the NGOs complied and decided not to cross the picket line but requested meetings off-premises. Others (among them Jubilee 2000 and Save the Children UK) were prepared to have meetings inside the Bank.[81] Friends of the Earth-US originally endorsed the protests, but later regretted this position and wrote to the Bank that they had done so because of concerns 'that there would not [otherwise] be enough emphasis on the issues since many of the groups involved in organizing the [protest] activities do not necessarily have an expertise with the institutions'.[82] Playing into Wolfensohn's division of reasonable and knowledgeable NGOs with expertise versus naïve dreamers, Friends of the Earth set themselves apart as the expert NGO, without which the other protesters could not arrive at a well-balanced view. When the protests turned partly violent, they distanced themselves from the coalition.

---

[80] Clark, 'The World Bank and civil society. An evolving experience', p. 123.
[81] John D. Clark, *Worlds Apart: Civil Society and the Battle for Ethical Globalization* (Bloomfield: Kumarian Press, 2003), p. 123.
[82] Email from Friends of the Earth to the World Bank Group as quoted in Clark 'The World Bank and Civil Society', p. 124.

Oxfam dissociated itself from these protests even more clearly. Coined as a 'radical force' by Wolfensohn, Oxfam Great Britain's Policy Director, when asked about the violent protests, said that '[t]he political space around big international meetings has been hijacked by those who want to commit violence. ... It is counter-productive. They are taking the spotlight off those who want positive change'.[83] But the NGO did not only criticize the means of the protest – Oxfam International even went so far as to delegitimate its core message. In its strategic plan, the organization wrote: 'The isolationist and protectionist tendencies on display in Seattle, Washington and other public demonstrations against the international order show that short-sightedness and selfishness are not exclusive to politics, bureaucracy or business'.[84]

At a time when the movement against the World Bank Group was arguably at a peak, the President of the institution incorporated parts of that movement (the ones deemed 'reasonable'). These, in turn, discredited more radical groups as violent and uninformed, largely reinforcing the institutional division of the protest movement. The fact that such fragmentation did not occur in 1994 or other big demonstrations, when violent tactics had been employed as well, isolates specific practices of critique as contributing to fragmentation: precisely those organizations that were explicitly named by Wolfensohn as 'worth listening to' were the ones that antagonized the more radical ones, despite them having been co-organizers of such protests until that point.

2. North–South fragmentation

An even stronger enactment of the fragmentation occurred in the anti-debt movement. The hotly debated structural adjustment policies had been changed around the millennium as a response to public pressure. From then on, the World Bank Group replaced Structural Adjustment Funds with 'country strategies' and 'policy lending'.[85] These successes by the anti-debt movement led to a split in Jubilee 2000, the large coalition of debt campaigns.[86] The moderate parts of the campaign were happy with the outcome and retreated from the movement in 2000. In hindsight, many of

---

[83] *Financial Times*, 7 Decemer 2001, quoted in Clark, *Worlds Apart*, p. 161.

[84] Oxfam International, 'Towards global equity: Oxfam International's strategic plan, 2001–2004' (Melbourne, 2000).

[85] World Bank Administrative and Civil Service Reform Thematic Group, 'The World Bank's Poverty Reduction Support Credit (PRSC) – a new approach to support policy and institutional reforms in low income countries', *Working Group on Administrative & Civil Reform*, Vol. 1 (Washington DC, 2001).

[86] Priska Daphi, Felix Anderl, and Nicole Deitelhoff, 'Bridges or divides? Conflicts and synergies of coalition building across countries and sectors in the global justice movement', *Social Movement Studies*, 21, 1–2 (2022), pp. 8–22.

the activists I spoke with told me that these changes turned out to be 'only rhetorical' (Interview, Philippine NGO), or a 'superficial change of names' (Interview US NGO). Big parts of the movement had already seen this coming in the year 2000. Quoting from an activist newsletter that was widely read at that time, activists assumed that the World Bank Group wanted to 'rename, repackage and expand adjustment lending'.[87] Additionally, there was an initiative to cancel some debt of highly indebted poor countries (HIPC). This came arguably as a success of the international anti-debt campaigns. However, not everybody was content with this solution: while the radical share of the critics was not satisfied with these changes and even intensified the protests, representatives of the Jubilee 2000 campaign complained that anarchists' campaigns on third world debt at the World Bank Group's Annual Meeting in Prague 2000 had damaged their efforts by constricting the space for lobbying inside. They hence felt 'used' by the demonstrators.[88]

To understand why institutionalized parts of the movement antagonized radical anti-debt groups, their shared history is crucial. The coalition's participants from the Global South had founded 'Jubilee South' – to the dismay of the Northern, especially British debt relief campaign (Jubilee 2000). They had done so because they

'felt that our perspective as southern movements was not faithfully reflected ... or expressed in how the Jubilee movement was shaping up internationally, and secondly we felt very strongly that the southern voices and movements should be in the frontlines of this campaign so that the other groups will not be speaking for us.' (Interview, Philippine NGO)

Jubilee South complained that the HIPC initiative's list of 'poorest countries' was largely defined by what the World Bank Group and the IMF considered to be the poorest countries, based on indicators that the Southern activists rejected. These activists argued that the one-off slashing for this limited number of countries would neither solve systemic problems of international injustice, nor help the countries that were missing on the list despite their debt. The concept of HIPC seemed rigged to them because "in the eyes of the creditors you're only in a debt crisis if you can't pay, never mind that you can't do anything else. And then it was also clear to us that it was yet

---

[87] Nancy Alexander, Sara Grusky, and Sameer Dossani, 'News & notices for IMF and World Bank watchers', Vol. 2 (Washington DC, 2001), 1; see also Bretton Woods Project, 'PRSPs Just PR', *Bretton Woods Update 23* (London, 2001), 3, available at: {http://www.brettonw oodsproject.org/publications/23-2/}.
[88] Ann Pettifor quoted in Clark, *Worlds Apart*, 162.

another way for these institutions to impose economic prescriptions and conditionalities on countries" (Interview, Philippine NGO).

The Jubilee South coalition reacted more sceptically to the opportunities which their Northern peers embraced:

> Past experiences have taught us what kind of 'participation' takes place in WB/IMF. ... No matter how these processes are to be undertaken, as long as countries are indebted and reliant on external infusion of capital, as long as the WB and the IMF are big lenders and have a lot of say about a country's credit worthiness, as long as we have governments run by the elites, the IMF and WB will still exercise tremendous influence on government policies. In fact, many South countries' economic managers do not have to be persuaded to follow the neo-liberal economic paradigm, as they have so internalized this paradigm. Furthermore, in the end [these programs] are still to be approved by the WB and IMF.[89]

These groups saw the World Bank Group's proposal of debt cancellation as a form of charity but demanded an act of justice instead. Activists from the UK and Germany, which had good access to the World Bank Group's relevant bodies, disagreed. They thought that the HIPC initiative was their great success, which should be openly endorsed.

Now, in a movement fighting for the rights of highly indebted countries in the Global South, the activists from Jubilee South were not ready to have the Northern activists speak for them. They cherished the slogan 'nothing about us, without us'. The Northerners were, however, the ones being invited into the institutions. On a preparatory meeting, these issues had been widely discussed and "it was really the UK and Germany" that opposed Jubilee South's wish for representing their own cause. Especially the leading figure of the British Jubilee 2000 campaign was perceived as hostile, claiming to be able to speak for the whole movement because the Northern governments had to be pressured and, furthermore, "she was very explicit in her claim for speaking on behalf of not just the Jubilee 2000 UK but, and I quote, 'the 206 million people who have signed the petition'" (Interview, Southern NGO). This successful petition had been initiated by Jubilee 2000 UK and was not supported by Jubilee South because it demanded a one-off cancellation for the poorest countries.[90]

---

[89] Extracts from the paper presented in 2001 by Lidy Nacpil, Secretary General of the Freedom from Debt Coalition and International Coordinator of Jubilee South. Available at: {http://cpcabrisbane.org/Kasama/2001/V15n3/ISC_Debt.htm}.

[90] See Advocacy International's web page on Jubilee 2000, available at: {http://www.advoca cyinternational.co.uk/featured-project/jubilee-2000}.

The confrontation of Northern and Southern groups on the issue of debt policies resulted from differences in political positions. It escalated, however, because of the opening-up of the World Bank Group towards some selected parts of this transnational movement: while Jubilee South was outside of the World Bank Group's Annual Meetings in 2000 and Spring Meetings 2001, the leaders of the European movement were inside, working on their political victory. Being convinced that this was a vital opportunity for debt cancellation, they took the chance against the profound objections of those hailing from the countries that were indebted – thereby destroying the trust of these activists. Their press statement, which was openly directed against these outside activists, finally sealed this separation.

3. The World Bank diffuses into NGOs or creates new ones

Beyond the processes of fragmentation that followed from the preferential treatment of some NGOs, the World Bank Group also directly interfered with the 'civil society' spectrum. The institution created close links with NGOs, for instance the World Resources Institute (WRI), a research organization that officially works in more than 50 countries, and employs 500 experts who address topics like food, forests, water, climate, energy and cities.[91] Andrew Steer, who became President and CEO of the WRI, used to head the civil society team in the World Bank Group before taking over this position. One of my interview partners put it like this:

> 'What the World Bank does is that it recycles people that 'help out' NGOs everywhere. ... Like Andrew Steer: you know, I used to lobby him, when he was at the World Bank for many years and now he's the head of the World Resources Institute, and Manish who was with the World Bank ... went to head the Bank Information Centre and now he works for Andrew Steer.' (Interview, US activist)

Manish Bapna left the World Bank towards BIC in 1997. Andrew Steer left shortly afterwards and was replaced by John Garrison in 2001, who was then deeply involved in founding the CSPF (discussed previously). Steere and Bapna symbolize a new, unhesitating, posture towards changing from the World Bank Group to its (not so) critical watchdogs; moving from the World Bank Group's civil society team towards heading an NGO that lobbies the World Bank Group, towards a think-tank that operationally supports it.

Besides the staff swaps, the World Bank Group during Wolfensohn's era also strongly invested into the expansion of staff responsible for dealing with 'civil

---

[91] See the website: {http://www.wri.org/}.

society'. One activist demanded that I do a count: "The World Bank and the IMF have both gotten very smart. I want you to do a count – in your paper, you have to do this. How many people the World Bank pays to interface with civil society" (Interview, US activist). Insinuating a conspiratorial plot, this particular interview partner felt like these moves were part of a strategy on the part of the institutions to actively undermine their critics. There is, however, nothing secret about the World Bank Group's civil society strategy. Wolfensohn created an environment in which, increasingly, lobbyists were allowed entry to talk to their former – and possibly future – colleagues. This had an impact on the tone that those inside-activists were using, talking to former peers rather than an unknown 'other'.

More clearly indicative of a direct exertion of influence of the World Bank Group towards activist circles was the foundation of its own civil society: "Probably one of the most significant factors in civil society relations with the World Bank was the establishment of the Center for Global Development (CGD), which is almost entirely a collection of former staff members, officials of the different multilateral development banks" (Interview, US NGO). The CGD acts like a regular CSO, but with policies that come suspiciously close to the ones propagated by the World Bank Group. For instance, "it was one of the organizations that opposed the safeguard movement [which] was just seen as a real money loser" (Interview, US NGO). The CGD, although sometimes critical of the World Bank Group, unsurprisingly places efficient work of the institution high on its agenda. Therefore, it fights for the relevance of classic development funding and is afraid that, with too many social and environmental safeguards, the institution will lose out against other development banks with less complex guidelines – an argument that is very close to the one by the World Bank Group management (see Chapter 7).

The creation of 'civil society' and its forum

I have shown that (a) staff from the World Bank Group started to take on jobs in advocacy NGOs and vice versa, and (b) the World Bank Group actively supported the creation of new NGOs, which thereupon more or less critically monitored the institution's work. All this started or accelerated in the late 1990s with a big push by Wolfensohn for a more open World Bank Group. Another major building block for that strategy was the creation of the Civil Society Policy Forum (CSPF). But for that idea to succeed, there was an obvious need for a certain number of (ideally moderate) activists to identify as 'civil society'. An activist from a faith-based African NGO who has been attending the meetings for 16 years, said: "Before 2000 we had protests on the streets when the World Bank had its annual meeting. Then Wolfensohn came and said: let's bring them inside. That's what created the CSPF". When I asked her what civil society did before 2000, she answered: "There was no 'civil society'. That was created by Wolfensohn." I inquired: "What else was there when there was no civil society?" Her reply: "There were a number of social movements that met here to protest." This statement nicely illustrates that the 'opening-up' of IOs has to be seen in a bigger context: first, it does not only have effects on the institution's policy-making process. Getting access to the institution also changes those subjects who make use of it.[92] Second, this incorporation is only part of a bigger constellation without which scholars miss the socio-political meaning of this institutional transformation.

When the institution had to cut short its 2000 Annual Meeting in Prague with 15,000 protesters blocking the building, there was a substantial need to 'do something' in the face of a perceived radicalization of resistance. In the words of a staff member of the World Bank civil society team: "The Bank realized ... wait a minute! We have to – let's listen to the civil society folks, rather than them demonstrating outside and disrupting our meetings. Why don't we invite them into the Bank and create a space, let's hear them out" (Interview, World Bank Group manager).

So, in 2002, the CSPF was officially born. Much smaller in scope at that time, "they had like maybe five, six sessions" (Interview, World Bank Group manager). After this first year, it quickly grew in size and scope. One should not underestimate the rupture that this new forum created regarding the World Bank Group's external relations: "I think I should also attribute a little bit to the Wolfensohn era at that time: You know, we had the Washington Consensus, Wolfensohn also spearheaded some fresh thinking into Bank at that time". The creation of the CSPF, as well as the moderation of parts of the movement, happened as a result of, but also *in parallel* to, a growth in radical protests outside the institution. It is important to have this in mind because it lays the foundation of the fragmentation of the World Bank Group's critics that the following chapters will trace more analytically.

---

[92] Tucker, 'Participation and subjectification in global governance'.

6

When a Contentious Process Opens Up: Extractive Industries Review

Over a period of twenty years, a massive transnational social movement against the World Bank Group shrank to a largely tamed advocacy network. Could this have been avoided? In the long-term history of the movement, it is evident that solidarities broke over time, and that the fragmentation happened in interaction with the institutions of open global governance which integrated some critics, leaving the prior protest movement out of steam. But it is harder to pinpoint the decisive processes, *the how*, of this effect.

In this chapter, I therefore zoom into one specific conflict: resistance against the World Bank Group's funding of extractive industries projects. The process resembles what I described previously, albeit in a condensed form. The succession from protest on the streets to an opening-up of the institution, which leads to the integration of parts of the movement, and hence to a fragmentation of resistance, can be observed yet again. What had to remain speculation in the previous chapter, due to the long timeline and potentially endless external factors, shall be systematically reconstructed for this case. I first describe the transnational protests against extractive industries projects from the late 1990s until shortly after the year 2000. Then, I trace the process resulting from this resistance (2000–2004), James Wolfensohn announcing the Extractive Industries Review (EIR), its preparation and actual work, and the clashes that occurred between the institution and its critics, as well as among the critics during that review. Consecutively, I present the recommendations of the EIR secretariat resulting from the consultations, how they were received in the World Bank Group, and their partial and evasive implementation. Based on this, I reconstruct the movement's fragmentation during the process.

A transnational movement against extractive industries projects

Extractivism and development have been a couple for decades now. The idea of growth and progress based on the exploitation of natural resources is deeply enshrined into developmental models of the 20th century. Additionally, when the World Bank's go-to policy of structural adjustment became increasingly delegitimized in the 1990s, investing into oil, gas, and mining projects promised a new productive avenue for poverty alleviation through the private sector. However, many of these projects had devastating consequences for the local populations. Scandals regarding involuntary resettlement and environmental issues, a serious lack of accountability, and newly acquired scientific knowledge about climate change rendered the topic increasingly contested.

In response, a decentralized and transnational movement against the World Bank Group's financing of extractive industries formed from the mid-1990s. It can be traced alongside the contention around one specific project which culminated around the millennium: the Chad–Cameroon oil pipeline project, a campaign that is still remembered by activists as a 'paradigmatic case'[1] for a civil society protest campaign, which was carried by hundreds of NGOs, protest groups and transnationally networked individuals. The World Bank Group's plan to invest with ExxonMobil in oil exploration and large-scale pipelines in Chad and Cameroon was rejected by environmental and human rights groups around the world. Due to previous experience with such projects, as well as the unstable situation in Chad under military government, hardly anyone in civil society believed in the promised poverty reduction for the local population. Exxon's Director General, who held that developing countries should avoid environmental controls to encourage foreign investors, did not help to build confidence.[2] Today, there are still huge differences of interpretation regarding the project's performance. A top World Bank manager told me in 2016 that "from a business perspective, this was a very good project. The Chad buying tanks from the money, that's of course unfortunate" (Interview, World Bank Group manager). While all activists I spoke to drew on this project as a catastrophic idea that involved huge environmental risks and especially involved social disruption, the World Bank Group still argues that '[t]he project was a pioneering effort between

---

[1]   Introduced as such on the Urgewald Conference: Multilateral Financial Institutions – What progress concerning human rights and accountability? In Berlin, 16–17 March, 2015.

[2]   *Wall Street Journal* 14 October 1997, quoted in Martin Petry, *Wem gehört das Schwarze Gold? Engagement für Frieden Und Gerechtigkeit in der Auseinandersetzung mit dem Erdölprojekt Tschad-Kamerun – Erfahrungen eines internationalen Netzwerks* (Frankfurt am Main: Brandes & Apsel, 2003), p. 25.

IFC and the World Bank to demonstrate that large scale crude oil projects, when designed to ensure transparency and effective environmental and social mitigation, can significantly improve prospects for sustainable long-term development'.[3] These vastly differing opinions as to what a successful development project looks like make the Chad–Cameroon Project a good example illustrating why the protests were so vigorous: the institution was unwilling to reflect on its role; with the effect that the movement was increasingly growing.

This campaign was initially launched by a small number of individuals.[4] A Chad specialist made available project documents to the Environmental Defense Fund (EDF). This NGO was able to land a first success: the plan to finance the oil project via IDA, the World Bank's share of official development assistance (ODA), was halted after public scandalization. US Congress became convinced that money would not go into poverty alleviation. The EDF employee responsible at the time told me: "As important as the internationally networked campaigns are, the decisive thing for the World Bank is what is happening in the US" (Interview, European NGO). Unlike in other World Bank member states, the US Congress has a direct influence on what the funds of the US contribution to the World Bank are used for. Therefore, targeting US Congress has been highlighted as crucial by many of my interview partners.[5]

But outside the US, too, the movement grew and gained momentum. In June 1997, organized by Les Amis de la Terre, 20,000 postcards were sent to the World Bank from France. The postcard read: 'World Bank – money pump for oil companies'.[6] In Germany, Urgewald and World Economy Environment and Development (WEED) had persuaded the Federal Ministry of Economic Cooperation and Development (BMZ) to reject IDA funding. The long-standing World Bank manager Calderisi remembers that the public rejection of the IDA as a financing mechanism brought tangible problems to the World Bank: 'In November 1997, after a visit to Stuttgart, Mr. Wolfensohn accepted to finance the project with the bank's own funds. This has necessitated a certain amount of gymnastics by our financial experts'.[7] This bought valuable time to do further research on the project

---

[3] See {https://www.ifc.org/wps/wcm/connect/008265b5-f5cc-4679-b73e-16f870ce4 df3/ChadCamProjectOverview.pdf?MOD=AJPERES&CVID=jaLpjwb}.

[4] Petry, *Wem gehört Das Schwarze Gold?*, pp. 25–32; see also Rich, *Foreclosing the Future.*

[5] See also Park, 'Changing the international rule of development to include citizen driven accountability'.

[6] In French, the pun with Africa pump/money pump works better: 'Banque mondiale: Pompe A'frique des Compagnies pétrolières' (see Petry *Wem gehört das Schwarze Gold?*, p. 34).

[7] Quoted in Petry, *Wem gehört das Schwarze Gold?*, p. 37.

and sparked additional momentum. Amnesty International, Bread for the World, Eirene, Misereor and other rather mainstream NGOs were now on board.[8] The public discourse had taken a turn for the benefit of the critics and the campaign work in Chad and Cameroon was expanding with the help of new partners. Throughout the world, there were so many decentralized protests that Wolfensohn could no longer escape the conflict: "He couldn't go anywhere in the world, and give a press conference – in Japan ... no matter where – without being asked directly about the Chad Cameroon project" (Interview, European NGO). While the movement was critical of extractive industries in general, that particular project had the biggest impact. "The EIR process was indirectly triggered by the campaign against the Chad–Cameroon project", recalls one of the central protagonists (Interview, European NGO).

At the same time, the World Bank Group was in the focus of campaigns by indigenous communities denouncing the land grabbing they suffered from.[9] The institution's resettlement guidelines were still negligent then, whole villages frequently being relocated by force in order to implement extractive projects. Huge mining projects such as Freeport and Newmont in Indonesia had triggered social and environmental crises, which were publicly attributed to the co-financing World Bank Group (Interviews, Indonesian NGOs). The organization stood in the crossfire from numerous anti-extractivist movements with various geographical and political priorities.

The pressure culminated in 2000, when 16,000 people demonstrated against the Annual Conference in Prague. In addition to concrete concerns such as the resettlements and environmental devastation, the protests called into question the capitalist development concept in general.[10] Apart from the very specific issue of extractive industries, these protests can therefore be seen as a vital part of the Global Justice Movement, the campaigns on extractive industries feeding smoothly into the movement's overall concerns. In addition to the often disastrous consequences for local populations in project areas, extractive industries have been of great importance for the larger movement at the symbolic level, since they embody a colonial dimension of contemporary 'development policy': unfair global distribution of resources exploited in poor countries such as the Chad to serve the rich in the global North. The World Bank Group management could not ignore the pressure of this argument any longer in 2000.

---

8   Petry, *Wem gehört das Schwarze Gold?*, pp. 37–8.
9   Marcus Colchester and Emily Caruso, *Extracting Promises: Indigenous Peoples, Extractive Industries and the World Bank* (Baguio City: Tebtebba Foundation, 2005).
10 See {http://www.theguardian.com/business/2000/sep/28/imf.economics}.

I will now trace the process that evolved as a reaction to the aforementioned protests. I will first outline how the World Bank Group officially reacted by introducing the EIR, arguing that the aim of this decision was to calm down the protest. This is captured with the mechanism of incorporation. Subsequently, I explain how the EIR was organized and implemented. Highlighting the contestation between different critics, I describe one especially contentious workshop in Bali where most activists decided to leave the consultations. After that, I elaborate on how the specific setup and procedure of this deliberative process resulted in clashing expectations and contributed to the fragmentation of the social movement actors which I analyse alongside the mechanisms of professionalization and economization.

The Extractive Industries Review: incorporation

At the fiercely contested Annual Conference in Prague, Wolfensohn responded directly to virulent criticism and announced the establishment of a review which would appraise his organization's role in the oil, gas and mining sectors.[11] This came as a surprise to other high-ranking members of the World Bank Group management. One, who participated in the press conference together with Wolfensohn, described the situation as such:

> 'There was Wolfensohn with three or four of his Vice Presidents ... and then 40, 50 NGOs and they were scolding him again: "Mr. President, the World Bank shouldn't be involved in that" – and then the three of us almost got a heart attack when Jim Wolfensohn said: "Okay, we'll do a study and a review of this". ... Oh my god!' (Interview, World Bank Group manager)

Many NGOs perceived this reaction as a huge success (Interview, European NGO). They left Prague happy to have made this possible. Knowing the terrible situation in the field, they were convinced that an independent study would conclude that extractive projects are detrimental to development. At the same time, however, they were anxious whether Wolfensohn had made this move only to clear the air. Indeed, it seems plausible that Wolfensohn saw the EIR as a tool to calm down the public outcry, as already in the case of the World Commission on Dams (WCD) which had just released its report. When comparing the two similar initiatives, it is especially apparent that Wolfensohn repeated the

---

[11] Emil Salim, 'Striking a better balance. Vol. 1: The World Bank and extractive industries. The final report of the Extractive Industries Review' (Jakarta, 2003), p. 1.

move to outsource contention to a neutral body yet anticipating a less problematic outcome.

The WCD (1997–2000), or 'damn commission' as it was called within World Bank Management (Interview, World Bank Group manager), had also been a reaction to protests – and, since it officially stated the negative effects of World Bank Group projects on local populations, it represents an embarrassing chapter for the World Bank Group.[12] In the words of a World Bank advisor, who worked as the WCD's institutional counterpart, the process had been "dominated by rather aggressive and impolite NGOs, so the others lost interest. So, then the report became unbalanced. ... This thing was not acceptable" (Interview, World Bank Group manager). The institutional design of the EIR process was thus more top-down: a secretariat with World Bank Group staff and only one 'eminent person' who should lead the process (see Figure 6.1). The institution looked for someone who was "not only trusted by all sides but could also be trusted to have the authority, to edit the report in a way that would be palatable or digestible by the Bank's board". This eminent person was Emil Salim from Indonesia. He had earned a PhD in Economics and had served as a minister both under Suharto where he was, among other things, responsible for development planning and the environment, and under two democratic governments after that.[13] Furthermore, he had been on the United Nations (UN) Commission 'Our Common Future' which had published the 'Brundtland report'.[14] He could be expected to be a moderate and did not seem too close to NGOs. When Salim met Wolfensohn, the latter told him directly that he needed someone who could restore peace with NGOs (Interview, EIR Secretariat). The secretariat was staffed with 6–7 managers plus many short-term consultancy contracts. It consulted hundreds of civil society activists, government officials, and industry representatives. It ended with the finalization of the report.[15]

This strategy by Wolfensohn to appease hostile NGOs by letting them deliberate with companies, governments, and World Bank Group staff under the auspices of Emil Salim can be categorized as a form of incorporation.

---

[12] The World Commission on Dams, *Dams and Development*; Klaus Dingwerth, 'The democratic legitimacy of public-private rule making: what can we learn from the World Commission on Dams?', *Global Governance* 11 (2005), pp. 65–83.

[13] He was one of the 'Berkeley Mafia' and could hence be trusted to be not too far off the neoliberal economic policies of the World Bank Group. Naomi Klein, *The Shock Doctrine: The Rise of Disaster Capitalism* (New York: Picador, 2007), p. 83; see also Emil Salim, 'Recollections of my career', *Bulletin of Indonesian Economic Studies* 33, 1 (1997), pp. 45–74.

[14] Gro Harlem Brundtland, *Our Common Future* (New York: United Nations Organization, 1987).

[15] Salim, 'Striking a better balance. Vol. 1', p. ii.

Figure 6.1: Institutional design of World Commission on Dams, Extractive Industries Review

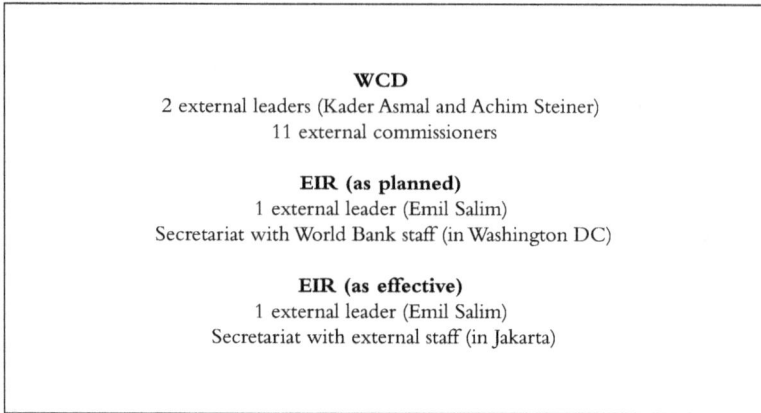

WCD
2 external leaders (Kader Asmal and Achim Steiner)
11 external commissioners

EIR (as planned)
1 external leader (Emil Salim)
Secretariat with World Bank staff (in Washington DC)

EIR (as effective)
1 external leader (Emil Salim)
Secretariat with external staff (in Jakarta)

Source: Author

Wolfensohn reacted to criticism of World Bank practices by opening-up the institution's procedures. NGOs and affected people were promised institutional access. Crucially, this case is also one of the few where an instrumental purpose behind this opening-up can be proven. As testified by Wolfensohn's statement towards Emil Salim, his major aim behind the invitation of NGOs was not to learn something about the World Bank's practices and possibilities of reform but rather to tame the critics. The incorporation was hence driven by a tactic of *active cooptation*.

Implementing the review

On July 19, 2001, the EIR was officially launched by James Wolfensohn. It was institutionalized under the auspices of the IFC Division on Mining Oil, Gas and Chemicals, which was a shared division by World Bank and IFC.[16] As Salim recalls, the secretariat had already been set up when he started his new job in 2002. While Salim continued to live in Jakarta, the secretariat was based in Washington DC. He was expected to visit every three months to review the work that had been done, and to give directions for the next three months. At first, he accepted these conditions, "because I didn't know the way the World Bank was working at the time" (Interview, EIR Secretariat). After three months, however, when he returned to Washington DC for the second time, he felt that there was too much focus on World Bank documents instead of insights from the field. "I didn't feel it was independent". Salim's perception of the job started to change. "If I wanted

---

[16] Salim, 'Striking a better balance. Vol. 1', p. 1.

it very easy, it would have been: you come, once in a quarter, you discuss, you agree on the work being done and you go back home and finish. But the content, I guess, I wasn't very happy with".

Salim came up with the idea that the secretariat needed to be in Jakarta, staffed with independent personnel, not remunerated by the World Bank. He reached out to NGOs and perceived one name as widely accepted: Chandra Kirana. She was an expert on extractive industries, came from Indonesia, spoke very good English, and was well-versed with the priorities of the World Bank Group and its critics. When he went back to Washington DC, Salim demanded the secretariat to be relocated to Jakarta and the World Bank staff be fired. He remembers facing a standoff regarding this decision, which he finally won by threatening to step down. Part of the resulting compromise was that the financial administration remained with Clive Armstrong, a World Bank manager, and Rashad Kaldanay, the leader of the aforementioned division in the World Bank Group. The management of the EIR secretariat was now in the hands of Kirana.[17]

In October of the same year, the first planning workshop with all stakeholders took place. Government representatives from developing countries as well as donor countries, high-ranking managers of oil, gas and mining companies, World Bank Group staff, and NGOs met in a hotel in Brussels. The atmosphere was heated. A World Bank manager with the unfortunate name James Bond, was in the focus of some more radical groups who ridiculed him repeatedly. Some Asian activists laughed at him being stuck in an elevator, shouting "James Bond does not even know how to use an elevator!" (Interviews EIR Secretariat, Indonesian NGO). In my interview with him, he expressed frustration with some of those groups who he deemed too stubborn to understand the issues at stake. The nonetheless productive atmosphere was enabled by Emil Salim's initiative to bring all stakeholders to the table. In opposition to what the World Bank had had in mind, he initiated a number of 'multi-stakeholder consultation workshops' to take place in Africa, Latin America, the Middle East, and the Asia Pacific, all of which attended by local civil society, especially affected people and indigenous communities, NGOs, business, governments, and academics (see Figure 6.2). All of these groups had the opportunity to speak out or hand in written statements.[18] The aim of the review was to assess the circumstances under which World Bank Group investments in extractive industries could contribute to poverty reduction.

---

[17] Salim, 'Striking a better balance. Vol. 1', p. 4.
[18] Emil Salim, 'Striking a better balance. Vol. 2: Stakeholder inputs: converging issues and diverging views of the World Bank Group's involvement in extractive industries' (Jakarta, 2003).

Figure 6.2: Multi-stakeholder workshops of the EIR

•   Latin America and the Caribbean, in Rio de Janeiro, Brazil, 15–19 April 2002;
•   Eastern Europe and Central Asia, in Budapest, Hungary, 19–22 June 2002;
•   Africa, in Maputo, Mozambique, 13–17 January 2003;
•   Asia and the Pacific, in Bali, Indonesia, 26–30 April 2003;
•   Middle East and North Africa, in Marrakech, Morocco, 29 June–2 July 2003.

Source: Salim, 2003, p. 2

Salim told me that he was completely free during the process, and nobody was controlling his moves or dictating him what to do. Thus, his team organized the participatory workshops,[19] and especially the one in Maputo made a deep impression on him: "It was very sad. The way the local people, the indigenous people, were not consulted at all. But also, the local governments, they were more cooperating with the business" (Interview, EIR Secretariat). He saw that mining companies were supporting military governments against the people; "there was no development!". While Salim had not held a negative view of the role of extractive industries in development, he developed this view during his fieldtrips. It is quite remarkable to look at his choice of words. He told me about a "corrupting elite" that wanted to perpetuate its power and would even go as far as to support civil war. It should be re-emphasized here that Salim himself had worked for an autocratic regime and is known as a pragmatic politician. The insights he gained from the workshops must therefore have changed his view dramatically. "Shocked" as he was, he asked the companies: "What is the position of business? And they said: Well, we do what the government wants" (Interview, EIR Secretariat). Unsatisfied by that, he asked: "but what does the World Bank do?". Again, the answer left him disbelieving, for the managers would argue that they did not have permanent staff in the field and therefore could not monitor everything that was going on at the project site: "And there is a sense of: we abide to the ruling government." After telling me that, Salim sighed and added: "I felt something: it's not for the people. And then we talked to the indigenous local people … my God! Then all the stories come. In conclusion: This is a non-renewable resource, used not necessarily for development but for perpetuating the ruling elite."

The EIR secretariat was trying to even out power imbalances between transnational corporations, World Bank and affected people. During field

---

[19]   Emil Salim, 'Striking a better balance. Vol. 3: The World Bank and extractive industries. The final report of the Extractive Industries Review. Annexes' (Jakarta, 2003), p. 8.

visits, Salim saw the need for this since he himself found the dialogue with the oil and mining companies rather difficult. Referring to their power, he said: "You go to the office and this table is really from here to there ... fantastic, very powerful. And big offices. And going there, I'm not very comfortable". Henceforth, he understood the reluctance of other stakeholders to speak to business and tried to make them feel as welcome as possible during the workshops.

Contestation: the Bali walkout

Despite these efforts, during the consultation in Indonesia, Salim's home turf, the majority of critics withdrew from the consultations in protest and organized a collective walkout. These activists felt that they were not being taken seriously. An employee of Wahana Lingkungan Hidup Indonesia (WALHI),[20] who read the official statement of withdrawal at that time, remembers: "Our aspirations were not well addressed. We didn't want to be a justification of the process or hijacked" (Interview, Indonesian NGO). This came as a surprise from the EIR Secretariat's point of view, given that civil society had so far been very engaged in the process. But especially Asian NGOs had a lot to lose in this process, first and foremost their credibility as brokers for the poor. With Salim as a former representative of the Suharto regime, the situation was especially tense for Indonesian NGOs. They were perceived as extremely critical by other participants (Interviews Industry, EIR Secretariat). To complicate things, Emil Salim had founded WALHI while still Minister for the Environment.[21] Many were thus struck that the representative of WALHI read out the statement of collective withdrawal. Afraid of Salim's reaction, the activist was relieved to see that he "only took notes and pictures the whole time" (Interview, Indonesian NGO). Because of his proximity to WALHI, there were (and still are) rumours that Salim had initiated, or at least endorsed, the walkout in order to have more leverage against the World Bank Group. But the reaction I received from his assistant speaks against such an interpretation. When I asked about the walkout, she became quite angry, although it was 14 years after the incident, calling the Indonesian NGOs "dishonest" (Interview, EIR Secretariat). Furthermore, the NGO leaders cite other reasons for their protest, among them that

---

[20] Friends of the Earth Indonesia.

[21] Nadya Karimasari, 'Transnational environmental and agrarian movements influencing national policies: the case of palm oil plantation in Indonesia', MA Thesis (The Hague: International Institute of Social Studies, 2011), p. 16; Nancy Peluso, Suraya Afiff, and Noer Rachman, 'Claiming the grounds for reform: agrarian and environmental movements in Indonesia', *Journal of Agrarian Change* 8, 2–3 (2008), p. 384.

the representatives of indigenous groups were fearing for their safety after an Indonesian delegation led by Solidaritas Perempuan (SP) (Women's Solidarity) was exposed to a violent confrontation during a field visit to Batu Hijau,[22] where they claimed to have been "attacked by sixteen men with long knives and with baseball rackets" in front of the Newmont field office (Interview, Indonesian NGO). The situation was cleared by the police, but the fear did not vanish because "these people were hired by the company. And two or three attackers were in the consultations". These were sincere allegations, which are denied by all the members of the EIR secretariat whom I spoke to. In contrast, they emphasize that some of the urban NGOs "instrumentalized" indigenous peoples' groups to provoke a walkout by civil society (Interviews EIR Secretariat, World Bank Group management). Today, it is difficult to establish whether these incidents happened or not, but they were at the least present as rumours and influenced villagers who refused to continue making statements, fearing physical violence as a result (Interview, Indonesian NGO).

Another reason for suspicion about the process was a circulating draft of EIR recommendations. Salim and his team deny that such a draft has ever existed and called it "fake" (Interviews, EIR Secretariat). Yet, just like the violent thugs, whether factual or fake, the draft negatively influenced trust into the process. Many Asian civil society participants argued that this draft was far too weak and not in line with what had been promised to them by Salim and his team. Therefore, a majority decided that they would not support the EIR any longer, a decision that was contested within civil society in the Asia Pacific region. At least one activist from Oxfam Australia went as far as to apologize to the EIR secretariat, pointing out that she would rather have remained in the process. But in solidarity, all the assembled Asian-Pacific activists rejected to continue.

Caught by surprise, Salim and his team wrote a letter to the NGOs and offered to organize separate meetings to clear the air, but they had decided and left the consultations. Most groups and individuals from other world regions, who had already participated in the process, were now in a delicate position. Either they could also withdraw from the process in solidarity with their Asian colleagues, or, in an attempt to save the process and its logic of inclusivity, remain and therefore give credibility to Salim and his expected recommendations. On an international civil society meeting in Amsterdam, they debated the issue and, finally, decided to remain. Too much work had been invested already, and, most importantly, the NGOs trusted the report to become worth it.

---

[22] Batu Hijau (in Sumbawa, Indonesia) hosts one of the world's biggest mining projects, Newmont.

Clashing expectations: professionalization and economization

The atmosphere at the workshops was often tense and shaped by misunderstandings. Representatives of the institution and its critics were often on entirely different pages in terms of what the reasons for and possible outcomes of the process were, and henceforth also what the procedure should look like. Affected communities typically saw the EIR as a litigation; business and World Bank staff, on the other hand, rather saw it as an exchange of views. While the former, therefore, testified and made their indictments, convinced to persuade the 'eminent person' to stop these harmful projects, industry representatives and World Bank Group managers were not ready to discuss the general need for investment in these projects, but felt already generous to discuss the 'how' of them. One prominent participant reported an "acrimonious vibe" that went back to a misunderstanding of the critics, "because the EIR wasn't going to shut the World Bank business down" (Interview, World Bank Group manager). Since this was, however, what many critics wanted, the World Bank Group management tried to move the discussions in a less radical direction by appealing to the NGOs' sense of reality, competence, and eagerness to 'influence something'. On the one hand, World Bank Management and business representatives perceived disruptions as 'helpful' for the further perfection of operations. On the other hand, they attempted to formalize discussions and to channel them towards a productive and pragmatic mode, sometimes openly communicating towards the transnational activist network what they perceived as professional advocacy and what they, on the contrary, perceived as ruthless ranting, detached from reality, poorly informed and hence without any influence. Both of these ambiguous sets of practices set in motion the mechanism of 'professionalization'. Some of these practices are strategic, some are expressions of a changing perception of self and other that develops over time in a managerial bureaucracy.

These processes happen all but smoothly. One of the representatives of the mining industry remembers

> 'a lot of very strong feelings, which was, you know, pretty understandable, given some of the stories that were coming out. But I think … just for people to have a way of bringing their issues and concerns to the table and for people to listen … . I think that was enormously helpful.' (Interview, industry)

Especially, she felt that the format made it possible to channel some of the emotions and make them productive together, because it gave the industry a means to appropriate these grievances: "You know, advocacy, or activist groups to come to these workshops whereas before, they said they would not engage with the industry. But you had to go meet with people and say: 'The mining industries made some really bad mistakes, but if it's going to do better... .'" The industry representatives were ready to admit some wrongdoings, an olive branch handed to moderate NGOs which were labelled as professional and which actually 'got stuff done', in comparison to those who only complained. For many critics, this was not how they had understood their role. Their answer to the review's question (under what conditions can extractive industries projects contribute to sustainable development?) was: under no conditions.

Yet, institutional staff and industry representatives were constantly channelling discussions towards a common, pragmatic mode: they admitted some wrongdoings and then asked everybody to look forward instead of backwards. This puts pressure on the critics because they feel a chance to make a difference, but only if they engage on the terms set for them by their opponents. Everything else is portrayed as counter-productive. One member of the EIR team, for instance, called out the Asian-Pacific civil society community and said: "I can really see why civil society is fighting for indigenous people and victims etc., but you still have to play straight" (Interview, EIR Secretariat).

Playing straight means to play along the institutionally set rules for dialogue and to ask reasonable questions, like "How do we now go forward from here? Cause I mean there is no point just always looking backwards" (Interview, Industry). If critics did not comply with this style, they were shamed for not being interested in real progress or they were labelled as bad negotiators. For instance, one representative of the World Bank Group in the final evaluation workshop in Lisbon recalled that "for the most part, the people on the NGOs and civil society ... weren't particularly professional" (Interview, World Bank Group manager).[23] She felt that for them, the main issue was to prove they were right. "But I would call them almost sanctimonious, at times". She complained that the advocates, especially those of indigenous groups, spoke eloquently about their feelings, about their habitat, or the land that they lived on. "But it was very divorced from the conversations that we needed to have. It was almost like mystical at times". When referring to the NGOs on the other hand, she remembers that "the calibre was often not equivaling to the calibre on the corporate side". Professionalization was instantiated by pressuring NGOs to be "reasonable". One major institutional figure in the EIR told them:

---

[23] After the multi-stakeholder consultation workshops, one final workshop was held in Lisbon from 11–13 December 2003 to discuss the completed EIR report.

'I myself came out of civil society and I am very pro sustainability, human rights, social justice, etc. And even with those principles, it was so unreasonable that I told them: 'If I didn't have my principles, I actually want to write this pro-industry'. Because, here you are, given a process that is open; and this is how you are behaving … .' (Interview, EIR Secretariat)

The critics were exposed to the choice of either being 'reasonable' that is to professionalize, or to be unreasonable and to spoil the process which was there to help the principles they stood for. The way the accusation is framed clearly puts them at the receiving end ("here you are, given a process"). They should be thankful to the institution for being invited. But nevertheless, they misbehaved – a language reminiscent of parenting. The critics needed to be trained in professionalism from the viewpoint of their adversaries. A member of the CAO told me that very often the interactions between World Bank and NGOs were superficial, and she always hoped that the critics would say something like: "Okay, there are proven ways of managing these risks. How many people do you have working on this? How much do you … so … clearly focused on implementation." This would have been effective advocacy from her point of view. And since she understood herself as neutral, she would also communicate these strategies to critics so that they would become better, that is more professional.

The implication of these ideas for professional advocacy is that matters of principle should not be part of the discussion. Rather, critics should focus on how to perfect implementation, expecting that everyone stands for, or at least accepts, the same principles. This also leads over to economization (discussed later): an argument that was used repeatedly against the 'unprofessional' critics was that the industry representatives were using their valuable time. One of them, visibly upset, asked his opponents: "Why do you not believe that we are here in good faith? Do you think I have nothing better to be doing?" (Interview, World Bank Group manager). One World Bank staff member recalled that this really struck her, because he was the chair

'of an incredibly large company. A very busy person. But this was important. And he was there, in Lisbon for, you know, a matter of days. I mean, the idea of getting him to be spending that much time on any issue … And they didn't seem to appreciate that. They had the week to be there. They had all the time in the world. … That's what I mean about not always being realistic, or practical in some respect.'

What she describes as not being 'realistic' can be theorized as a way of economizing the debate. In combination with the previously-described presupposition of ends as givens through the representation of the institution as bearer of the same principles ("sustainability, human rights, social justice, etc."), a specific rationality is defined as realistic, while other ways of looking at a problem are degraded. The confirmation of what already is was expressed through an openly communicated disbelief towards its critique. Furthermore, the logic of time-pressure from the corporate world was attached to importance, while the critics were perceived as less important, having "all the time in the world". Their unwillingness to confirm with the terms of debate and its pragmatic, goal-oriented character was portrayed as political die-hard and uncompromising. Yet, the underlying goals of the goal-oriented debate were not up for debate themselves. The ends were already clear, because they must be oriented at the global knowledge that the World Bank Group produced. Critics were associated with a partial logic and an "unwillingness, to even admit that there were some positives taking place here" (Interview, World Bank Group manager).

The pressure put on critics through economization was exacerbated in the Bali case, where they were blamed to have committed a moral mistake:

'Walking out? Well, people have flown, taken time from their schedule … . And again, that level of sort of disrespect … for the process, and for the fact that you've actually come together. So, you can disagree and maybe not come to an agreement. You might not finalize something, but walking-out is almost childish, unprofessional.' (Interview, business)

This quote shows how professionalization and economization complemented each other. For the EIR to have a positive outcome, the institution was ready to learn, yet only from critics who adopted the positive and forward-looking terms of debate. Everything else was framed as an irresponsible critique and used as proof for the partiality of its reasons opposed to the global wisdom that the debate was striving for. This worked through quantification by bringing the time investment of the participants into the debate as a currency. Those who did not honour it were labelled less important. This combination of professionalization and economization had the effect of portraying the institutions as open, learning, and forward-looking but also calculating and time-oriented and therefore rational, while the critique was framed as futile, misdirected and overreaching.

The outcome: recommendations for the World Bank Group

After the Bali walkout, the non-Asian activists remained committed to the EIR; the withdrawal of Asian critics did not further disrupt the process.

The final report was submitted in December 2003 and presented inside the World Bank Group, first to IFC and then to the Board of Directors.[24] Salim was not opposed to extractive industries per se. However, what he had observed in practice during the EIR did not strike him as sustainable. Salim had seen a greedy elite only interested in short-term gains and uninterested in long-term development:

> 'The local people in Africa, Latin America, my God, very sad. I was shocked! How is it possible? That's why I came to the idea: The balance in extractive industries is very much in favour of business. The business protected by the government. Therefore, we proposed: You, Mr. World Bank: Strike a better balance!'

'Striking a better balance' became the title of the report. It called for a general reversal of the World Bank Group policy towards renewable energies, beyond the concrete conditions for extractive projects. The report built on a perceived consensus during the consultations on 'the need for increased transparency of payments and revenues as a means to achieve better poverty alleviation outcomes in the extractive industries sector'.[25] But beyond transparency, the EIR included far-reaching demands. From today's perspective, three of these recommendations stand out, as they strongly shaped the terms of debate around the World Bank Group's further project management. Wolfensohn, when reflecting on the EIR later commented: "I must have been drunk. How could I have agreed to something like this?"[26] First, extractive companies were required to 'publish what they pay' and for governments to 'publish what they receive'. This broad call for more transparency had immediate impact. It led to the Extractive Industries Transparency Initiative (EITI). The second far-reaching recommendation is the Free Prior and Informed Consent (FPIC) of affected people, especially before resettlement measures. This recommendation remained among the hottest topics for over ten years and has only been implemented in 2016.[27] The third major recommendation was for the World Bank to stop

---

[24] Salim, 'Striking a better balance. Vol. 1'.
[25] Salim, 'Striking a better balance. Vol. 1', p. 13.
[26] Quoted in Rich, *Foreclosing the Future*.
[27] The IFC implemented it in 2012 for category A (high-risk projects). The language of World Bank Group reports often veils loopholes to outsiders. For instance, the World Bank Group agreed to adopt the EIR recommendation of revenue transparency for 'significant' projects. 'Significant' in this context means more than 10 per cent of government budget. Bank Information Center, 'EIR implementation status report: World Bank Group commitments on revenue and contract transparency' (Washington DC, 2006), p. 2, available at: {http://www.bankinformationcenter.org/wp-content/uploads/2013/01/EIR_Implementation_Status_Report.pdf}.

all investments in oil projects by 2008. The review's question – under which conditions can extractive industries help to alleviate poverty? – was therefore answered with 'under no conditions' in the case of crude oil. This recommendation was adopted at the end of 2017.

Salim highlighted that extractive industries can contribute to poverty alleviation only *if* three enabling conditions are fulfilled:[28]

- pro-poor public and corporate governance
- effective social and environmental policies
- respect for human rights

He demanded to rebalance institutional priorities, that is, to adjust the internal incentive structure from cash flow towards sustainability. The World Bank Group had not expected these demands. One of the managers told me that, at first, he had endorsed Emil Salim as an "excellent choice" and, later, got caught by surprise when he drifted off from the expected. According to him, the lack of the eminent person's institutional integration had led to the unrealistic recommendations, which could not be implemented. Because of that, this manager "did not take the process seriously" any more in the end (Interview, World Bank Group manager).

Back to business as usual? Legitimation and regulation

When I asked Emil Salim how he felt about the EIR, he said he was "very sad". Another member of the EIR team also told me they were "disappointed" about the World Bank Group's handling of their recommendations. Staff members of the relevant World Bank and IFC departments, in contrast, argued that the EIR had a major impact on the institution's future operations (Interviews, World Bank Group managers). Why such an enormously diverging interpretation?

Although some changes in the policies on extractive industries did occur because of the EIR, the implementation of the recommendations was very selective. The World Bank Group management first actively aimed at a dilution of the EIR recommendations and, when this was unsuccessful, tried to sweep the most challenging recommendations under the carpet. Yet, no new protest movement emerged in response to this. This missing outrage has to do with the overall constellation of complex rule being actualized here: the transnational activist network had already been exposed to the institutional mechanisms of economization, incorporation, and

---

[28] Salim, 'Striking a better balance. Vol. 1', p. 45.

WHEN A CONTENTIOUS PROCESS OPENS UP

professionalization during the EIR process. Furthermore, the World Bank Group's official response letter and the ensuing discussions regarding the EIR recommendations were guided by the mechanisms of legitimation and regulation, further instantiating complex rule.[29]

When the EIR secretariat had finished its report, it was circulated among World Bank Group management and Executive Board. Salim was first invited to discuss the draft with IFC where he received strong opposition. IFC managers scolded him for his recommendations, claiming that they were "impossible". Salim persisted that "it is the truth". But he felt that his opinion was not valued at all. "They were insistent on it to become more pro-business". The management staff pressured him to revise the draft. But he was not afraid because he directly reported to the President. "I was firm, because I knew that Wolfensohn was involved, so I did not need to bow to them". After that, however, he was spontaneously invited to meet Wolfensohn in Paris. To the surprise of Salim, Wolfensohn reacted furiously to the recommendations. "He tried to talk him out of the coal thing" (Interview, World Bank Group manager). From an insider, I received the information that Wolfensohn brutally cursed at Salim and gave him the choice: either the report would become more "balanced" toward business interests, or the World Bank Group was not going to publish it. Salim argued said "balance" was already skewed towards business. The World Bank Group needed to listen to its critics, otherwise there wouldn't be any balance. This statement provoked Wolfensohn to engage in a lengthy discussion as to what "balanced" meant. He said that he received complaints from businesses. Salim countered: "Exactly: You get the reports from business, but you never receive a report from the NGOs, especially the indigenous peoples. That is my biggest complaint! The business can get into your office, have your ear, you will listen. But you never listen to the indigenous people. This is precisely what we want to change." "Difficult", Wolfensohn responded. "I cannot accept it".

The next disappointment for Salim happened in the Board of Directors, chaired by India at the time. The governments represented in the meeting were not at all happy with his findings, arguing that they needed extractive industries for growth and employment. Furthermore, they complained about the process in which they felt the voices of the governments had not been heard sufficiently.[30] Salim had hoped to find an ally in the Indian Director, but much to the contrary, developing countries in particular rejected his

---

[29]   In the following 'Management Response'. World Bank Group, *Striking a Better Balance. The World Bank Group and Extractive Industries: The Final Report of the Extractive Industries Review. World Bank Group Management Response* (Washington DC, 2004).
[30]   World Bank Group, *Striking a Better Balance*, p. 3.

report. The Board of Directors supported Wolfensohn in his decision that the report could not be published in the form it had been drafted.

Salim remained firm and Wolfensohn's threat was carried out. The report is, until today, a poorly designed Word document – and stands out in contrast to other shiny World Bank Group reports with colourful pictures on the front page. The EIR thus remained only an external expertise and was not officially published *by* the World Bank Group.[31] It went directly to the Board of Directors which, in the same session, received the draft *Management Response* that had been written by World Bank Group managers simultaneously to the EIR process. In this Management Response, the language was much friendlier than the witnesses of the exchanges between Salim and Wolfensohn could have anticipated. Most of the EIR recommendations were welcomed, although the language remained more abstract than in Salim's report. There was striking deviation in terms of policy, however, especially regarding two core points in which the Management Response interpreted findings of the EIR on page 1:

- Extractive industries *can* contribute to sustainable development, when projects are implemented well and preserve the rights of affected people, and if the benefits they generate are well-used.
- There *is* a continuing role for the World Bank Group in supporting extractives provided its involvement supports poverty reduction and sustainable development.[32]

Although the detailed response does deliver on many of the EIR recommendations, these core insights distort the EIR's message. While Salim had outlined very specific conditions under which extractive industries may contribute to development, the draft Management Response turned the structure of this argument around and highlighted the exception as the rule, citing that extractive industries *can contribute to development* as the core take-away message. Management therefore "decided not to disengage in funding extractive industries even with the absence of several enabling conditions enumerated in the Eminent Person's Final Report".[33]

The core recommendations of exiting oil until 2008 was not taken up and the otherwise high stakes for engaging in extractive industries

---

[31] Although it was later uploaded to the website: {http://documents.worldbank.org/cura ted/en/961241468781797388/Striking-a-better-balance-the-World-Bank-Group-and-extractive-industries-the-final-report-of-the-extractive-industries-review}.

[32] World Bank Group, *Striking a Better Balance*, p. iii, my emphasis.

[33] Victoria Tauli-Corpuz, 'Preface to the second edition', in Marcus Colchester and Emily Caruso (eds) *Extracting Promises: Indigenous Peoples, Extractive Industries and the World Bank* (Baguio City: Tebtebba Foundation, 2005), I–II.

seemed almost ridiculed by the Management Response. NGOs and parliamentarians therefore called it "inadequate", argued that it "fails to commit to most essential conditions".[34] This also held for other core EIR recommendations, the most striking example being the FPIC. Salim had called the search for consensus prior to any resettlement measure an absolute basis for the World Bank Group's work on extractive industries ('the social license to operate'). The Management Response agreed that FPIC was necessary. However, in the document, FPIC translates into 'free prior and informed *consultation*'.[35] The guideline was diluted from consensus to holding consultations, taking the emancipatory power out of FPIC. Such mitigations of the EIR recommendations can also be found in other areas of the Management Response. In general, the World Bank Group agreed with the report and initiated various processes, such as an annual review of all extractive projects, and promised to develop new safeguards for the IFC based on the EIR.[36] At the same time, central recommendations were mitigated and concrete demands, such as the establishment of a permanent ombudsman for the publication of information, or a new, independent complaints mechanism, were rejected with reference to existing mechanisms.[37]

Like Salim's choice of process, the EIR recommendations turned out to be spectacular – and surprisingly fundamental to many critics. The technical character of the Management Response was therefore even more disappointing, especially for affected populations. This was also communicated by the involved critics. Wolfensohn responded to this criticism with a letter to Salim in which he wrote:

> I do not necessarily accept, as some groups assert, that unless the report's recommendations are adopted in their entirety, the World Bank Group will somehow have failed in its response. Our obligation is always to take into account the legitimate views and interests of all stakeholders, as well as our own best judgment, and to do what is right for the world's poor people.[38]

---

[34] World Bank Group, 'Comments Received on the Draft Management Response to the Final Report of the Extractive Industries Review: Staff Report by the Oil, Gas and Chemicals Department' (Washington DC, 2004), pp. 5–7.

[35] World Bank Group, *Striking a Better Balance*, p. v.

[36] World Bank Group, 'Comments Received on the Draft Management Response', p. 5.

[37] World Bank Group, 'Comments Received on the Draft Management Response', p. 25.

[38] James Wolfensohn, 'Letter from James Wolfensohn to Emil Salim' (Washington DC: World Bank, 2004), available at: {http://siteresources.worldbank.org/INTOGMC/Resources/eirfaq.pdf}.

Legitimation

The constant legitimation of practices is a central mechanism of complex rule, characteristic of it being organized as a reflexive order of justification. In the following, I outline that (1) arguing with complexity and (2) rhetorical disarming shaped the way Management approached its critics in the time after the EIR's completion.

(1) The most frequent practice of legitimation in the case of the EIR is arguing with complexity. This happened in 2004 as a part of promoting the Management Response as the right message, and it happened in retrospect in all my interviews with managers as an answer to critical questions. The groundwork for this argumentative resource was already built into the EIR's design: when Salim was hired as eminent person, the World Bank Group decided to also ask the three in-house evaluation groups to review the institution's performance in extractive industries.[39] The same job was hence given to two parties. In the inhouse evaluation report,[40] recommendations were less divergent from existing practice, although often agreeing with the problems described by the EIR. Furthermore, shortly before these processes started, the International Council for Mining and Minerals (ICMM) had organized a review themselves and, therefore, the EIR's introduction irritated industrial figures, who argued to have completed just this exercise already (Interview, World Bank Group manager). Finally, the CAO was running an inquiry into extractive industries projects as well.[41]

These parallel processes are usually invoked when questions regarding the non-implementation of the EIR are raised. Had there only been the EIR, the non-identical proposals in the Management Response could be judged as deficient in that they failed to take up some of the issues raised in the EIR. As a response to various evaluations, the Management Response could not answer affirmatively to all EIR recommendations because the situation was 'more complex than that'. One responsible manager at the time drew on the parallel processes as a reason for not accepting some of the critics' demands: "Civil society wanted us to ... do things in the EIR, but I didn't

[39] Operations Evaluation Department IFC Operations Evaluation Group (OEG) and MIGA Operations Evaluation Unit (OEU).

[40] Andrés Liebenthal, Roland Michelitsch, and Ethel Tarazona, 'Extractive industries and sustainable development. An evaluation of World Bank Group experience' (Washington DC: World Bank Group, 2005).

[41] Compliannce Advisor Ombudsman, 'Extracting sustainable advantage? A review of how sustainability issues have been dealt with in recent IFC & MIGA Extractive Industries Projects' (Washington DC, 2003), available at: {http://documents.worldbank.org/cura ted/en/886741478094865899/A-review-of-how-sustainability-issues-have-been-dealt-with-in-recent-IFC-MIGA-extractive-industries-projects}.

want to pre-empt this parallel process which was also a consultative process, so a lot of the details were left for that" (Interview, World Bank Group manager). The plurality of evaluations and their respective recommendations worked to immunize the World Bank Group against criticism. This was a conscious decision by the responsible managers at the time to balance potential outcomes of the EIR after the bad experiences of the WCD. The manager with the idea to bring up a second, internal, evaluation recalls that "operational Management strongly supported the idea of a parallel OED/OEG Review because it was believed that this would provide an objective assessment. And this would complement the consultation report on stakeholder views" (Interview, World Bank Group manager). This double structure portrayed the EIR as less objective because it was 'only' gathering stakeholder views, while the internal evaluation would collect 'objective' data, hence diminishing the EIR's original purpose. Responding to my surprise regarding the parallel processes, a manager said: "it's very complex", not specifying whether he meant the issue itself or the double structure they created. One of the managers I spoke to said that once the EIR report had been handed to the Board, he had stopped taking the process seriously because he had felt that the EIR was too simple in order to appreciate the complexity of the topic (Interview, World Bank Group manager). In this case, the legitimation of the self (non-fulfilment of recommendations because of complexity) worked through de-legitimation of the recommendations (not complex enough).

While this aspect of institutional complexity as rhetorical device was strategically put in place, others are side products of organizational culture and came handy for legitimation on the way: consider the multi-layered process of decision-making in the World Bank Group. While, from the perspective of the EIR team, Wolfensohn was perceived as spoiling the process of adoption and implementation after they handed in their daft, most of the involved managers highlight his fight for the very recommendations inside the Executive Board, where they remember him brokering a compromise that was still more progressive than many countries had been willing to accept:

'It went through two rounds at the board, that was the role Jim Wolfensohn played, shepherding it through the board. So, we had our first meeting where he agreed – "Okay, we heard you, we'll change things and come back" and I freaked out. I said, "what are you meaning, what are we gonna change? I've been coming through this consultative process three years, we gonna do another three years?" But he kind of calmed me down afterwards, you know, so we went back to the board and made really minor changes, but enough for them to feel like: we heard them, and here's the final, final report.' (Interview, World Bank Group manager)

This experience of Wolfensohn as actually saving the process by navigating through the minefield of the Board is a typically contradictory attribution of agency from different perspectives. Since so many individuals and departments were involved in responding to the EIR, the institutional complexity worked as a tool for legitimation in which knowledgeable actors told the critics that they should be happy with what they got because "we", who the critics saw as spoilers, actually pushed this agenda against institutional resistance.

In the case of FPIC, this is especially astonishing: I talked to *all* decision-makers in the relevant department of the World Bank Group, and they unanimously endorsed FPIC but argued that there was reluctance inside the management structures of the institution. Since I talked to those managers who had a say in this process, it is possible that either they retrospectively rationalize their view, or that they may have privately held the belief that FPIC was good, but they all thought the others would not yet be ready. This is an enlightening example for how they argued towards critics: we want the same as you, and we will push the agenda as far as possible. The critics were then left with the difficult judgement whether they were faced with an ally or a spoiler because they could not discern where this 'institutional reluctance' was actually located. The argument of institutional complexity hence worked as a legitimation tool for managers, positioning themselves as progressive allies without, however, any means for critics to hold them accountable, because actually tracing the institutional pathways would be 'too complex'.

Over and over again, the World Bank Group staff emphasized that "there is no monolithic IFC that makes its own decisions for the Bank". This point has been theorized by organizational sociology[42] and frequently embraced by IR scholars.[43] The view that IOs "are anything but monoliths, and as each component is subject to variations and various power positions" is of course correct.[44] But as the example of FPIC has shown, it also provides a

---

[42] Rick Delbridge and Tim Edwards, 'Inhabiting institutions: critical realist refinements to understanding institutional complexity and change', *Organization Studies* 34, 7 (2013), pp. 927–47; Gayl D. Ness and Steven R. Brechin, 'Bridging the gap: international organizations as organizations', *International Organization* 42, 2 (1988), p. 245.

[43] Julian Junk and Frederik Trettin, 'Internal dynamics and dysfunctions of international organizations – an introduction to the special issue', *Journal of International Organizations Studies* 5, 1 (2014), pp. 8–11; Tine Hanrieder, 'Gradual change in international organisations: agency theory and historical institutionalism', *Politics* 34, 4 (2014), pp. 324–33; Barnett and Finnemore, 'The politics, power, and pathologies of international organizations'; Dingwerth, Klaus, Dieter Kerwer, and Andreas Nölke, *Die Organisierte Welt: Internationale Beziehungen Und Organisationsforschung* (Baden-Baden: Nomos, 2008); Swati Srivastava, 'Assembling international organizations', *Journal of International Organization Studies* 3, 1 (2013), pp. 72–83.

[44] Richard Jolly, Louis Emmerij, and Thomas G. Weiss, *UN Ideas That Changed the World* (Bloomington: Indiana University Press, 2009), p. 35.

good hiding place for actors inside the organization. Strikingly, professionals even refer directly to theories of organization to justify the institution's slow or non-existent responses. "We're not going to change who or what we are, or the decisions we make or the philosophy that we hold because of those processes, that's just never gonna happen, that's against every rule of organizational sociology" (Interview, World Bank Group manager).

(2) The mechanism of legitimation is also observable in rhetorical disarming, such as in the schmoozing of civil society actors, the construction of a common goal, and the anticipation and dilution of criticism. All of these were frequently practiced during the EIR. Referring to the parallel review on extractive industries compiled by the OEG/OED/OEU, for instance, one of the authors highlighted to cooperate with 'civil society', but with the reasonable part of it, and therefore claimed to reach more legitimate conclusions than the EIR could.[45] This is remarkable because the EIR itself was mainly a stakeholder consultation, involving dozens of industry representatives, government officials and NGOs and affected communities on all continents. The inhouse evaluation, in contrast, was legitimated by the power of two individuals, Arvind Ganesan and Michael Rae, because they work for 'reasonable' NGOs. The World Bank Group at the time elevated specific individuals and organizations as 'reasonable' civil society – and, by that, legitimated their process as participatory, at the same time decreasing the value of the independent EIR and its process.

Besides this rhetorical elevation of moderate NGOs, managers at the time also tried to rhetorically disarm their critics by constructing a common goal and highlighting the great pains to which they went to reach it. An example I encountered repeatedly is to make the point that working for the World Bank Group itself is already a sacrifice and, therefore, criticizing these individuals is misplaced. One of the managers involved in the EIR said:

'People like me ... made a conscious choice to leave a good career in industry to come to the Bank, because we believed in development, and we thought there's something deep. We've lost legitimacy – why? ... Why are the people furious about the Bank? You know, we go out to these terrible countries, and we catch malaria, and we do all this because we do really want peoples' lives to be better, how come this is not reflected?' (Interview, World Bank Group manager)

---

[45] The OED/OEG/OEU evaluation covered the following individuals: James Cooney (Placer Dome, Inc.), Cristina Echavarría (International Development Research Centre), Arvind Ganesan (Human Rights Watch), Michael Rae (WWF) and David Rice (British Petroleum).

As I collected from NGO participants of the EIR, this argument was held against them time and again: "we all fight for the same goal here"; "are you not for development?" With this rhetorical trick (conscious or not), the self is legitimated by the construction of a common goal with critics.

A third way of rhetorical disarming is the anticipation and dilution of criticism. One long-time advocate against the World Bank Group's environmental policies who had not participated in the EIR told me that he felt reassured in his decision to refrain from the process because the Management Response was the classic rhetorical move he had expected: "to endorse the general goals … but then there were very specific operational goals, … very specific operational recommendations which they did not accept. [But the] more specific operational recommendations were what we needed because everyone can agree: 'oh we believe in inclusiveness and participation'" (Interview, US activist). Looking back at the EIR, one experienced activist told me that this would be a good example for the "remarkable readiness for self-critique" inside the higher ranks of Management (Interview, US NGO).

The EIR process had a disarming effect. Before critics could even complain within the consultations, managers would already state how they perceived own mistakes and readily listened to the horror stories of affected people, assuring them how much they cared. One of the former staff members responsible for interaction with civil society told me that this was a strategy to legitimize the institution, the rationale being that complaints will be taken into the institution and rationalized: "It's the classic answer of that kind of institution: 'Yes, you're right, there is something true in what you say – but …'" (Interview, World Bank Group manager). This was not necessarily a tactic by all involved staff but possibly honest openness. Retrospectively, with many of the recommendations not implemented, it nevertheless had the effect of disarming critique which was encountered constructively and hence had no need to scandalize issues.

Regulation

I have shown how the World Bank Group management reacted to the EIR with a response that fell short in many decisive aspects. To explain why this did not cause a bigger mobilization of critics, I have argued that the institutional approach was characterized by legitimation practices. Beyond the discursive legitimation, however, the process of responding to the EIR was regulated to a great extent, limiting the possibility of critique considerably as I will show in the following. With regulation, I refer to the mechanism through which the organizational form of the managerial bureaucracy is instantiated in global governance (next to professionalization, discussed previously). It is observable in institutional practices of creating rules as well as the ordering and disciplining of critique.

The most heavily contested issue in the EIR was FPIC, a good example of how the World Bank Group regulated its approach. The Management Response's diluted version of FPIC (free prior and informed *consultation* instead of *consent*) had led to an outcry among the participants and leadership of the EIR. The Management's public justification of the diluted version in the years to come was shaped by a retreat to the logic of rules, highlighting that it was right (in a legal sense) to commence with resettling people without their free prior and informed *consent*. A phrase that managers used repeatedly was the judicial concept of 'eminent domain'. When asked about the grievances of local people and forced resettlements, World Bank managers often referred to this concept:

> 'That is something called 'eminent domain' in most jurisdictions. And just because one person doesn't want to sell his house or whatever, you are not going to stop the metro line or maybe relocate it somewhere else, when instead of one person you have hundreds or thousands of people affected.' (Interview, World Bank Group manager)

This logic persists until today.

The World Bank Group President Kim said in 2016 (see Chapter 8), "Everyone who came with an airplane or on a highway profited from the resettlement of other people. That's called eminent domain in rich countries". This comparison to the domestic sphere seems adequate but, *de jure*, this concept does not apply in the context of projects operated by the World Bank Group. It is a right solely reserved to the sovereign state. The institution itself has no jurisdiction and hence can also not execute eminent domain, a fact that visibly frustrates World Bank Group managers who refer to the concept as an abstract comparison – something they say one would 'normally' expect. In referring to this legal term, at the same time, they circumvent the competitive wording applied by the critics, namely 'forced eviction'.[46] Avoiding the clearly negative connotation of the latter term, the institutional staff usually speaks of the more neutral 'resettlement'. Referring to eminent domain creates an imagined legal space in which the problematic resettlements of the World Bank Group become 'right', because a majority profits from it. This utilitarian logic is not spelled out on moral but on legalistic grounds, with reference to a legal norm that does in fact not apply in the given context. Yet, by referring to this concept as a 'normal' background against which to measure the own actions, the contestation which had been initiated on moral grounds by critics ('suffering') is transferred to a rule-based logic ('in most jurisdictions').

---

[46] See also: {https://www.icij.org/investigations/world-bank/about-project-evicted-and-abandoned/}.

In the end, FPIC (C as in consent) was rejected with reference to these (partly imagined) rules. The wording was taken up, however, and the World Bank Group from that point on required FPIC (C as in consultation) and operationalized this with 'broad community support'. The compromise was adopted and heavily influenced the policymaking of the years to come. This is especially visible in the IFC Performance Standards, which were reviewed in 2005. As one manager told me, the IFC Management was even opposed to the compromise formula ('broad community support') in the beginning, because they wanted to stick to a formalistic procedure to 'get stuff done'. Visibly proud in an interview, the internal broker of the compromise formula told me how he convinced the sceptical IFC Management:

> 'I had a bit of an argument, if you will, at that time with my seniors and the IFC who were reluctant even to accept that. And I said, "Tell me something! You really gonna do a project if you can't, in all honesty, say you have broad community support?"'[47] (Interview, World Bank Group manager)

Being oriented to rules was privileged over the moralistic claims of critics. A bureaucratic culture was slipped over the EIR's recommendations and blurred them beyond recognition. During this process, the ordering and disciplining of critique was put in place by explaining this logic to the critics and by highlighting that critique has to be formulated according to this regulated, bureaucratic logic oriented at the current rule book; only then could it exert real influence. This point has been described with theories of organizational culture: referring to specific rhetorical and normative standards that people working in the institutions become used to, and by which they demarcate the self from other organizations or the general environment.[48] Some influential staff members refer to the idea of organizational culture and environment as if they had read these sociological textbooks:

> 'If a minister of finance comes to us and tells us something in a language that we can understand it's easily digestible by the Bank, a decision

---

[47] FPIC (C as in consent) was later adopted, in the IFC Performance Standards review 2012, however only for indigenous peoples, and in the Safeguards Review of the World Bank in 2017, although only for 'affected indigenous peoples/Sub-Saharan African historically underserved traditional local communities'. The World Bank, 'Environmental and social framework' (Washington DC, 2017) p. 79.

[48] Weaver and Nelson, 'Organizational culture'; William G. Ouchi and Alan L. Wilkins, 'Organizational culture', *Annual Review of Sociology* 11, 1 (1985), pp. 457–83; Sarfaty, *Values in Translation*.

can be made and some accommodation. But if somebody comes along and complains about this and that, it's much more difficult for us to a) understand and b) do something about it. This is because very often those things are beyond our scope of authority or influence and basically difficult to digest, to internalize.' (Interview, World Bank Group manager)

What this evaluator describes could be interpreted as a form of 'pathology' of the institution.[49] Yet, some managers also turn this observation around, expecting critics to adopt the organizational logic. Recommendations that demanded to change this logic (for instance to say "No" to coal, discussed previously), were therefore perceived as irresponsible. Only those recommendations that were 'digestible' by the institutional culture were seen as 'realistic' recommendations.

From this regulated perspective, the outcomes of the EIR were a huge success, signified in the World Bank's and IFC's pledge to implement FPIC (C as in *consultation*) and broad community support. These impacts, however, seen from the perspective of many critics, were perceived as disappointing, if not circular: for them, this move towards consultation meant that their consultation led to more consultations, but not to tangible changes in the mining policies, or their termination. Yet, as will be elaborated in the next chapter, some of the professionalized NGOs indeed came to see the value of these gains during the process of consultation, endorsing the institutional rules and its formalized bureaucratic culture and enjoying the growing opportunities for participation.

---

[49] Barnett and Finnemore, 'The politics, power, and pathologies of international organizations'.

7

Fragmentation in Contestation: The Movement during the EIR Process

During my interviews, I was struck by how explicitly the World Bank Group managers named the calming down of critics as a consequence of the EIR. When, for instance, I asked an IFC official in the mining department how interaction with critics evolved after the EIR, she said that "its constructive most of the times, I don't think that there is a big adversarial tension going on". How is this possible, bearing in mind that almost all involved critics perceived the Management Response as falling completely short of Salim's recommendations and their wishes? Asking World Bank Group managers and their critics this question, I received strongly diverging answers. The former would usually explain the lack of mobilization with the substantial progress made in institutional policies: "I think civil society saw that we made some substantial changes, improvements. Of course, they didn't get everything they wanted, but I think they felt: 'Well, let's at least work with these guys, let's use them to influence the industry'. ... And so that's what I think happened" (Interview, World Bank Group manager).

Activists, on the other hand, typically gave an alternative account of what happened, and claimed that they were simply too frustrated to continue, because things seemed so useless and ineffectual after the non-acceptance of the EIR recommendations in the Management Response. One activist who was strongly involved in the process, and who seemed very passionate about it in the interview, demonstrated her deep frustration with institutional politics as follows: "I don't really know. They changed their safeguard policies and I didn't review whether they are stronger or weaker. I stopped following the process. ... and I guess in a way you could say I am disillusioned, but you could also say I am just more realistic now".

Referring to the frustration, she commented: "I think the disappointment with the EIR was that nothing was really implemented, except the EITI" (Interview, EIR Secretariat).

Contrasting these two contrarian explanations of the demobilization of critique puts a question mark behind both. It seems unrealistic that the critics were so satisfied with the implementation that they stopped mobilizing, only to then tell me collectively that "nothing" was implemented. On the other hand, it also does not seem plausible that they were simply tired and frustrated and went home, instead of doubling-down on the institution in case they would have felt betrayed. So, what did really happen to the resistance during and after the EIR?

My claim is that by engaging in the EIR, the critics entered a constellation of complex rule by playing along the five governing mechanisms reconstructed in the following. These allowed them to gain exceptional institutional influence, hence the progressive recommendations, but also fragmented the movement, demobilized their base and de-radicalized their repertoire so that protest against the ensuing non-implementation was not possible anymore. Entering the EIR, an arena of *open global governance* par excellence, the critics became divided among themselves, the result of which was the crumbling of their resistance.

Economization

I have shown previously that the World Bank Group management – strategically or not – economized the EIR process by dividing global from particular knowledge, presenting ends as (economic) givens, and actively quantifying discussions. To hold up my hypothesis that the governing mechanisms are instantiated by institutional as well as resistant practices, we should be able to observe how, through the course of events, parts of the critics accepted a neoliberal governing rationality, while others delineated themselves from this economized logic, in effect creating fragmentation among critics.

The economization of critique in the form of accepting a neoliberal governing rationality was a core pattern during the EIR, specifically in the adoption of economic and technical language by critics. A good example was given to me by one advocate whose organization uses situations in which governments or companies are suddenly opening-up due to public pressure to lobby them with reference to their reputation. "But we have to argue on the basis of the long-term interests of these actors: when there is a blockade, it will be expensive for you" (Interview, US NGO). The critics thus utilize the language of their adversary to convince her of a line of action, the outcome of which they would support.

An even stronger indication of the economization of critique is when not only the adoption of language but an adoption of ends can be observed. One process that stands out in this regard is the programmatic reorientation of NGOs along the guidelines of big foundations. I refer to an influential NGO with the following example, which has been named to me by various activists who all asked for confidentiality. In 2004, this NGO reshuffled its staff structure in an attempt to adapt to a changing funding environment.

> 'I don't know what possessed [the head of this NGO]; they threw out the whole staff that was there, that were all very radical and gifted. And they hired, younger, less radical, more inexperienced people, and then combined with that ... the donor funding changed. And, you know, if you asked [X] about working on anything, they would say: "Oh sure, just show me the money flow."' (Interview, US NGO)

Activists from various strands of the movement acknowledged that many of the critical NGOs changed during the time of the EIR:

> 'if you asked anybody ..., what they were standing up to, they would tell you neoliberalism. I mean, there was one force and civil society was looking at the structure of power in driving neoliberalism. And that turn, that was just completely emasculated, you know, to a point where you had dedicated donor streams to three issues.' (Interview, US NGO)

The approach that this activist described as "brown–nosing foundations" was a turn of tactics that started after 9/11 and has been continuing to this day.[1] There are two distinct features to this trend. The first is a tendency in foundations to earmark money and concentrate on a few specific issues. Second, they have increasingly been cutting the funds available to organizations working on international finance and development.

Alongside these context factors around the EIR, some dissident activists also observed the participants of the process being increasingly oriented towards a neoliberal logic. One of the critics of the EIR contrasted the difference in repertoire in comparison to the 1980s. But what he found more staggering than the comparatively mild protest tactics, was the adaption of mainstream goals by activist groups during the EIR:

---

[1] Some big donors, notably the Ford Foundation, changed their funding schemes significantly after 9/11, referring more to securitized issues and less to international finance and development (Interviews NGOs).

'Transparency was not our major goal, I think if you look at a lot of civil society groups now, transparency is their goal, as opposed to stopping projects that destroy natural systems, tropical rainforest and possibly relocate indigenous peoples or take over their ancestral territory. ... Now, the goals have shifted.' (Interview, US activist)

The emphasis of 'transparency' as a goal is only meant as an example in this quote, but it is important in the context of the EIR. The most far-reaching and positive outcome according to both World Bank Group management, the EIR team, and – most significantly – also according to many critics, was the EITI, a new entity with the goal of establishing transparency on revenue flows between governments and extractive industries companies. The tactical benefit of demanding transparency on revenue flows was, as one involved activist told me, that "this is something that the private sector wanted, too. This is one of the reasons why there was a concrete outcome" (Interview, US NGO).

Extractive industries companies wanted to be publicly credited for money that they were giving to governments in developing countries. More importantly, they wanted contract transparency for their investments in this risky business. The involved critics therefore saw a possibility to coalesce with business on the question of revenue transparency, a tactic that worked retrospectively in the eyes of those who endorse EITI. This success was bought with an economization of language and, in the case of transparency, the adoption of a non-controversial goal at the expense of more radical ones.

Delineation from economized logic

There are many debates among critics regarding how far one should rhetorically approximate the economized logic of the institutions to convince them of specific reforms. This is an important tactical question, and most NGOs are aware of the need to divide labour on that front. More politically loaded is the question whether some of the 'civil society' groups are still representing the affected people or whether they serve the interests of capital because they have been subjugated to the neoliberal logic of their former opponents. The most striking division during the EIR was between the big international advocacy organizations on the one hand and local or national anti-mining activists on the other. Members of the latter faction in Indonesia referred directly to the previously-discussed transparency agenda to explain their general scepticism towards the EIR.

Some of the organizations, one activist claimed, would lose track of the "people's resistance" on the ground in these consultations, focusing on transparency and other lofty goals. He emphasized that his group focused on the communities around extractive industries projects and how to improve their lives. He did not believe that these communities profit from abstract discussions on transparency like in the EIR (Interview, Indonesian NGO). Furthermore, he added, his organization would generally refuse to speak with someone like Emil Salim, an economist and government representative of Suharto's New Order.

It is important to put the EIR in a historical context here: the World Bank Group strongly supported the modernist developmental regime of Suharto until its fall, and contributed to its survival.[2] The World Bank's country office (and the US embassy) would regularly serve as targets of Indonesian anti-regime protests, not only because this was an indirect way to criticize the domestic regime, but also because Suharto's dictatorship was, in their view, strongly coupled, both ideologically and financially, with what they perceived as a Western imperialist world order (Interviews, Indonesian activists). Emil Salim, a Chicago-trained economist and representative of the regime, was unacceptable to many in the Indonesian movement. For these groups, Salim moderating a supposed change process in the World Bank Group's extractive industries policies – the most symbolic part of the exploitative capitalist order – was not a trustworthy constellation. They abstained from the process and sometimes challenged other groups who were willing to engage with the institution.

Regarding the aim to achieve transparency, many activists think that the EITI is a "big scam" (Interview, European NGO), and even moderate groups increasingly agree with this judgement: in an internal evaluation paper on international advocacy of a big German donor organization that I confidentially received, the evaluator writes about EITI in the context of a Sub-Sahara African country:

> Instead of continuing to focus on [more pressing issues], many have jumped on the new fashionable themes and by that thrown advocacy into disarray. EITI and PRSPs were sexy, there was fast money, international support, the possibility to travel to distant countries and to receive posts in state forums. For the young coordinators … these were things that, in the context of economic precarity, were of great interest. (My translation)

Cheap travel is a theme I heard several activists refer to and complain about. 'Free plane tickets', sleeping in fancy hotels and getting free food during

---

[2]   Anna L. Tsing, *Friction: An Ethnography of Global Connection* (Princeton: Princeton University Press, 2005), p. 70.

the consultations was assumed a motivation for some to attend the EIR. Presumably, these speculations about other activists are more of a symptom than a cause for the fragmentation of critique, but it needs to be taken into consideration, both as 'objective' factor as a material motivation for activists, and as a derogatory interpretation of activists' motivation to only attend because of the financial benefit. It fragments the movement in that there is a suspicion towards others who might only be 'here for the money'.

These allegations are often made towards activists hailing from the global South. They are accused of enriching themselves by fellow activists from Southern countries, but mostly from European or US colleagues. Only few activists from the North were able or willing to acknowledge their own economic privileges. One said that "it's quite seductive to jet around the world from one conference to another and fighting injustice. You know, I've been there myself, what I call fighting poverty business class" (Interview, NGO). These ruptures were fought so bitterly, because the strategic and the tactical dimensions overlapped with personal animosities, often created by the economic privilege of some individuals.

These accusations, coupled with a tactical choice of NGOs to side with companies on some issues (transparency), and hence toning down the language, created economized subject positions for those attending the EIR. Others, especially radical anti-extractive groups observed this behaviour with disbelief and anger. This climate, fuelled by a general context in which NGOs economized in accordance with funding needs, was one factor why a post-EIR standoff on extractive industries between the World Bank Group and 'the movement' was non-existent.

Incorporation

The second mechanism leading to fragmentation, incorporation, is observable in both the shifting from protest (outside) to lobbying (inside), and the elevation of individuals. The former is most obvious in the case of the EIR. The transnational protest movement's practices shifted from protest (outside) to participation (inside). After the contentious Annual Meeting in Prague when, to the surprise of many, President Wolfensohn announced a review of all institutional practices in the extractive industries, large parts of the protest movement enthusiastically endorsed the institutionalized form of interaction and put great hopes into the EIR. I have described these processes already and showed how participation in a pre-configured space arose at the expense of more disruptive repertoires. This increasingly conformist repertoire was, however, not without controversy.

The previously discussed Bali Walkout shows awareness within parts of the movement regarding the question whether participation was useful or not. "Inclusion is a very general term. So, it's easy to go through a pro forma process, you know, it changes nothing" (Interview, US activist). Comments like these show the contempt with which parts of the movement see participatory processes like the EIR retrospectively. They argue that the consultations did not result in policy changes and, in the case of the Indonesian movement, were even concerned for the safety of participating community representatives. The ensuing debate on whether to leave the consultations was extremely contentious. In the end, most of the Asian activists present at the Bali workshop decided to drop out. Many of my informants remember that the debate created a rift between the supporters and the opponents of the EIR, which has not been bridged until this day.

In retrospect, many activists agree with the decision to exit the process, even among those who opted for remaining at the time. The lacking implementation of EIR recommendations has thus contributed to a scepticism towards participation in general: asking me rhetorically why anyone in a position of power should change their behaviour, an activist joked: "certainly, based on a meeting with a bunch of low-budget NGOs who claim that they're standing for human rights and refer to all these UN treaties" (Interview, US activist). Such a purely power-based understanding of how to influence IOs ridicules the logic of deliberation which underlies processes like the EIR. The same individual told me:

'Some NGOs have gotten sucked into a process of endless meetings with people in the World Bank. [But] the only leverage and the reason why some changes took place is that some organizations, maybe more in the 80s or in the 90s, were quite effective in mobilizing the US Congress. It's through threatening to cut off their money.' (Interview, US activist)

Regardless of whether this activist's assessment of the situation is correct,[3] it shows how the division on the question what effective advocacy looks like was provoked by the very opportunity to participate inside the institution.

These ruptures on the question whether to participate in the EIR or not were occurring time and again during the consultations. The counterparts in the institution were sometimes annoyed by these discussions: "The types of NGOs who come here, they are too engrossed into their own community issues" (Interview, World Bank Group manager). They put this down to the critics being too strongly attached to specific issues in contrast to seeing 'the bigger picture': "they want to represent their communities, but that means they are very narrow. ... Some of the NGOs don't have the bandwidth to deal with the breadth of issues they today have to be able to deal with to

---

[3] But see Pallas and Uhlin, 'Civil society influence on international organizations'.

have a discourse" (Interview, World Bank Group manager). But during the EIR, competition occurred not only between specialized NGOs trying to privilege their issue. The critics had a serious discussion on the format of participation itself (Interviews EIR Secretariat, Indonesian NGO).

Elevation of individuals

Among all this unrest among the critics, a 'Civil society advisory group' was founded to work with and make special reports to the EIR secretariat.[4] The 'civil society representatives' who were elevated into such a position experienced a difficult situation during the EIR, trying to push for institutional change through their privileged access while not losing track of the other activists. One of these individuals explained to me that, from the perspective of World Bank staff, her organization was among the ones that "you could actually talk to" (Interview, US NGO). Emphasizing her strong effort to remain critical, she added: "Although they might say that they couldn't talk to *me* [laughs]." Turning serious, she added that parts of the critique by other activists, who challenged her and her organization to be coopted, were not unsubstantiated:

'[We] had a partnership with the World Bank during this time. You know, so I was in a very precarious situation myself because, you know, I was aware of the fact that [anonymized] needed to keep its good relations with the Bank. But even within, … my colleagues like in the UK wanted to push much harder on things than my colleagues in the US because it was the [US branch] that had the partnership.' (Interview, US NGO)

From the perspectives of the three elevated individuals in the advisory group whom I spoke to, the activity was worthwhile. They were closely integrated into the EIR team, handed in commissioned reports, and were even closely consulted in the drafting of the final report.[5] Some of my informants claim that the strong emphasis on climate change in the EIR report was added in a last-minute move by the advisory team who brought in the rebellious World Bank manager Robert Goodman to make their case (Interviews, US NGOs). The end-result was thus stronger and more progressive in their view *because* of their elevated status. Others expressed a different view. Activists told me about a required trade-off if one wanted to be respectable to World Bank managers. In accordance with the activist whose NGO was one of those

---

4   Salim, 'Striking a better balance. Vol. 1', p. iv.
5   Salim, 'Striking a better balance. Vol. 3', Annex 4.

that "they could speak to", other critics complained that these NGOs put too much emphasis on being respectable: "you can say, 'shut down the Bank' and say that it's exploiting the Third World, or you can appear respectable and get a job with WWF or whatever and say you're a serious person, you're not one of those people shouting at the Bank" (Interview, US activist).

The elevation of some, in the form of special access, or in being trusted by World Bank Group officials, created tensions inside the advocacy coalition. Accordingly, one of the members of the advisory group told me that she did not feel the trust of other, more radical, groups during the EIR:

'I didn't have really strong relations with a lot of the other advocacy organizations and because I represented one of the big NGOs, ... I don't wanna use the word 'trusted', [her NGO] don't reach out to some of the smaller groups, very much. Because they're so big, they kind of just go in on their own, and so it was a little bit ... I was in kind of a funny role.' (Interview, US NGO)

Referring specifically to the contention in Bali, she added: "I really wasn't part of the walk-out and I wasn't, I mean, I knew of course that they were gonna do it, but my memory isn't serving me very well, I can't remember the discussions" (Interview, US NGO). For her as an elevated individual and part of the advisory team, walking out of the consultations was not an option. Other members of big international NGOs also felt they were put in a difficult position, as symbolized by an Oxfam employee who did not leave the Bali consultations but remained silent for the rest of it to show respect to both the World Bank Group and its critics (Interview, EIR Secretariat).

The issue of trust was also brought up from the other side of this rift. More radical critics mockingly spoke about the individuals in big international NGOs whose goal, according to them, was being well-respected by the institution and sitting at the table with the important people: "But the people who just wanna be respectable and go to meetings and you trust them with the key to the men's room, or the ladies room when they go to World Bank, that's something worse" (Interview, US activist). Calling these individuals "Swabian Spießbürger" (also to mock the author of this book), this activist dissociated himself from their approach and opted for rejecting fora like the EIR.

Aware of such accusations, one of the criticized individuals replied to my inquiry: "You can't just do all the things that need to be done through street protest. ... You have to have governments, you have to have enlightened business leaders, you have to have reformist presidents of international institutions, even if they only inch forward very slightly, they've still done that" (Interview, NGO). The divisions resulting from the EIR have sustained beyond the EIR process. Many frustrations and allegations are around to this day. In my interviews, I sometimes felt like the wall in a game of squash where activists shot back and forth via me as an anonymizing messaging service. It remains impossible for me to tell whether activists got their opinions about participation from a perceived failure of the EIR or whether they contributed to its failure because of their beliefs.

Most World Bank Group staff reported to have better relationships with many civil society participants of the EIR than they did before. One told me that, although the EIR had been contentious,

'a result I believe was to enhance the appreciation by World Bank Group staff working in the extractives area of the views and roles of NGOs, even in some cases their courage and integrity. Relationships post the EIR were much more productive even though some NGOs felt that they had not got all they wanted from the process.' (Interview, EIR Secretariat)

The 'productiveness' alluded to in this quote is a good marker for categorizing critics on one or the other side of the rift. Those who agree endorse the participatory spirit of the EIR and often were elevated by that in some form. Those who precisely see this productiveness as a danger were also the ones who did not attend the EIR or left it during the process.

Legitimation

Next to incorporation, the reflexive order of justification is (re)produced by the mechanism of legitimation. While on the institutional side I have observed this in arguing with complexity and rhetorical disarming, it can also be traced in resistant practices, namely when critics legitimate themselves with reference to the institutional order, that is in the attempt to deliberate within a given system's logic which is taken for granted. Demands are, then, already framed as a compromise instead of confronting the opponent with 'unrealistic' demands. Many of my interlocutors grant that a process towards arguing within the given institutional logic has taken place: "I wouldn't disagree with the move towards a sort of more insider, professionalized – it's not really a debate, you know, engagement, let's call it constructive engagement, it's a general trend throughout the world of civil society" (Interview, NGO). Beyond this, I want to show that legitimation as a *process* has taken place within the EIR, meaning that 'constructive engagement' was not only an effect of prior legitimation but constituted by the constellation of complex rule during the EIR.

One component of this mechanism is how the advocates in the EIR reacted to 'arguing with complexity': legitimating the process by referring to institutional complexity to evade allegations. My impression from talking to the activists, who were exposed to these legitimating practices, is that they have worked. Activists who were strongly involved in the EIR learnt during difficult and complex discussions how many issues had to be considered: governance, the environment, human rights, development. This had the effect of enlarging their respect and understanding for the EIR secretariat, which was "in a very funny position because they could never satisfy anyone basically. They won't gonna satisfy the Bank, they won't gonna satisfy private sector, and they won't gonna satisfy civil society" (Interview, US NGO). Thus, they argued towards other NGO members and activists to be more understanding towards the EIR team and keep in mind that they tried their best in a complex field of governance: "Sometimes civil society … needs to take a step back and understand negotiations a little bit better" (Interview, US NGO). Reflecting on this statement, she added later in the interview: "which might be easy for me to say because I'm not a person living next to a coal mine, who just had their home destroyed, you know, it's easy for me, an American, asking people to be more accepting of the issues". This reflexive epilogue already hints at her experience of being shamed by other activists for being too understanding based on her privileged North American position.

Criticism of the deliberative approach within a given institutional logic was common, especially from anti-extractive activists hailing from the countries where actual projects were implemented. They had little time for approximating the World Bank Group rhetorically and especially no understanding for compromises based on an institutional logic, which they found entirely false. Within these groups, I heard a lot of disregard of Northern NGOs, who were seen as satisfied with small corrections in the World Bank Group's safeguard policies, while they themselves had participated in the consultations to end the financing of extractive industries entirely.

But also within the Global North, more radical groups complained about how reformist NGOs approached the consultations. They still saw them as coalition partners but struggled to accept the compromise-oriented character of their tactics, claiming that to be effective, one needed aggression and fun,

'not this Judeo-Christian guilt and all that. … Some of the worst people are the Scandinavians and the Dutch, they're kind of self-righteous and that kind of thing. I kind of enjoyed it. If it's a job, it's not pure enjoyment, [but] there's a lot of fun going after the World Bank, and just causing as much trouble as you could. … All these people said, "Oh, you have to propose solutions, in order to be credible". But I liked the pure aggression part of it.' (Interview, US activist)

Unsurprisingly, there was a considerable estrangement between the two factions represented by these quotes. The former argued that the EIR needed the support of civil society to be taken seriously and to acquire enough leverage to push Management to accept the recommendations. The latter argued in favour of withdrawal from institutionalized interaction and wanted to focus on protest again. Those parts of the movement who, over the course of events, internalized the institutional logic, and hence believe in the legitimacy of the World Bank Group's practices, measured success at the baseline of what was already there. Disappointment was seen as natural, because the maximum demand could never be achieved:

'When civil society first read the final report, they were disappointed … each group has their own agenda and so of course not everybody was happy, but I pleaded with them and said, "It is much stronger than I expected it to be. So, we have to come out and support Emil, we have to be united, and we have to support him because it's really the best we're gonna get."' (Interview, US NGO)

This individual was on the side of those who saw the EIR as a success although she was "very frustrated" with the Management Response and the lacking implementation. Nevertheless, she used the document a lot in the following years. "I referred back to it all the time" (Interview US NGO). The EIR report was a useful advocacy tool for her and her Washington DC-based NGO.

The two groups of the original movement that completely disagreed with this interpretation were, on the one hand, affected people and their direct advocates in affected countries, for whom the advocacy tool seemed worthless (Interview, Indonesian NGO). On the other hand, there were radical groups from within the North American or European movement who found the institutionalized logic unconvincing and even mocked those who saw reports like the EIR as success: "You have to go to meetings but to win, which means stopping that project … , they don't have this, maybe it's a bit too old fashioned, testosterone, macho approach …, but I think you've got to have a better predatory instinct" (Interview, US activist). With mutual accusations evolving after the EIR's publication, the chances for further unified mobilization decreased.

Professionalization

Institutionally, I observed professionalization, the fourth mechanism of complex rule in global governance, in a new management style that accepted disruption as innovation. On the side of critique, it can be detected when 'civil society' shares responsibility of institutional governance tasks. In contrast to that, critics delineated themselves and continued to stress the need for spontaneity and direct action. In Chapter 5, I traced professionalization by showing how an activist was shamed as a sell-out for his move from Oxfam to the World Bank in the 1990s, while a similar move from Oxfam to the IMF was welcomed by colleagues 20 years later. In the following, I show how such change processes occurred even within the short time span of the EIR.

The EIR was shaped by a division between those who wanted to accuse the World Bank Group of its failures – "almost like in a trial" (Interview, World Bank Group manager), and an increasing share of activists who saw an opportunity in the process and therefore wanted to contribute in a serious and reasonable fashion. Many of them were increasingly sceptical towards the 'noble things' they had called for during the 1990s, when they had been oriented mainly at the own, internal, ideological coherence and hence had failed to gain stronger institutional impact (Interview, NGO). The result of these thoughts was an increased readiness to share parts of the governance burden in the EIR, at the dispense of radical opposition.

The most obvious sign of this trend is the participation in meetings with extractive industries companies and World Bank managers; and even more so the participation of individuals from the movement in the advisory panels mentioned previously. The responsible IFC evaluator told me that "we actually selected … some of the relatively more progressive companies and also some of the more, what we considered reasonable civil society organizations" (Interview, World Bank Group manager). These so called "reasonable" NGOs were respected during the EIR process by their peers in more radical groups and enabled the relatively smooth running of the consultations (besides Bali) through their hinge function, motivating others to play a professional, hence constructive, role in the process.

But the EIR secretariat itself played an equally important role in this regard. Salim's secretary Chandra Kirana had been an influential civil society activist in Indonesia before joining the secretariat and was widely respected and trusted among NGOs (Interview, Indonesian NGO). Not only was her own move to the EIR a form of professionalization which continued after the EIR with a job at the World Bank and contracts with EITI. During the EIR, she was in steady contact with the civil society representatives, who attended the consultations, urging them to contribute to this process and share a burden of the governance responsibility.

It is useful to assess professionalization from the eyes of World Bank Management because they had to make the distinction between professional and unprofessional critique frequently to assess what was worth being considered. Many of them state today that the EIR has changed their views of civil society (Interview, EIR Secretariat). While beforehand, the critics were mainly seen as ideologues, the process revealed to them that many of the critics' arguments were based in reality and that the NGOs "have become better" (Interview, World Bank Group manager).

When a World Bank manager thinks that NGOs or activists have become "better", this is a solid indicator for a professionalization of the latter. When asked about the meaning of the term, this interlocutor explained: "They have understood the Bank better and invested in understanding the Bank". In explicating who the 'good' NGOs are and what qualifies them, he mentioned "IUCN, Oxfam, WWF and so on: they actually have economists that work with some of our staff and try to put things in such a way that the Bank can do it" (Interview, World Bank Group manager). While overlapping with the process of economization, this quote shows that World Bank Group staff indeed take notice of external critique, but constantly evaluate what is 'digestible' and what is not. The non-digestible input is frequently framed as unprofessional because it does not link to existing frameworks and policies and is therefore seen as purely negative or utopian. Among the World Bank Group staff whom I spoke to, there seems to be a strong consensus that, for the aforementioned reason, 'professional' NGOs are more effective than others in their influence on the institution. Referring to the EIR consultations and what effects these had, one manager told me:

'some like Oxfam, IUCN and so on are quite sophisticated, and effective I would say. Getting the Bank to pay attention to things that they also regard as important and they're quite compatible with what we're, we the Bank, are trying to do. And others like, whatever, the International Rivers Network or the organization of the displaced people from Brazil[6] for example, who have valid grievances ... but they haven't figured out how to deal with the Bank.' (Interview, World Bank Group manager)

The World Bank Group staff frequently complained about critical movements with too narrow an agenda and made judgements as to which organizations were reasonable and which ones were ill-informed. This had two major effects during the EIR. First, some NGOs tried actively to sound 'reasonable' and well-informed by linking their demands to existing policy frameworks. Second, World Bank Group staff mentioned to me that they learned from the EIR how to actively exclude the 'non-professional' critics through either filtering out in the process of accreditation, or by filtering them out cognitively during the process. The following quote by a formerly high-ranking staff member is evidence of this. He mentioned that the institution

---

[6]   She refers to the Movimento dos Trabalhadores Rurais Sem Terra (MST).

has become much better at pre-selecting the 'reasonable' ones through accreditation processes, and

> 'that the Bank, even amongst the accredited, has learned the techniques of, you know, looking like you're treating the advocacy guys who have a one-topic issue the same as the guys who already put a lot of resources into thinking through this. But ultimately, you're giving the second more, and we weren't able to do that initially, I think that's probably the biggest weakness of the EIR, the fact that we under-resourced the effort in talking to the serious NGOs because we needed to spend the time, well, talking to that one guy.' (Interview, World Bank Group manager)

From the perspective of some critics, this looks unsurprisingly different, and they made the case for spontaneity and direct action during and after the EIR. Although many were retrospectively surprised by the openness towards their issues in the EIR report, they felt that only specific positions were heard and respected by the participating companies and World Bank staff (and affirmed by the Management Response), and hence an uneasiness about participating proliferated. This feeling erupted in the Bali Walkout, which – an exception to the overall process – was decidedly *unprofessional*. This is also how World Bank staff perceived it: "the walking-out is ... almost, sort of childish ... unprofessional" (Interview, World Bank Group manager). This interpretation of the walk-out as an anti-professional move is plausible, especially when recalling the difficult position this brought the individuals from big NGOs into. Discussing their role in the interviews, many activists strongly disagree with the World Bank staff's appraisal that those 'professional' NGOs are more effective: referring to a comrade at the WWF involved in the EIR, one activist told me: "they employ a lot of good people. But [he] was under the restrictions of the bureaucracy and ... those kind of things at WWF" (Interview, US activist). Therefore, they urged fellow critics to refocus on activism. The lack of policy results from the EIR reaffirmed their mistrust in the professional approach of NGOs.

Regulation

Regulation is the second *organizational* mechanism of complex rule. It fragments critique by creating rules, ordering, and disciplining critique. I have outlined earlier how World Bank Group staff regulated the discourse around the Management Response to reconnect the options on the table with the specific rules of the game in which they felt less vulnerable. A regulation of the mode of interaction to happen in an institutionalized consultation is not surprising. It was openly communicated as an aim by the World Bank

Group in its civil society strategy of 1998: '[to] convey to external parties more clearly if there is need for confidentiality or other special requirements during the consultation on draft policies – and exclude those NGOs which are not willing to play by mutually agreed rules'.[7]

In the following, I additionally make a more counter-intuitive argument about the mechanism of regulation in suggesting that parts of the critics also fuelled it: by endorsing specific institutional rules and engaging in acts of self-policing, they co-produce the increasing grip of institutional rules and the consecutive limitations arising from them. Other critics reject this regulated approach and would rather have the system fall than to subsume themselves under its rules; they want to play a different *game* altogether. The division resulting from these different approaches was the final factor contributing to the fragmentation of critique during the EIR.

Why do critics submit to institutional rules? According to my interviewees, two motives were instructive during the EIR, careerism and idealism. Activists wanting to appear 'respectable' in front of institutional counterparts may serve their careers either by receiving an offer to work for the institution, or by being quoted and frequently invited which may, in turn, elevate their status inside their NGO. However, the motive to endorse institutional rules may also be driven by an idealist agenda – if the respective activist sees an opportunity and thinks that within these rules, more gains can be achieved than without them. But those who did not opt for playing along the rules would later often incriminate those who did with careerist motives. In practice, however, the two often fall into one and make up a pattern in which it is almost impossible to distinguish one from the other. One of my interviewees put it that way:

'Basically, what happens is that we all want to be part of the club. And if we want to stay part of the club, we have to obey the rules … . So, it is a form, it's a form of cooptation, it happens over time in certain ways but it's not overt, and it wouldn't work that way. I think it's very difficult to resist if you're in [anonymized NGO], to resist these invitations, because you want your message to be heard.' (Interview, NGO)

This quote is a good example of the internal dynamic in NGOs at the time, or even within the minds of single activists. They constantly weighed the opportunities created through the EIR against the potential dangers of losing their independence and credibility. Yet, during the EIR consultations, almost

---

[7] World Bank, 'The bank's relations with NGOs: issues and directions', *Social Development Papers* (Washington DC, 1998), p. 15.

all critics involved in the protests agreed beforehand that the rules underlying this process were worth being played by. This has to do with the specific institutional design of the EIR (discussed previously) and the consultations being external to the World Bank Group with their institutional staff also having to submit to the same rules. Except for the Bali workshop, the critics hence endorsed the specific institutional rules set for and by the EIR.

Playing along the institutional rules included acts of self-policing and mutual disciplining. These acts are especially visible where they fail, and that is what happened in Bali. Before the walk-out, "there was quite a tension between us" (Interview, Indonesian NGO). Some of the present activists urged others not to break the rules that were created for all. Some of them were impressed by the amount of moral shaming that they received from World Bank staff. Many activists were convinced by their logic: if you join a game and agree to the rules, you cannot leave in the middle of the process. Respect for the rules and the other participants was hence one of the major arguments that opponents to a walk-out made. In this case, these rule-abiding advocates lost the internal contestation on the means of critique, but in all other consultations, they won or did not even have to argue, because the logic of playing along the institutional rules was agreed upon by all attending activists.

This largely harmonious process along the institutional rules ended when the Management Response and the justification around it drew on a regulated approach to legitimate significant changes to the EIR report or the non-implementation of core recommendations such as FPIC. Many of the activists who had played along understood this move as a violation of rules and felt betrayed. Yet, even then, the core group of the activists, who had accompanied the EIR from beginning to end, were so invested into the process itself that they did not move to a more radical repertoire. They continued to lobby along institutional channels. Through turning to legislative bodies, activists tried to weigh in on the regulated approach of the institution. After receiving the Management Response, they tried to build up pressure on the World Bank Group by involving parliaments. In the European context, for instance, an NGO coalition led by Urgewald managed to induce both the German Bundestag[8] as well as the European Parliament[9]

---

[8]   Deutscher Bundestag, 'Antrag: für eine nachhaltige Rohstoff- und Energiepolitik der Weltbank' (Berlin: Deutscher Bundestag, 2004), available at: {http://dipbt.bundestag.de/doc/btd/15/034/1503465.pdf}.

[9]   European Parliament, 'European Parliament Resolution on the World Bank-Commissioned Extractive Industries Review – B5-0171/2004, 29 March 2004' (Brussels: European Parliament, 2004), available at: {http://www.europarl.europa.eu/sides/getDoc.do?pubRef=-//EP//TEXT+MOTION+B5-2004-0171+0+DOC+XML+V0//EN}.

to debate the topic and adopt resolutions in favour of a comprehensive implementation of the EIR.

The call for a different approach to critique, drawing on street protests and direct action, was largely absent even after the disappointing results of the Management Response. During the consultations themselves, a constant consideration between those who endorsed the rules and those who were in favour of breaking them took place. Yet, in the bottom line, regulation as a general process was less contested than the other four mechanisms of complex rule. Consider the heated atmosphere at the first planning workshop in Brussels where activists openly mocked the World Bank manager stuck in an elevator. These extra-institutional provocations increasingly lost traction during the process, in favour of a concentrated and serious mode of conversation oriented at institutional reform (Interview, EIR Secretariat). Most strikingly in this context, the participants, first, respected the procedural rules of the consultations, and, second, oriented their inputs at the institutionally possible, both of which indicates an increasingly regulated approach.

An increasing investment into the process by rule-following critics led to a disengagement with those groups who did not join the process and who hence did not undergo the process of gradually trusting institutional rules. Irritated about those who did, these dissident groups increasingly stayed away from the advocacy towards the World Bank Group. Other topics gaining traction around the same time (such as the Iraq War), they became less active on matters concerning the World Bank Group (Interview, US activist). Thus, the overall advocacy towards the World Bank Group had transformed towards a largely regulated approach.

8

Uncontentious Politics? The Civil Society Policy Forum

In 2002, the World Bank Group introduced the Civil Society Policy Forum (CSPF) which has since then been an integral part of its Annual Meetings. This institutionalized forum of interaction contributed to the successive fragmentation of the movement. In the following two chapters, I will show how. The CSPF publicly stages the processes of interaction between institutions and its critics. Observing the forum, I show that we still see the mechanisms of complex rule at play more than a decade after the EIR – even among the small and specialized transnational activist network that remained active when the fragmentation of the bigger movement had already taken place. Open global governance did not only contribute to a division between radical dissidents and moderate opponents. Rather, the mechanisms of complex rule can be observed until this day and they even fragment moderate critics who are still attending the CSPF.

At the CSPF, World Bank Group staff and their critics meet to discuss the guidelines and problems of institutional development policy. I engaged in a participant observation; a method particularly useful for research focused on process rather than outcome.[1] Accordingly, it is a matter of illuminating the organizational culture as well as the thinking and acting of those people who work in the organizations.[2] However, the method is also confronted with problems, access being the most immediate one in formalized institutions in which the possibilities of participation are usually limited. For this study, access was facilitated by the fact that the World Bank Group and the IMF organize

---

[1] Birgit Müller, 'Introduction – lifting the veil of harmony: anthropologists approach international organizations', in Birgit Müller (ed) *The Gloss of Harmony: The Politics of Policy-Making in Multilateral Organisations* (New York: Pluto Press, 2013), p. 4.

[2] Julian Eckl, 'Zooming in dissolves the taken-for-granted: towards a political anthropology of international organisations', in Sarah Biecker and Klaus Schlichte (ed) *The Political Anthropology of Internationalized Politics* (Lanhham: Rowman & Littlefield), p. 67–94.

the CSPF in a decidedly open manner; the event being the flagship of its 'opening-up' to civil society. The following refers to the Annual Meeting of the World Bank Group and the IMF in Washington DC in October 2016. I was officially registered and had expressed my interest in a scientific study.

Relevance

The IMF and the World Bank Group co-organize their Spring Meetings and Annual Meetings. Since 2002, a program for civil society actors has been part of these events. This forum takes place during the meeting and is held at the same location (usually Washington DC). There is no legal basis for the forum, there are no official rules in terms of its organization,[3] and it varies in length between two and six days.[4] The preparation of the CSPF and the information campaign around it are handled by the World Bank's Civil Society Team.[5] The meetings regarding the IMF are taking place in the IMF building, and the meetings on World Bank Group issues are situated within World Bank premises across the street. In 2013, the CSPF moved to the smaller World Bank building. Some say this has contributed to a separation from the institutional proceedings: 'NGOs talking to NGOs' is a formulation that I encountered frequently. Fewer managers make their way to the CSPF than in earlier years when it was spatially integrated into the Annual Meetings. Even more frustrating for NGOs, journalists, too, tend to abstain. They had usually dropped into one or two sessions of the CSPF to also get 'the civil society perspective'. Since the two are spatially divided, fewer journalists take note.

Despite that problem, the number of participants has grown considerably over time. This is in line with the World Bank Group's general tendency of greater operational collaboration with CSOs through their involvement in Bank-financed projects at the country level. The Civil Society Team proudly presents the rising numbers participating at the CSPF as proof of its relevance, and for the improved relations between the World Bank Group and civil society more generally. In a blog post from 2012, the leader of the civil society team made this direct link:

A record number of CSOs participated in the recently concluded Spring Meetings in Washington. Over 550 civil society

3   Peter Van den Bossche, 'NGO Involvement in the WTO: A Comparative Perspective', *Journal of International Economic Law* 11, 4 (2008), pp. 722.
4   Jan Aart Scholte, 'Civil society and IMF accountability', CSGR Working Paper (Warwick, 2008), 19; World Bank, 'World Bank – Civil Society Engagement: Review of Fiscal Years 2010–2012' (Washington DC, 2013).
5   Deborah A. Bräutigam and Monique Segarra, 'Difficult Partnerships: The World Bank, States, and NGOs', *Latin American Politics and Society* 49, 4 (2007), pp. 152.

representatives ... – 200 more than in 2011 – attended the Civil Society
Program. ... Of these, the Bank and Fund sponsored 29 CSOs / Youth
Leaders and Academics ... from developing countries. ... The growing
number of CSOs attending the Bank/IMF Meetings reflects a historic
trend in improved Bank – CSO relations. In addition to having ready
contact to Bank officials, what seems to be driving this increase is the
fact that the CS Forum offers an independent and credible space for
policy dialogue. CSOs are encouraged to determine the topics, format,
and panelists for their own sessions, and this has led to substantive and
frank exchange of views in areas of common concern.[6]

The quality of the meeting is therefore seen as creating a 'real' dialogue
with substantive discussions, as well as representing a plurality of topics and
actors, the latter being economically sponsored for improving geographical
representation. But it is not a given that the engaged discussions at the CSPF
reach the ears of managers, much less affect policy. This depends strongly
on the way the respective Civil Society Team tries to convince managers to
listen to the critical voices (Interview, US activist).

In my interview with the former World Bank Civil Society Team leader,
he reported his team's efforts to convince influential staff members to
accept the CSPF's importance, and if possible even to show up. Because of
this difficulty, some activists think that the CSPF "is really kind of a joke
[because] the World Bank has organized the civil society forums so that civil
society is just speaking to itself. Its message doesn't permeate beyond the
walls of the civil society forum to journalists or to officials." (Interview, US
NGO). I did see World Bank Group staff at the CSPF. Most of them were
invited by NGOs to sit on a panel in which direct interaction took place.
Some of them brought colleagues and stayed for informal discussions or to
attend other panels afterwards. These managers constantly emphasized how
important the exchange with civil society is for them. They highlighted
the role of CSOs as middlemen and women between Management and
the 'beneficiaries', the latter being also referred to as 'affected people' if
something goes wrong in a development project. The role of civil society is
said to be, furthermore, one of external innovation and democratic control.
It takes over the role of checks towards the institution. "Without civil
society", one of the World Bank managers said at the CSPF, "we would
lose track of the local people and forget the perspective of those that are
actually affected by the projects".

---

[6]   See John Garrison, 'Why are increasing numbers of CSOs coming to the spring meetings?'
      Blog post on the World Bank website (5 February 2012), available at: {http://blogs.worldb
      ank.org/publicsphere/why-are-increasing-numbers-csos-coming-spring-meetings}.

Proceedings

The CSPF is organized in panel sessions. CSOs can apply with suggestions and the program is put together by a team of the institutions in cooperation with an 'interim working group' of 'civil society representatives' (discussed later). There are several possible subject positions: institutional staff – mostly referred to as 'Management', staff members of the institutional complaint mechanisms, and experts from third organizations. NGO workers and other advocates from 'civil society' take different positions, some operating as 'experts', some rather as 'activists'. I roughly detected a difference between 'critical' and 'affirmative' CSOs based on their performance, clothing, habitus, and forms of critique. While at the World Bank Group panel sessions, there would usually appear one 'affected' individual to report from their local communities and give subjective accounts of their suffering, by that also bringing a spirit of protest or at least dissent to the meeting, the IMF sessions were highly technical. Civil society representatives and IMF staff were all introduced as 'experts' by the moderators there.

The atmosphere was comparable to a big academic conference, including the discussions as well as the networking efforts. The old days of massive protests against the institutions only appeared in narratives of participants. Disruptive protest was absent. In front of the World Bank headquarter, one [sic!] protester distributed leaflets against IFC involvement in water privatization. Nevertheless, the 'critical' part of the participants drew actively on these earlier experiences and presented themselves as leftover from the old movement. Their critique of the neoliberal development model was still fierce, and they constantly contemplated the methods of their interventions, as I will discuss.

I will now describe two panels that capture the mode of interaction as it played out on the CSPF 2016. The first was organized by the CAO, the second by the Operations Policy and Country Services (OPCS) department of the World Bank. I selected two panels organized by the World Bank Group to be sure to capture actual interaction, since many of the self-organized panels of CSOs were hardly attended by institutional staff and thus rather resembled civil society networking or strategy events.

From accountability to action?[7]

The CAO Panel 'From accountability to action: the role of management' is a discussion panel between the CAO himself (Osvaldo Gratacos), the

---

[7] For better readability, I use present tense for direct observation. The segment 'From accountability to action' has been published in German. Felix Anderl, 'Entwicklung als Motiv für Herrschaft und Widerstand. Kohärenz und Fragmentierung während des Zivilgesellschaftsforums der Weltbankgruppe', *Peripherie: Zeitschrift Für Politik Und Ökonomie in Der Dritten Welt* 38, 150/151 (2018), pp. 219–44.

new appointee of the Green Climate Fund's (GCF) independent redress mechanism (Lalanath de Silva), a member of the World Bank Board (Jason Allford), an activist from BIC as civil society representative (Kate Geary), and the Director for Development Results and Accountability at the United States Department of Treasury (Daniel Peters). The session is situated in the largest of the four seminar rooms available for the CSPF inside the World Bank building. As two informants from the World Bank Civil Society Team had told me, the meetings either organized by 'critical' civil society with controversial advocacy aims or by the World Bank Group around critical issues are always the most attended ones, while sessions organized by affirmative groups around non-controversial issues are usually quite empty. The CAO session is no exception to this rule. There are approximately 50 people in the audience, most of them from NGOs, but also from academia (myself and at least two other scholars I know), and from World Bank Group management. They can typically be distinguished from each other by dress code: while World Bank Group staff are generally wearing a suit or pantsuit, CSO folks go with shirt and jeans, or sometimes a blazer. In some rare cases, activist wear T-shirts ('Cut the Carbon'); most advocates, however, usually stick with more subtle attire.

The atmosphere is outspokenly friendly: the speakers smile at each other and shake hands before the panel starts. They help each other setting up the PowerPoint presentations, which are projected onto three oversized screens behind their panel (see Figure 8.1). Jason Allford, who sits in the middle, functions as a moderator. The audience is having coffee or water and cookies from the modest buffet outside the room. People speak to each

Figure 8.1: Preparations for the CAO Panel at the CSPF 2016

Source: Author

other, but there are few welcoming and small-talk scenes, because it is the third day of the forum and most networking efforts have been concluded already. To my right sits a staff member of the Inspection Panel whom I later meet for an interview. An activist from a German NGO sits on my left. He is a valuable companion to me during the whole CSPF and offers concise explanations of 'how things are done here'. It is his twelfth annual meeting, and he observes the entire proceedings without raising his word publicly. He introduces me to key stakeholders of the World Bank Group and its critics. At this forum session, he taps my shoulder and points at two people in the room whom I "should definitely speak to" (one from the CAO, one from an NGO). Around us, the noise level has decreased, and the panel begins.

The session is opened by Lalanath de Silva who used to work for the ADB's compliance panel and announces that she is therefore acquainted with CSOs and their work. She relates her current job to the IFC's work. This may have to do with the fact that her spot had actually been earmarked for a member of IFC Management (the program read: 'IFC management—tbc'). As I was told by several sources, getting Management for these appearances is very hard; in a constellation that is almost certainly going to criticize the 'role of management' (title of the session), it is easy to imagine why nobody would volunteer to sit on the panel taking the blame. In the subsequent discussion, however, a senior IFC manager actively takes part from the audience (discussed later). De Silva proactively describes some problems that 'Management' usually faces in such projects: since they do not usually implement directly but leave this to the borrowing state or other clients, they do not interact immediately with critics and only engage reactively when problems are already identified. She underlines that this is insufficient and that real relationships cannot be created in such a mode of interaction. She underscores this argument by giving insights into complaint processes where early engagement of Management has led to a less confrontational form of conflict. Therefore, she calls for responsiveness to civil society complaints starting at the project design stage, not just later when things have already gone wrong. Listing factors such as internal human resources, and perverse incentives (cash outflow), she explains why Management does not speak out at the project design phase before harm is being done.

The second speaker presents a scene that can be observed on almost every panel with critical participation: The 'civil society representative' (official program), Kate Geary, introduces problems that affected communities have with accessing the complaint mechanisms: filing a complaint is very complicated, documents are often not available in local languages, and IFC staff will not listen to complaints even if they are filed properly. If investigations take place, they take very long, and the damage is already done by the time the CAO has come to a verdict on the case. Furthermore,

Geary complains that the CAO is often seen as last resort, and the World Bank Group does not change its development model despite the large number of project failures. Although she welcomes the work done by the CAO, she attests a severe lack of cultural change throughout Management, especially in the IFC, and in particular regarding projects with third party involvements. These projects are, in her language, 'secretly' funded by the IFC but implemented by commercial banks or other intermediaries. She complains that often it is not even possible to trace that the IFC has stakes in these projects and the communities and CSOs do not know that a complaint could be filed.

To illustrate what that means, she points to a man in the audience who is a member of a community affected by one of these projects (a thermos development). He speaks in Hindi and someone else in the audience translates for him. The story he offers is one of destruction resulting from 'development': The Tata Mundra 'Ultra Mega Power Plant'[8] has depleted the fishery yield in the area, destroyed big parts of the environment, and as a result caused thousands of community residents to abandon the place. His main point is the experience with IFC, the financing institution. He complains that the community has never received the report by the CAO, and he mentions a feeling of abandonment in the community, because IFC did not even send a visitor to the community after the several complaints that were filed.

The session's chair, Jason Allford, is now in the delicate position of responding to the community member's presentation. As several activists during the forum pointed out to me, these are the situations they want to create: bringing the important people into situations where they must listen and respond, and potentially follow up on cases later on. Allford comments: "It's really hard to react to such a specific case, but it's great to hear about these cases". Despite this remark, he does not refer to the story but rather elaborates on complicated discussions within the board, highlighting the fact that the various interests of the borrower countries have to be catered to. He then adds that "all board members" are committed to human rights and are happy about the work of the CAO, also mentioning that a cultural change within the World Bank Group, especially IFC, necessarily takes time and that there are specific people inside the institution that "need to be supported".

Alford hands over to the next speaker, Daniel Peters from the U.S. Treasury Department, who is responsible for an external view on the process of complaints. He is regularly in touch with the IFC in his function as envoy to

---

8   Official project description. See the project website: {https://www.tatapower.com/bus inesses/projects/national.aspx}.

U.S. Congress, where he explains and defends the work that has been done by international financial institutions and answers questions of Congressmen and women who decide on the funding, partly based on this exchange. The question he addresses to Allford is: "Why don't you want complaints to come in?" He argues that from the point of view of MDBs it might sound paradoxical, but that the filing of complaints, especially early ones, would make cases and their problems accessible before they escalate.

Peters draws a picture of a World Bank Group (and its Board) that tries to deny problems and suppress complaints as long as possible, concluding: "When formal complaints arise, it's important for Management not to be defensive. That still happens too frequently, it becomes a legalistic back-and-forth". Peters claims to understand why this happens: "I defend the MDBs in front of the Congress, and I tend to be defensive, too". Nevertheless, he adds: "but it's strange since the MDBs enjoy immunity. Well, the IFC can technically be taken to court but that's gonna be thrown out". Peters then refers to the role of the Board: Ideally, he claims, meaningful dialogue would take place between Management and the affected communities, meaning that the board would not have to play a role. But if that is not happening, "the board also has a responsibility and has to dig in. It's difficult and the board members have a lot to do, but it stops with the board. Members should take that seriously and take that role". Since he visibly addresses Allford with his statement, the latter reacts directly by saying: "Yes, and I would add that sometimes in the board, we talk about Management as if they are something else. But we are the governors of this institution".

The next speaker is Oswaldo Gratacos, CAO. He embodies his very mandate of being neutral and independent by means of his look and performance: on the one hand, with his fine suit, oiled hair, and self-confident gestures, he resembles a banker or a businessman. On the other hand, he casually chats with the CSO members before the panel and starts his presentation by greeting an elderly lady in the audience, who turns out to be Meg Taylor, New Guinea's former ambassador to the US and Olympic contender in Pentathlon. He thanks her and describes her as "such a crucial person in the accountability process". Building on her as an individual, he explains that "accountability is not an outcome but a state of mind". Asking the question "so, what is the role of Management?", he outlines a multi-disciplinary task that should not be confined to times of crisis. Disclosure is "key and number one" according to his understanding of accountability. "We [the CAO] don't have to be around for that". As the second most important issue he mentions stakeholder engagement. Again, he calls for a proactively caring and accountable Management. "We should be the last resort. When everything else has not worked. We cannot be the first entry point".

In contrast to this ideal role of Management, he then goes on to describe the actually existing performance: "We see the frustration from communities, we see the frustration of CSOs if Management doesn't acknowledge findings". He refers to the many reports that CSOs collect from affected communities, stories like the one presented earlier on the Tata Mundra project, or – more politically charged – the reports of his institution. At a minimum, he argues, Management should respond with consultation.

Directly addressing Management, he outlines a procedure that they *should* follow; one that leaves me quite baffled when hearing that it is not a standard procedure already: the files have to be read; responses and action plans should be clearly stated; if you do not agree with the claim, say why; provide a time-frame of how the project will be altered (if so); provide lessons-learned. While he says all that, two Management members sit in the audience, shaking their heads in a concerned way. Both immediately raise their hands when Gratacos' input is over, since now is the time for statements from the audience.

The first of them is Morgan Landy, head of the IFC's Transactional Risk Solutions Department. He says that he would like to bring in "the IFC perspective". He stands up for his comments, takes the microphone and positions himself next to the panel, facing the audience, a move that will be repeated by his staff member who speaks afterwards. The other members of the audience usually remain seated when asking their question or simply stand up in front of their chairs. Landy therefore distinguishes his position from the one of a regular session participant. He starts his comments by highlighting how important the accountability mechanism is "for us" in terms of institutional learning: "The CAO is a key part of who we are". This wording is striking since the CAO's boss had just used a language of us (the CAO) and them (Management), clearly marking his institution as independent. Landy goes on to argue that CAO is "best in class", which would make him proud and help IFC to get better.

I risk a quick glance at the person seated next to me who works for the Inspection Panel (apparently *not* best in class), who gives me a look that I interpret as a slightly annoyed "whatever". Landy presents himself as open towards including CAO "early in the process as a mediator", rather than the current setup, where IFC lets CAO "do its thing after everything is ruined". He clearly marks this as a change by referring, on the one hand, to staff members who "in the past" were less sure about CAO involvement in early stages, but also, on the other hand, the CAO's part. He argues that in the last years, signals from CAO had not been clear, and therefore IFC staff members were not sure how to engage.

This conversation, which now looks like a contest in justification between Landy and Gratacos, each representing and justifying their respective institution, seems quite odd for an outsider like me. One might wonder why such debates on basic working principles are only held here and now, and in public. Landy goes on to justify the IFC's performance by first reiterating how important "social and environmental issues" are. He refers to the 80 people who work on these issues in the institution. Two weeks a year, he explains, "we have a meeting and are going through CAO cases" to track lessons learnt. These are consecutively posted on the website. Second, however, he also highlights the restricting external factors: "Our shareholders are asking us to go to harder places and more complicated environments, sometimes stepping into land conflicts that have been going on for centuries". With this statement, his gaze directed at the community representative from India, Landy finishes his intervention.

The chair gives word to Carla Garcia Zendejas from the Center for International Environmental Law (CIEL), whom I already know from previous panels. Despite the academic name, her organization is clearly an advocacy NGO and Zendejas is among the most outspoken of the critics at the CSPF. She argues in favour of an early warning system within the accountability process. Referring to her work in monitoring pipelines, she suggests that a change in mentality is necessary. Management should feel empowered to internally raise an issue and point out flaws in a project. She claims to know people in IFC who do not dare to raise their voice internally, and therefore hide that something is going wrong, leading projects into much bigger disasters than necessary. Directly addressing Landy, she asks: "How can we engage with people who might be punished inside?" Justifying her own work, she adds: "There are people in here who want to make a change but seem to need us in order to put a finger on the thing."

Although the question was directed at Landy from IFC Management, ED Alford takes the word and says: "In here, what you said is usually framed as incentive. A very important question is thus: What incentives are there for staff to say when something goes wrong?" He then wants to give the word to Landy who, however, passes on the microphone to Aaron Rosenberg, Head of Public Affairs at IFC. He explicates that there are already 30–60 days of consultation phase for every project before it is suggested to the board and that these projects are published on the website for comments. He agrees with Alford that the issue of incentives is important. But he also adds: "We are a development bank; thus, development has to be first." He continues by speaking about IFC's new CEO, Philippe Le Houérou, with whom he thinks this will be the way to go, since "he is all about development".

While my NGO friend directs a tortured smile at me – what else should the CEO of a development bank "be about"? – Rosenberg recollects a recent seminar on agribusiness, with 20 people from IFC in the room – as many as there were CSO representatives. After a dramatic pause to underline this apparently remarkable fact, he adds that "half of them [were] investment managers". The story hence serves as an illustration of internal learning processes: It is difficult, but we have understood the message. If even the investment bankers at IFC now understand that "it's about development", the organization is on the right track. This input is concluded by an enthusiastic closing statement: "Let's help our clients and everyone get to a better place".

Everybody is equally unhappy

The second panel discussion that I want to zoom in on was organized by the OPCS division of the World Bank. Shortly before the CSPF, the World Bank's Board of Executive Directors had approved a new Environmental and Social Framework (ESF) which, according to its own presentation 'expands protections for people and the environment in Bank-financed investment projects'.[9] Critics had strongly complained during the time of drafting the ESF, and called the Management's new approach a 'rollback'.[10] The World Bank then promised to take up the criticism, but after the final draft, critics still said it 'diluted' standards that had already been in place.[11]

The session being dedicated to 'the New World Bank Environmental and Social Framework: Opportunities and Challenges for Implementation', a heated debate was expected, and the room is accordingly packed. However, the program already gives an indication that the organizers wanted the session to become as little controversial as possible: none of the notoriously 'critical' NGOs are invited as speakers. Aside from two World Bank managers, one speaker represents the US Office of Accountability, another one hails from a Washington DC based policy think-tank, and El Mahadi Abdel-Rahman from a Sudanese NGO. The session is moderated by Faith Nwadishi, Founder & Executive Director of the Koyenum Immalah Foundation (KIF). She acts as civil society representative in the international board of the EITI, an institution founded as a result of the EIR (see Chapter 6). She and Abdel-Rahman are outstanding examples of 'civil society representatives' who are elevated by the World Bank Group and seen as 'coopted' by many others. Both of them are financially supported by the World Bank Civil Society

---

[9]   See press statement of the World Bank, 4 August 2016, available at: {http://www.worldb ank.org/en/news/press-release/2016/08/04/world-bank-board-approves-new-enviro nmental-and-social-framework}.

[10] See among many Human Rights Watch, 4 August 2015, available at: {https://www. hrw.org/news/2015/08/04/world-bank-dangerous-rollback-environmental-social-prot ections}.

[11] See press statement by the Brettonwoods Project, 23 September 2016, available at: {http:// www.brettonwoodsproject.org/2016/09/world-bank-approves-new-diluted-safegua rds/}.

Team to attend the CSPF.[12] The whole session is live-streamed via YouTube, and warm lunch is provided for all attendees after the session.

Hartwig Schäfer, Vice President of the OPCS, opens the session. He looks very pleased, a bright smile on his face. He introduces the topic and thanks everyone for taking part in the long process of consultations on the new safeguards. As an outsider, I am surprised that he is *not* claiming that the safeguards are very good. Rather, he uses phrases like "they have something for everybody", stressing the big role of compromises and the geopolitical difficulties that the World Bank was faced with (alluding to the rise of the AIIB). He also refers to a difficult situation in the Board of Directors where different countries have very different agendas. Again, he does not have to call out "China and India" for most people present to know that especially these countries are said to oppose stronger social and environmental safeguards and would rather have more legroom for big scale projects. Schäfer therefore highlights the role of multilateralism and explains that there had to be something "in there" for all the 184 countries.

He argues that the new ESF is a success because "everybody is equally unhappy". This is the exact formulation used by the World Bank Group's President Kim in the "townhall meeting" with civil society (discussed later). Schäfer introduces the implementation phase. Self-confidently facing the audience, he raises his voice and adds: "All the stakeholders have to be ready: recipients, borrower countries, partners like you". His final remark is on the "localization" of these safeguards, a delicate topic since the safeguards are, by definition, standards set at the centre, and the borrowing countries need to stick to them in order not to lose the projects. Some borrowing countries have therefore likened the safeguards to conditionality of the 1980s and hence tried to weaken them in the process of the new ESF. Advocacy NGOs, on the other side of the spectrum, support an expansion of the safeguards and see them as a major step away from the old neoliberal development logic, or at least its cushioning. Schäfer omits these political implications in favour of highlighting that the capacity building for ESF will be delivered by and in the borrower countries, highlighting their gains in autonomy created by this measure.

Now, Mark Alan King, Chief Environmental and Social Standards Officer of OPCS, enters the stage. He gives an overview of the process in which the new ESF came to life, highlighting its inclusivity. "We went to 60 countries", is a sentence that he stresses by pausing before and after. He sketches how his team met with "borrowers, bank, and partners," outlining the agenda for each of them. Regarding borrowers, it was about making these countries

---

[12] I received the list of the supported CSOs from the World Bank Civil Society Team. I am very grateful for their support and repeated interviews.

aware of new requirements. For this, a "knowledge portal" was created. The second player involved, the World Bank itself, receives more time in his report, showing that it is not self-evident for every staff member to simply adopt new safeguards and act accordingly.

King outlines how the new ESF is "mainstreamed" within the institution. He promises to "lift the quality of safeguards staff" by making sure that everyone working with safeguards will have to be accredited in order to really know them and know how to handle them. Later at lunch, an activist will ask me the rhetorical question: "What was before that? Anyone could work on safeguards without a clue? It's incredible!" King goes on to argue that part of his work is to send signals that safeguards work is a very important part of the World Bank. "We want to make [staff] aware that safeguards specialists have a future here," thus also turning to the issue of incentives in the organizational culture.

King draws the picture of a cooperative spirit in which all involved actors have an interest in spreading and applying the new ESF. It is all for the better, contestations around the ESF's content are not mentioned. Instead, he lists more and more potential practices that sound like a beginner's guide to governance: "Develop guidance notes"; "have working groups come up with drafts"; "share with other colleagues"; "publish on a special website for review"; "organize feedback loops and expert workshops"; "best practice methodologies"; "tools and checklists to create a more consistent approach to the projects.". *Internally*, he promises "change management". *Externally*, he wants to involve stakeholders and their "knowledge resources". For this, a Memorandum of Understanding ("MoU") has been signed with the IUCN, and trade unions with "in-country knowledge". These groups are supposed to help with training of staff and of borrower countries. "Undoubtedly", he adds, "there will be teaching problems", without, however, specifying which ones. He also highlights that a first meeting was held "with CSOs that approached us". He ends by emphasizing that "these are the kind of partnerships we are looking for".

Only a well-informed participant of the session could know that the two NGOs attending this meeting were BIC and *Sightsavers*. While the latter is rather a charity than an advocacy organization, BIC used to be a nodal point in the resistance against the World Bank Group policies. Although they began to develop towards a less radical watch-dog organization already in the mid-2000s, being called a "partner" in a process that most resistant actors find highly flawed, must feel like a provocation towards the more critical stakeholders in the room.

Michele de Nevers, the next speaker, represents the Center for Global Development, a think-thank that I introduced in Chapter 5 as example for a spin-off institution of the World Bank Group which is formally independent but closely connected to the institution. In line with this observation, she used to work for the World Bank Management for 30 years before joining this "civil society organization". She stresses the leadership role of the World Bank Group in the social and environmental accountability process: "The Bank is snow-white and the other MDBs are the seven dwarfs". However, she is concerned about the "relevance" of the MDBs. With a plethora of opportunities for cheap credits and investments for developing countries, she worries that these might prefer those less complicated opportunities to the disadvantage of multilateral institutions which insist on stiff safeguards. A "focus on implementation" could change this, as she argues. Therefore, the "country systems" which the ESF aspires to, are the right approach in her regard.

The use of "country systems" effectively means that national legal provisions of borrowing countries replace the application of the institution's social and environmental standards, which in turn reduces the institution's degree of obligation and instead obliges the borrower to organize implementation alongside vague social and environmental standards. Such a "localization" of safeguards is normatively desired by many to counter Southern countries' suspicion of being governed from afar. Nevers, however, shows that this change also has a second dimension, which she finds "very welcome": flexibility in implementation. She argues that it is understandable for Management to desire a moving-away from high risk-projects, but that the World Bank needed to double down on them, giving forestry and dams as examples: openly facing the audience with a concerned gaze, she asks: "What role can the Bank play in development if not by being risk-taking. Borrowers have so many means to access funds, the Bank is getting irrelevant if they don't go in there."

By saying this, she delivers an independent justification for "high-risk" projects that the two prior speakers, who still work for the World Bank, did not pursue in their statements on the same topic. Although they also praised localization, they did not make the causal connection between the institution's move to country standards and more risky projects. The person in the adjacent seat from a critical NGO, visibly agitated, whispers into my ears: "The only thing that they think about is that the Bank shouldn't become irrelevant. But wouldn't it be relevant as a standard setter for *social development?*"

After this, Bill Kennedy, Director of Accountability at the US Overseas Private Investment Corporation (OPIC), starts his presentation very colloquially, by greeting everyone and highlighting his familiarity with the process. "I have 30 years of experience in writing, reviewing and updating environmental and social safeguards". Also, he adds that "we" [OPIC] do a lot of co-financing with IFC. Referring to his long-term stay in Germany, he presents a 'German wisdom': "Vertrauen ist gut, Kontrolle ist besser"[Trust is good; control is better]. The three Germans in the room engage in heavy eye-rolling. I catch myself participating in this exercise, although to that point I have not yet made up my mind regarding Kennedy's role on the panel. His message is that monitoring of the ESF will be the most important issue. He criticizes that, so far, monitoring has often been left to junior staff. Additionally, the cost of monitoring the ESF is often not budgeted in projects, marginalizing it in the phase of operationalization.

After two representatives of World Bank Management and two independent speakers, who are arguably close to the World Bank, Yahia Abdel-Rahman El-Mahadi, Managing Director of the Sudanese Development Initiative, is introduced by the moderator as "the voice of the civil society". He himself repeats this distinction by saying: "I want to speak here for civil society". In his presentation, he bemoans a gap between "global programs" and "local problems" and pleads for a necessary alignment. He refers to guidance notes for projects ("glad to hear they exist") but adds that "on our level", they are usually kept on the shelves or websites.

He makes clear what the abstract discussions on "country level systems" can effectively mean in practice: the borrowers must engage with stakeholders on their own terms, but what if these terms are corrupted or non-existent? "I come from a country where the state is extremely repressive: how do you rely on a borrower that is not likely to organize a real conversation with civil society?" In addition to this specific example of the Sudanese context, he adds that "even the Bank's own consultations could be done better. They need to be participatory. The views have really to be captured, not just lost in the notes". The guidelines should hence also capture how consultations are to be done. Furthermore, he alludes to the government-focus of World Bank staff. Sometimes, he narrates, people come from DC but they are engrossed by government officials and have little time to really talk to "local people in the field". Self-confidently, he emphasizes that civil society *can* play a role", if consulted properly. For this to happen, the World Bank country offices however need to have a sense of the civil society in the country. For this purpose, he suggests a mapping process during which "the right CSOs" to engage with should be identified.

After these presentations, the moderator, Faith Nwadishi, takes over the microphone and announces the rules for the upcoming open discussion. In a strict tone, she explains that there are 30 minutes for discussion, "but" [she adds], "the safeguards are already decided upon. Let's talk about implementation!" The first question comes from Mohammad Alhamin (WALHI). He problematizes the "country systems" approach in the new ESF since these systems are different in every country, especially, he adds, in human rights. His concern is that human rights defenders cannot really participate in authoritarian contexts. He therefore demands a "gap analysis" between country systems and the ESF: "How can civil society contribute if the national situation doesn't allow for that?".

The next question comes from Peter Bakvis, who works for the International Trade Union Confederation (ITUC). He highlights that "we have a lot of experience with safeguards with other banks", and claims to have learnt that early consultation of those who lack the specific institutional knowledge is paramount. Referring to the partnership with IUCN, he notices that the World Bank also lacks expertise in the labour sector and therefore asks whether a similar MoU is planned with the ILO or a trade union.

Carla Garcia Zendejas from CIEL asks the question that I had been waiting for already: "This new framework does not have a standard on human rights. How will you make sure human rights are respected and implemented?". In a final question of the first round, Ilana Berger (BIC) complains that guidance notes from earlier times are not systematically integrated into the ESF and asks how they will be integrated without needing "ten different documents" for one process.

It is obvious that all comments were directed at Mr. King. Accordingly, he takes the microphone and elaborates on the contentious issue of country systems, saying that "the Bank has to make a mental risk analysis". If there is not a free and enabling environment, he promises to engage with civil society:

'Really, we want to hear from civil society and we will find a way to engage them. ... We're very clear that there is an issue there. ... But there are for example colleagues from the umbrellas like BIC here, or Bankwatch in Europe, and they have good contacts to civil society". The cooperation with them will "create an island, or even an oasis of environmental and social standards in the projects within these countries.'

On this positive note, he hands the microphone to "Charles from Human Rights" [a member of the World Bank department on human rights] who adds that "this question" came up at the roundtable of board members. He admits that "the word [sic] human rights doesn't come up in the ten parts of the EFS". He explains this with the difficult multilateral process: "We didn't get a consensus with all 184 countries on the definition and meaning of human rights." However, he highlights that the draft safeguards the rights of affected people in all circumstances, even without explicitly mentioning human rights. Another staff member is handed the microphone and he adds, directed at the critics in the room, "We very much value your comments so far, and we will further consider them".

Nwadishi then opens the second round of questions. Stephanie Fried from the ULU foundation, probably one of the most outspoken and respected safeguards specialists among the critics, alludes to the criminalization and imprisonment of civil society in many contexts. I had observed her already in other contexts and noted that she tends to extend the limits of the thinkable by addressing very physical effects of World Bank Group policies and their failures to generate a debate that is less 'technical'. In this case, drawing on violent police forces in Indonesia as an example, she transcends the abstract questions on compliance and national safeguards systems by asking: "Will there be a security force risk assessment, and an assessment of armed forces in the borrowing countries in order to guarantee for the safety of affected people?". She further enquires, given that guidance is not mandatory and the rules for using country systems are vague, whether "there [will] be any kind of mandatory rules for consultation and resettlement? Our colleagues are afraid: Will there be any mandatory measures?". By this, she references the fears of critics that this ESF is a rollback and disentangles the safeguards, for instance on resettlement, that these organizations had fought for so hard.

Korinna Horta from Urgewald ties in with this comment and refers to large-scale infrastructure – so-called transformational projects – and their relationship with country systems. "Capacity building", she carries forward, "will be the holy grail" to make sure that the ESF works. Drawing on older experiences, however, she argues that capacity building is very difficult. She refers to the EIR, highlighting that "capacity" needs to be around already to really draw on such difficult frameworks on the local level. She then asks a somewhat complex question about sequencing: what will be there first, the capacity, or the country system going operational?

While she still elaborates this point, the moderator interrupts, telling her in a vigorous voice that she should come to a close and please only ask a question. When Horta continues speaking, Nwadishi drowns her out: "30 seconds and I will get you off the mic". This evokes another advocate to intervene. She stands up and, visibly trembling, speaks loudly towards the moderator: "I want to say to you: we have to remind ourselves where we come from as civil society. Everyone should have the right to speak here, and you should give them the necessary respect."

After this fight between three representatives of "civil society", Mr. King is granted last answers. He concludes by noting that "guidance is a funny species, it is not mandatory, but there is the understanding that it should be followed".[13] He highlights that the use of country systems is not at all vague in his opinion, since there is "an interpretation note on this, which is very clear". Again, he underlines that everybody's concerns were addressed during this process and that "the use of civil society is key".

---

[13] Maybe he read Onuf, *World of Our Making*, p. 86.

Hartwig Schäfer, visibly content with the meeting, concludes with an observation:

'In 1990, this meeting would have been impossible. When I came to the country where we implemented a project, I tried to get the heck out of there in order not to meet civil society [Garcia Zendejas interjects loudly: "We know!"]. Nowadays, this is real partnership. We work together and it is unthinkable to have such a reform process without civil society participation. I see this as real partnership.'

With this, the meeting comes to a close, and the participants enjoy salmon or chicken.

Economization

I will now turn to a more systematic analysis of my observations alongside the five mechanisms of complex rule. I detect the mechanism of economization in the division of global from particular knowledge which presents ends as (economic) givens, and actively quantifies discussions. At the CSPF, I observed the division of global from particular knowledge on numerous occasions when institutional officials had to react to a concrete story from the project sites, such as in the aforementioned example of ED Alford stating that it is hard to react to a "single story" and quickly changing to the next subject. A different way to react to a particular story is the rendering technical of discussions. I observed this quite regularly and want to illustrate it with the following example. In a session on public-private-partnerships (PPPs) where an NGO worker had given a presentation, outlining his fear that PPPs turned out more expensive than public procurement and were prone to corruption, an IMF manager reacted by switching first to a register of universal duty ("We all agree that the world has an increased infrastructure need"), and then quickly to an economic/technical repertoire, speaking of "contingent liability shocks", a "PPP Fiscal Risk Assessment Model", the "realization of efficiency gains", and the "mitigation of fiscal risk".

The division of the utilitarian and global knowledge from embodied or local experience is established in this example by not reacting to specific cases or problems but switching the scale towards the globe. On such an aggregated level, a 'need' for infrastructure is presumed with a formulation that includes everyone ('we all agree'). Only a partial, or *ideological* perspective could deviate from this statement. When this presumed consensus is established, the next step is devoted to technical descriptions, economic models, and policies. The step in between is eluded and thereby taken for granted.

I have often observed such an argumentative strategy combined with the moral convictions attached to 'development': we all want development (inclusive); and we in the World Bank Group (exclusive) know how to organize it. This latter point is underlined by technical terms or aggregated data, making it hard for critics to situate their point, especially those ones from the 'local' communities who have often not attended universities and are not used to the technical language of economic modelling.

Another feature of this switch of registers is that 'reasonable' critique can be separated from 'irresponsible' critique because by economizing issues, the ends (economic growth, infrastructure development) are excluded from a political discussion. Those who still question these ends will be encountered with technicalities. If these are put into question, the critic must be irrational.

When activists, for instance, demanded from the World Bank's President to divest from projects involved in water privatization, he reacted by elaborating the neutral and rational stance of the World Bank:

> 'I am not ideological whether the private sector or the public sector provides services. But I am very, very insistent that everyone gets access to water. So, the places where we have done privatization projects, it was because the access to water was absolutely awful. ... So, we are not running around the world trying to make money out of water privatization. ... In each of these areas [water, healthcare, education], we have very good examples of how price, quality, and access have all gone way up because of the participation of the private sector. And again: you can be ideological about this if you want and say: "Only the public sector!" But I would say, we can't afford to be ideological about it because in the end of the day it's about ending extreme poverty.'

In this quote, President Kim constructs an opposition between those who want to solve the problem of poverty and those who simply want to reaffirm their ideological stance. Poverty is by the same token rendered a purely economic issue which can be overcome by economic means, that is by technical interventions. Stakeholders who politicize the issue of poverty, for instance by arguing that the causes of poverty may be political in themselves and therefore not "solvable" by the given economic register, are deemed ideological and therefore not interested in real progress.

Another way of economizing an issue is to actively *quantify* debates. I observed this in a panel session organized by the IMF where an NGO member complained about the institution's lacking adaptiveness with respect to the Sustainable Development Goals (SDGs). The representative of the IMF reacted to this by playing back the ball to the critics, arguing that the IMF can only work with quantified goals: "Before we can really connect [our framework] to SDGs, we need them quantified. So please, all CSOs in the room, issue all the pressure you find appropriate on the institutions to quantify the SDGs".

This statement exemplifies well the logic that I encountered on numerous occasions, especially when 'affected people' report on grievances from project sites and Management reacts to these with a demand for quantification: 'how many proven cases of … ?'; 'what is the ratio of … ?' are typical questions. As several advocates told me in interviews, these questions constitute a challenge for them when trying to support affected people who would like to complain in front of the Inspection Panel or CAO. The claimants may hail from quite non-bureaucratized backgrounds, and the claims are partly not translatable into numbers, for instance when spiritual sites are destroyed for the sake of a development project.[14]

The economization of issues hence works by presuming the ends of development as givens, thereby excluding them from the discussion. Debates are rendered so abstract that 'everyone' agrees about these ends. In a second step, the means are elaborated in a highly technical and economized language which potentially intimidates non-economists and neutralizes the institution's approach so that that deviation must be 'ideological'. 'Reasonable' critique, on the other hand, remains within the means proposed by the institution: for example, the privatization of a public good.

Incorporation

The process that I conceptualized as incorporation has two observable implications.

(1) On the one hand, it comes along as an institutional 'opening-up' towards civil society.
(2) On the other, it is shaped by the institutional strategy to coopt social movements and NGOs.

Depending on the political perspective of observers, they tend to see only the former (liberals), or the latter (critical theorists). My point is that both processes take place and, although they sometimes overlap, they can be analytically separated: institutional access for CSOs is not yet a cooptation although it may lead to that. I speak of active cooptation when individuals from civil society are hired by the institutions, when specific individuals from among the critics are elevated into prestigious positions, or when material incentives are created for politically moderate organizations, or for organizations to become more moderate.

1. The creation and execution of the CSPF is an observable indication for 'opening-up'. Yet it goes even further than that, because the institutions also

---

[14] Ziai, 'Can the subaltern file claims?'

include civil society in the planning of the event: critics can make suggestions for the program, hand in ideas for panels, and they are consulted regarding sequencing, infrastructure and so on. The civil society teams in both the World Bank Group and the IMF make an enormous effort to accommodate the wishes of civil society in the preparations. The institutions' opening-up thus goes very far, and there is a strong effort by the responsible teams to make the most of the CSPF, yet the difficulty lies in providing the civil society access to high-ranking staff members.

For a rather contested panel on 'vulture funds', the IMF did, for instance, not even respond to emails. The same NGO had also organized a thematically less contested panel where they did not encounter these problems. The contentious panel was thus staffed with two members of Parliament (in order not to generate the situation of NGOs talking to NGOs). Opening-up thus refers to formal access, not necessarily to being heard, or exerting impact.

2. We can observe active cooptation, first, when individuals from the movement are hired and situated in institutional positions where they encounter their former colleagues, thus functioning like a buffer to their attacks. Second, I take as an indicator of active cooptation when material incentives are given for moderate organizations to the disadvantage of more radical ones. I want to illustrate the first logic by describing a meeting, which in the official program was announced as 'Future of the CSPF Session', where advocates openly discussed the format of the events with the two civil society teams of the World Bank and IMF, thus blurring the lines between institution and critics.

The session is led by the two civil society team leaders of the IMF and the World Bank Group. The former used to work for Oxfam before he moved to his new job in the IMF, the latter used to work for the ONE Campaign before joining the World Bank Group. These former civil society organizers now represent their institutions in front of their former colleagues, which brings them into a position of constant balancing of perspectives and interests. Before the meeting, they greet the NGO crowd in a friendly and intimate manner, hug some former colleagues and friends. At the same time, they must defend the institutions and think in a specific logic that is alien to their former colleagues.

At the meeting, the institutional control of access is discussed. After complaints from participants about the registration process, which was too restrictive for the taste of some critics, the World Bank civil society team leader (Edith Jibuno) explains that her team processed 2000 applications,

'but a lot of them were private sector or else: everybody that wants to go to the annual meetings comes to us and they try to get a civil society badge because they think this has the lowest barrier to entry. ... You want an open space, right. So, we create that, and people see that as the easiest space to get in. But we have to be careful. I got two

7am messages this morning about security issues, and my heart was in my mouth because I thought oh my God, they are CSOs, thank God it was other people. But we have to be careful. ... There are 1200 people here to whom I issued letters and I don't know where they are, and that's what keeps me up at night. And I just want you guys to understand that context.'

The World Bank has installed a person to whom most civil society members are sympathetic, and she has been given the responsibility to represent in front of the critics some restrictive institutional decisions. The atmosphere during that process feels much as if there would be no institutional staff around, although the institutional constraints, such as organizing security, prevail. Communicated by a person who acts like a peer, this restriction – although still made authoritatively – sounds comprehensible and unconfrontational.

The CSPF 2016 was shaped by moderators from civil society. When specific individuals from among the critics are elevated into prestigious positions, they soften external critique, because consciously or unconsciously their former peers will less likely engage in radical critique if they sit face to face with them. Because of this observation, I characterize this move as an active cooptation rather than only opening-up. In the next chapter, I analyse in detail what that meant specifically for critique at the CSPF. Now, it suffices to say that three of the panels that treated contested issues, as well as the largest event (the Civil Society Townhall Meeting), were moderated by an individual external to the institution (a 'civil society representative'), leaving the policing and creation of order to a person who is not employed by the institution. This person, in turn, may gladly take this elevated role, which does not only provide public visibility but also potentially brings economic value.[15]

To create material incentives for moderate organizations or for organizations to become more moderate is another process hard to separate from 'opening-up'. But upon closer inspection there is a big difference between creating the possibility of access for CSOs on the one hand, and purposefully selecting groups that the institution would like to be accessed by, on the other. Wandering through the annual meeting, my first impression was irritation about the number of uncontentious sessions. There are panels organized by Standard Chartered; the African Leadership Development Initiative, the Young Americas Business Trust; Junior Achievement Americas; Freedom House; Joy for Children Uganda. For an outsider, these panels look very similar to the ones elaborated on previously. Yet,

---

[15] The World Bank civil society team highlighted to me in interviews that these jobs are not paid. However, it is noticeable that the moderators of the 2016 and 2017 townhall meetings were on the list of financially supported individuals.

almost all these panels feature speakers from African countries for whom the flights and per diems were covered either by private companies or World Bank stipends.[16]

This inclusive move was, as far as I have discovered, not applied to outspoken critics but to individuals who represented civil society perspectives on rather conventional or affirmative panels of the organizations named previously. The funds allocated to make access more global thus create greater inclusiveness *and* a greater number of uncritical voices from civil society. The institutions sell this as a democratizing move in favour of an improved interest representation: in an interview, a high-ranking World Bank staff member told me that this measure balances out the radical voices which she deemed overrepresented at the CSPF. The problematic practice of selecting 'civil society' to the institution's liking did not occur to be problematic to her.

Legitimation

Legitimation works through the application of discourses that put institutional policies in a good light by way of normalizing practices and justifying reflexively their underlying thought structures. I want to single out two such processes here: (1) arguing with complexity, and (2) rhetorical disarming.

1. 'Everybody is equally unhappy' is an outstanding example for the practice of arguing with complexity, especially because it was used in exactly this formulation in three instances by three different individuals from higher World Bank Management. This formulation is self-legitimizing in the sense that outside critics can hardly demand more in a situation where all stakeholders have already compromised to an extent that everybody is unhappy about the outcome. It implies procedural fairness and burden-sharing in the production of a specific outcome, highlighting that a particular policy, if deemed problematic, cannot be blamed on the person who is justifying it at this very moment. Rather, the individual teams up with the critic, highlighting commonalities and equal dissatisfaction about an outcome, yet endorsing the higher principles which guided the process leading to a specific outcome.

Another practice that I observed in this regard is the highlighting of multilateralism as a complex 'background' to the work of the institution. When a critic in the session on the new ESF challenged the World Bank for not explicitly referring to human rights, the institutional representative explained this with the difficult multilateral process: "We didn't get a

---

[16]   48 CSOs were sponsored by the World Bank Civil Society Team. See online at: {http://pubdocs.worldbank.org/en/964781478211008057/AM-2016-CSPF-infographic.pdf}.

consensus with all 189 countries on the definition and meaning of human rights". Again, the complex process is to be blamed for the outcome. And since the process is connected to democracy, this decreases the pressure since the critics hold dear democratic principles as well.

2. Rhetorical disarming is the second set of practices that work as observables for legitimation. This includes the anticipation and dilution of criticism, as well as the outright schmoozing of critical actors. Beyond the several instances in which I alluded to this practice previously, I want to illustrate this with the rhetorical repertoire of one IMF manager, Mark Flanagan, who was the main speaker in a session on debt. He was the last speaker after input from critical NGOs, which challenged IMF policies rather fundamentally in several aspects. Within his 20-minute input presentation, he used all of the following formulations:

- "We have it on the radar."
- "We certainly agree."
- "We have it on our minds."
- "Intuitively, I agree totally."
- "Again, full agreement on that."
- "So, no disagreement on that."
- "We are determined to come up with something."
- "We'll do a better job at explaining it in the future."
- "If we sat in this room and had perfect information, we would not have a discussion. Concerning the ultimate end, we all agree."
- "On that aspect, we will have some more work to do, I'll be quite frank with you."
- "We are all for that."
- "In principle, there is no reason why we could not do that."

The anticipation and dilution of criticism can be observed in these formulations, which take up the critique and create an image of the IMF as an institution that is happy to accept criticism and will follow-up on it. In some formulations, he gives the impression that he already knew about a problem and his institution is just about to find the solution. This practice also draws on the generation of ends as givens as described in the part on economization. His inclusive language creates a situation in which all people in the room have the same goals. Problems are either externally induced ('information'), or they are currently worked on and will soon be solved. Rhetorically, the IMF's critics are disarmed because their critical points seem to have been taken up by the institution which, apparently, shares those concerns.

The speaker does not only share the concerns of his critics, he also very much endorses them as critical actors. He highlights in several parts of his presentation how dear he holds the NGOs that have just heavily criticized him and his institution. In the end of his talk, for example, he tells a critic: "Keep doing what you are doing: if we didn't disclose our DSAs [Debt Sustainability Analysis], they would be a disaster, so please keep it up. Accountability is so important." The external feedback is thus framed as making the IMF's work better and is hence a 'good thing' for the institution.

Professionalization

This approach to external criticism is also driven by professionalization as a mechanism of complex rule. It is based on a new management style that perceives external protest as productive irritation instead of an annoying and illegitimate cost factor. It bureaucratizes the behaviour towards critics, drawing less on emotions and more on formalities. Such professionalization can be observed, for instance, in the way Morgan Landy reacted to contentious points in the session described previously. He stated that the CAO was "best in class" and that the IFC was "proud" to have such a good complaint institution. This conveys a professional handling of problems. Problems exist and will always exist, thus external advice – and external complaints – are welcome tools to solve these problems. This handling of critique is in line with "New Public Management" literature, in which the culture of external consultancy is grounded. Management members of the World Bank Group and IMF react to critics by treating their criticism as if it were a free consultation for better management. The Management presents these critics as part of a network for development instead of antagonists.

The positive spin that is given to external irritation is also visible in the big room of manoeuvre provided to 'civil society'. Instead of locking them out, they are invited in, and even made responsible for organizing the civil society meetings inside the institutions. In the 'Future of the CSPF Session', NGOs meet and discuss how the CSPF should be organized in the future. As described previously, the NGOs discuss among themselves, while the two institutional representatives justify the current setup and caution if proposals seem difficult to accommodate.

During this meeting, a civil society working group was officially set up. It had so far existed as an 'Interim Civil Society Working Group' and was supposed to be responsible for keeping up communication with the institutions in terms of organizing the CSPF. The professionalization becomes especially visible in the process by which this working group comes about. An election is held which officially gives a mandate to a few individuals from pertinent NGOs. These can by now function as contact points for the institutions and in turn have to justify their decisions in front of their colleagues. As of 2017, this process even takes place online in a formal voting procedure. Consider the confrontational mode of contention that I described in Chapter 4. The creation of a proto-representative group of elected 'civil society' spokespersons who are in close contact with their counterparts inside the institution to organize a smooth running of dialogue is a formalization that would have been unimaginable then.

The process of creating 'civil society teams' in the institutions as 'contact points', or 'gate keepers' – depending on the view – is another such professionalization that works through *formalizing* relations. Critics are provided an official counterpart with an email address, an office, and a website. The CSPF itself is a project of formalization and an offer to those critics who are ready to join into the bureaucracy. Managers stream into the same room and discuss in a goal-oriented manner instead of hiding away and ignoring outside critics. When Hartwig Schäfer recalled his physical fear of the critics in the 1990s, he illustrated the successful steering of conflict from an "emotional" towards a "professional" affair.

The network-thinking underlying the examples of institutional staff signalling their openness towards critique and 'input' is a good indication for the depersonalized managerial approach that professional institutions are characterized by. Personal and political differences are bracketed in favour of expertise: contentious discussions are frequently closed with the dictum that "these are learning experiences". Conflicts are depoliticized. One can also observe this when focusing on the physical dimension of interaction: institutional staff will be listening in a concentrated, attentive, and open-minded manner, reacting friendly to allegations and they take time to shake hands and exchange greetings after the panels. This appeared almost unsettling to me since I had heard on several occasions in interviews outside the CSPF, from current or former World Bank staff, that "Management *hates* NGOs".

It is impossible to find out whether those ones who attend the CSPF are the share of Management who does *not* hate NGOs, or whether they just act like it. However, this does not matter regarding professionalization, because either way the visible procedures transport an image of a transparent and approachable institution open to criticism. If the other mechanisms may seem more plausible in terms of an establishment of institutionalized super- and subordination, this less apparent aspect is highly functional for the process of 'rendering managerial' in complex rule.[17]

Regulation

With the mechanism of regulation, I do not necessarily mean the creation of law, but an increasing trend to predefine processes of interaction according to rules. I thus observe this mechanism in the creation of new rules, the stricter

---

[17] Boltanski, *On Critique*, p. 136.

application of existing rules, or in the ordering and disciplining of critique through rules. The CSPF is full of (partly unspoken) rules. This is no surprise since this is one of the main characteristics of institutions. Therefore, I focus on the *process* of enclosing the possibilities of critique by the creation of rules or standardization of procedures which limit the possibilities to disrupt for those critics who choose to (or are made to) abide by them.

Several rules that fall under the category of regulation have already been alluded to in the previous descriptions, some of them seemingly trivial. The accreditation of actors, first, works alongside a rule-based procedure that critical actors must comply with. This process is getting ever more formalized. Under the auspices of the former leader of the civil society team (until 2015), so I was told in several interviews, activists could simply show up, register late or informally. He himself told me that his main goal was to open up the procedures for as many people as possible and to make access easy for everyone (Interview, World Bank Group manager). Increasingly, however, the process of accreditation is becoming a hurdle. Unfortunately, I could not get hold of the accepted and disallowed applications (1200 vs 800 according to the civil society team). Yet even when accepting the institution's claim that only security and stopping business from entering with CSO-card are the reasons for this formalization of entry, it forces applicants to associate with a formal institution. This requirement already rules in that it preconfigures the possible subjectivities present at the CSPF. 'The Global Justice Movement', for instance, is not an appropriate affiliation.

The conference format is another rule steering and by that limiting the possible repertoire of action at the CSPF. I have described two panels in detail already. The forms of protest are predefined to rhetorical interventions in a highly technical debate. Every scholar knows that sitting on a panel or listening to a panel has effects on what can and cannot be said. Additionally, the moderators of the panels meticulously guard the time and specific talking rules as well as in some instances the possible topics of conversation. The only way that critics had in mind in order to break with this mode was the 'walk-out', a means that they had practiced several times in previous years but not in 2016, although it was briefly considered (interviews with NGOs). This also shows that they perceive themselves to be guided by the institution's rules while the only way to circumvent them is to leave.

9

Fragmentation in Cooperation: Observing the Changing Practices of Critique

Attending the World Bank Group/IMF Civil Society Policy Forum, I observed in abundance the institutional practices that contribute to the fragmentation of critique. This is probably not surprising to any critical theorist or activist who has spent a while thinking through the problematic consequences of participation.[1] What may be more surprising, and more illuminating for the guiding question of this book, is how the practices of critique change throughout this institutional interaction. As in the case study of the EIR (Chapter 7), I will now go on to present the practices of critique alongside the mechanisms of fragmentation. I do this by drawing on one specific session of the CSPF and the ensuing discussions about it, in which these practices became specifically visible: the so called 'townhall meeting', public highlight of the CSPF. Christine Lagarde, Managing Director of the IMF, and Jim Yong Kim, Director of the World Bank Group, sit in a big circle with approximately 40 'civil society representatives', and another approximately 50 spectators (of whom I am one) seated in the back rows (see Figure 9.1).

I will describe this meeting in the following paragraphs, focusing on the observable mechanisms of complex rule. Instead of reproducing the contents (which are largely similar to the two sessions described in Chapter 8), I will first interpret the initial six minutes before the beginning of the actual debate. They already set the stage and framing for the whole meeting.

---

[1] Tucker, 'Participation and subjectification in global governance: NGOs, acceptable subjectivities and the WTO'; Julia Rone, 'The people formerly known as the oligarchy: the co-optation of citizen journalism', in Mona Baker and Bolette Blaagaard (eds) *Citizen Media and Public Spaces* (London: Routledge, 2016), pp. 208–24.

Figure 9.1: The Townhall Meeting 2016

Source: The World Bank on flickr: {https://www.flickr.com/photos/worldbank/sets/721576 74854832595}

I will argue that this specific format reproduces hierarchies and narrows down the possibilities of action for the attending critical actors to a very specific repertoire, which leads to a taming of those ones attending and, in effect, contributes to the fragmentation of resistance. I analyse the role of 'civil society' that is assigned to the participating NGOs, and especially the moderator, Faith Nwadishi, who is elevated as 'representative' of civil society in this specific format. After this, I analyse the critics' performance at the forum, and their reflections on this format, building on informal conversations at the CSPF as well as on interviews and online research conducted afterwards.

The townhall meeting in 2016 was more tightly managed than it had been in the previous years. Questions had to be handed in beforehand, and the moderator summed these up into thematic blocks that were thus predefined. Spontaneous questions outside these blocks were denied. Attendees could either raise their hands to ask questions, but only regarding these blocks, or they could tweet questions on the World Bank's website, where a live feed of these tweets was provided alongside the live stream of the meeting.[2]

---

[2]   The hashtag of the event was #AMCSO2016.

Townhall

The townhall meeting starts off with the representatives of the World Bank Group and the IMF flocking in late. All the other attendees had been seated around the enormous table already; only at one end, where Kim, Largarde and the moderator were expected, chairs remained empty. When these individuals enter the room, they are followed by their respective delegations who shall be placed behind them. These second-row delegations cover high-ranking management such as Hartwig Schäfer (World Bank), Philippe Le Houérou (IFC), and Mark Flanagan (IMF), exhibiting the meeting's significance to the institution. In between these powerful white men, an aide to President Kim is placed, eagerly preparing notes that she passes to the World Bank Group President during the session. While the institutional staff behind their bosses are still getting seated, whispering, and exchanging greetings, Nwadishi opens the proceedings. Visually, she stands out in contrast to the dark-blue business-dresses around her, with a colourfully patterned headscarf matching her eye-catching dress and a green scarf (an activist item) around her neck. I will reproduce a transcript of her opening statement here because it captures in five minutes (of spoken words) some fundamental processes that I have theorized before.

Nwadishi: Good evening ladies and gentlemen, my name is Faith Nwadishi, I'm an Ukwuani woman from Delta State, Nigeria. I'm the founder and executive director of the Koyenum Immalah Foundation. I am one of the two African members of the international board of the EITI, that's the Extractive Industries Transparency Initiative, representing civil society. Koyenum Immalah Foundation simply means: 'You cannot give what you don't have'. So, especially at this meeting, as colleagues, we will give as much as we have. We try as much as possible to be what we are. And as you can see, I am seated in between what we call in Nigeria the Oga and the Madam at the top [moderate laughs from the audience; Kim smiles; Lagarde laughs]. And when you mention the Oga and the Madam at the top, you're actually talking about the people who are in charge of affairs. So today, we are having a conversation with the Oga and the Madam of the World Bank and the IMF. So, colleagues, we'll try as much as possible to be brief, we have just one hour for this meeting. We'll go straight to the point. The entire objective of this meeting is to be able to get our issues across and get to hear from the heads of the two organizations. Let me also formally welcome Madame Christine Lagarde, the first female Managing Director and chairperson of the IMF, and Dr. Jim Jong Kim, the President of the World Bank, to this townhall. And also allow me, on behalf of all of us, to congratulate them for their re-election for their second term [polite applause]. As a child, I used to think that the World Bank was the commercial bank of the world [scattered laughs]. But now, I know better [she laughs]. I'm very humbled to have been considered for this very important task of moderating this civil society townhall at this year's annual meeting, and I thank the team that considered me suitable for this role, and would also like to thank all of us, our colleagues who have continuously made this happen. Indeed, the voices from the Global South have particularly been heard but still need to be louder and attended to, in the light of the rapidly closing space for civil society in many countries and regions that make up the global South. This is the voice that I represent here today. We have this townhall meeting. It is a townhall meeting ... as they say the simplest definition of democracy. This townhall meeting therefore is townhall for civil society, of civil society, and by civil society.

Permit me to set some ground rules for this meeting, considering that we have just one hour for this meeting, and we need to make the ultimate use of the time. Prior to this time, we have sent out emails, and colleagues sent their concerns. Following these emails, we were able to put all of these questions under eight categories. And the categories are these. Please, can you put that down. We have safeguards, citizens engagement, civic space and access to information, debt, climate change and energy, infrastructure, financial intermediaries, international taxation, poverty and inequality. We'll have two rounds of questions. The first four categories will come under the first round and these are the safeguards, citizens engagement, debt, climate change. I expect each speaker to speak for at least a minute or less [sic]. And please go straight to the point. No comments. If you begin to make comments, I will have to cut you off [smiles in the backrows of institutional staff]. And please don't take that personal, because we only have one hour for this meeting. If this time limit is not respected and I'm forced to cut people off; it is in our collective interest that as many people as possible can ask their questions. Be also advised that on Friday 7th, we're having the civil society meeting at 12. There is a working group that was set up, that I am also a member of, to look at issues around the Civil Society Policy Forum. Therefore, to open the questions, I will take the privilege of the moderator to ask the very first questions. And my very first question will go to Madame Lagarde. My question is: In recent years, including most recently in Chicago, you have talked about the need for growth to be more inclusive. Can you tell us why it is so important in the light of current global challenges and what the Fund is doing to make growth more inclusive and reduce inequality?

Lagarde: Thank you very much chair and congratulations for representing all your colleagues in the room.

In the following, I analyse this passage according to the five mechanisms alongside which open global governance divides and rules.

Economization

The economization of critique, which can be attributed to a neoliberal governing rationality (dimension 1 of complex rule), leads to a growing acceptance of an economistic mindset among critics. This is observable in a move from 'existential tests' to 'reality tests', the usage of economic and technical language, and the adoption of ends set by the neoliberal institution. Although Nwadishi does not go into questions of policy, all these practices are already observable in her brief opening statement, which subsequently shapes the way the townhall debate is structured.

First, she excludes existential tests from the possible tableau of action by predefining the pillars of discussion. The topics are henceforth always already set within the current paradigm. She legitimizes this with 'objective' constraints, adopting the logic of efficiency that excludes fundamental debates, or even comments, since "we have just one hour for this meeting, and we need to make the ultimate use of the time". This prefigures and separates what will be counted as 'reasonable' critique from 'irresponsible' critique which is situated outside these seemingly apolitical parameters. *Second*, she represents the political reason of governance and its economized and technical language which abstracts from positionality, personal grievance, or politicized polarization towards the best technical solution for 'everyone' by stating, for instance, that "it is in our collective interest that as many people as possible ask their questions".

More significantly, *third*, her question towards Lagarde shows how much the interaction between today's civil society with the financial institutions has changed in comparison to the advocacy of earlier years. As I elaborated in the previous chapter, such encounters used to be hostile. These antagonistic relations were shaped by diametrically opposed ideas on economic policy. It is no stretch to say that these encounters were often framed as a standoff between capitalists and anti-capitalists. Much in contrast, Nwadishi's question pays court to the IMF's policy: "In recent years, ... you have talked about the need for growth to be more inclusive. Can you tell us why it is so important in the light of current global challenges ...?". This first question, catering to the personal agenda of the IMF's Managing Director, is followed by a lengthy opening statement on Lagarde's side. Beyond this tactical choice, the question reveals that the adoption of ends, which I have theorized as a core practice of accepting the neoliberal governing rationality, has already extended very far. It is remarkable that the officially 'representative' figure of civil society, in the most high-profile interaction with the World Bank Group and the IMF of the year, sets the stage for self-promotion of the institution rather than outlining differences. Her 'why' implies a knowledge question that is to be answered with the wisdom of a teacher (the *madam at the top*) rather than by an opponent. More importantly, the question's content is affirmative rather than critical in that it does not question growth as an aim and affirms the IMF's plans to make growth 'inclusive' as the right policy.

Incorporation

The mechanism of incorporation is observable when practices of critique shift from protest (outside) to lobbying (inside), as well as in the elevation of specific civil society individuals. The latter practice is probably the most striking in the segment analyzed. Not only does the moderator herself stress several times that she is "the representative" of civil society. At the same time, she also represents the "voice of the global South". And she does not miss the opportunity to extend her thankfulness for this honour, stating that she is "very humbled to have been considered for this very important task ... and I thank the team that considered me suitable for this role", thereby also underlining that she is a representative by the World Bank's grace.

This practice, which I conceptualized as 'active cooptation' on the side of the institution and 'elevation of individuals' on the side of critique, has effects for the character of dispute between the institutions and the attending NGOs. The moderator plays soft on her counterparts, and, obviously proud, highlights to be seated in between 'the Oga and the Madam of the World Bank and the IMF'. She also does not forget to congratulate them on their election to a second term, a fact that numerous critical activists had considered a terrible choice.[3] Her only question being enabling rather than critical, she is paid back by Lagarde who, before answering the question, congratulates Nwadishi to her elevation. In this case, the domestication of critique thus works *through* an elevated individual who, in this session, also has the power to regulate others' style of participating.

Legitimation

On the side of the critics, legitimation is observable when they argue within the rules of the game. Maximum demands lose traction because the logic of the institution is either endorsed or thought to be impossible to circumvent. In both cases, one can assume a high degree of normalization and internalization. As Steffek argues, "taken for grantedness is the best indicator for a successful legitimation process".[4] In the townhall meeting, potential demands must be formulated as a question and have to abide by the preselected topics. More importantly, the framework of this session and especially the development model which the institutions pursue, is not put into question.

The actual observable in this regard, however, is a non-event. The mechanism of complex rule would be contradicted if critical actors had massive problems with the whole framework of interaction. Further on, I show that this applies to some of the critics who are astonished about the high degree of "taken for grantedness" observable in their peers. Such fundamental differences among the critics lead to fragmentation. Before heading to this point, let me give an example illustrating the observation of legitimation beyond the non-event.

At a panel just after the townhall meeting, co-organized by a well-known critical think-tank, the speakers (Managing Directors of the IMF, a politician, and an activist) were finished with their discussion. The first question from the audience began as follows: "I am really proud to be a co-sponsor of this panel, this is an outstanding conversation. The presentations have been so good." This comment came from a speaker who, in my interviews, had belonged to the most outspoken critics of neoliberal development. In her office, she told me that she used to be "totally diluted by the Bank. I wrote the participation strategy for the Board" (Interview, US NGO). Referring to the late 1980s, she reflected on her personal process of cooptation that she now claims to see through and is able to circumvent. The example of such a

---

[3] See, for example: {https://www.brettonwoodsproject.org/2016/09/one-man-one-vote-one-option-world-bank-set-coronate-kim-second-term/}.

[4] Steffek, 'The power of rational discourse and the legitimacy of international governance', p. 22.

reflected and experienced activist (who is, additionally, quite outspoken, and radical in her demands) can be taken as an indication of how far advanced the internalization of the institutions' and their participation policies' legitimation processes already are. Had I only interviewed her, I would have told a story of an activist who used to be coopted by the global governance institutions but then understood these logics and emancipated herself from them, reclaiming a radical anti-capitalist agenda. But observing her behaviour in interaction with representatives of the institution, I saw her arguing within the rules of the game. The far-reaching demands she told me about in private were not recognizable. This can, of course be due to both an endorsement of the institutional order, or because she thinks it is impossible to circumvent. Yet in contrast to the hostility reported from the early 2000s, her conciliatory tone is an evident embodiment of an interaction based on the logic of legitimate global governance. Irrespective of how the activist may feel about this in private, the meeting in effect is not contentious but technical, friendly, and cooperative.

Professionalization

I observe professionalization in the sharing of responsibility, that is the self-organization of 'civil society' for the purposes of the institution, or within its framework. Furthermore, I speak of professionalization when observing NGOization, that is a formalization of advocacy which goes along the lines of project logic, competition for funding, and the acceptance of the 'civil society' label.

Regarding the first practice, this townhall is informative as well-put by Nwadishi: "This townhall meeting therefore is townhall for civil society, of civil society, and by civil society." She also explains how the session was organized by her: "Prior to this time, we have sent out emails, and colleagues sent their concerns. Following these emails, we were able to put all of these questions under eight categories." The World Bank and the IMF have thus effectively outsourced the organizational burden of their biggest outreach event of their annual meetings. But this trend does not only refer to this townhall meeting, as the moderator is quick to add: "Be also advised that … there is a working group that was set up that I am also a member of, to look at issues around the civil society policy forum".

This working group has already been discussed, showing how the institutions delegate the task of organizing the civil society interaction to civil society, but guided by two institutional representatives who comment on the possibilities and impossibilities of ideas. Giving the activists additional access and creating the situation of an even more open IO, the blame for what goes wrong is also delegated to 'civil society', which is empowered organizationally, hence responsibilized (in the sense of Wendy Brown, see Chapter 3), and is happy to take on this task.

Second, Nwadishi addresses the participants with 'colleagues' several times, demonstrating that this is a working context.[5] She also introduces herself with a description of her positions ("founder and executive director", "member of the international board"), highlighting the professional character of the conversation. The audience, by this verdict, is to be imagined as a collective of "NGO workers" (with a salary) rather than "activists" (with a moral conviction).

Another example of professionalization can be observed in one of the questions directed at President Kim from a staff member of the Bank Information Center (BIC):

Activist: As other World Bank Presidents have left legacies for civil society in the past such as the safeguards or the partnership for social accountability, we appreciate your commitment in your first term, Dr. Kim, on citizen engagement and commitment on beneficiary feedback. However, recent evaluations of the indicators of the feedback in projects have shown that they're not really closing the feedback loop, and they're not leading to meaningful engagement, leaving your legacy as a leader for citizen engagement at risk.

Nwadishi: Question please!

Activist: So the question is: What will you do in your second tenure as President to ensure this legacy, ensuring meaningful engagement at the World Bank?

Nwadishi: I'm sorry but that was my first question to him!

Apart from the fact that the moderator interrupts the question and disallows it afterwards, the way the question is framed also tells a lot about the tactics of advocacy BIC engages in here. Instead of criticizing the head of the IO, the activist appeals to the President's legacy, showcasing positive aspects of his predecessors and by that trying to put pressure on him. This conscious empathizing with his career incentives is a sign for 'professionalized' advocacy in contrast to earlier, more radical, approaches drawing on scandalization and stressing the irreconcilable differences between the (bad) institution and (good) advocacy network.

Regulation

As elaborated in Chapter 4, with regulation I refer to the endorsement of institutional rules and, to that effect, the corresponding self-policing. In the opening statement, Nwadishi goes some way in introducing the institutional

---

[5]   On the email list of the European Network of MDB watchers, to give a counterexample, participants usually greet their peers with 'dear friends'.

rules and reaffirms the institution's hierarchies with great respect towards its leaders. Furthermore, she has internalized their custom to answer questions and dislike (especially long) 'comments'. She therefore does not only respect existing rules but asks the audience for permission "to set some ground rules for this meeting". Demanding that each speaker restrict herself to a maximum of one minute, she adds: "No comments. If you begin to make comments, I will have to cut you off." This is a notification that she implements with great vigour later in the session. As previously discussed, she also justifies this approach, when being challenged, and presents the rule-based character of advocacy as necessarily tied to reaching progress: "Yes, we are all civil society and what we do is, we give ourselves rules and we discuss according to them and make a difference and that's why we are change agents."

The policing of unruly critics is therefore taken over by the 'civil society representative' who, on many occasions, does not fail to mention the benefits for "all of us", thus signalling her belonging to the non-institutional side. This self-policing by civil society is welcome by Kim and Lagarde; so much so that Kim later, after she interrupts a speaker, comments: "You disallowed that question, thank you very much".

Fragmentation

The practices that I discussed with the example of the townhall's moderator evoked counter-reactions from critics. I will describe these reactions in the following, again along the mechanisms of complex rule. As I have argued before, the fragmentation of critique is the effect of interacting with institutions in open global governance, because it is structured in a constellation that I call complex rule. Fragmentation happens in a composite process through the aforementioned mechanisms. These mechanisms are observable both in institutional and critics' practices while the latter are contradictory at first glance. Exactly this contradiction is where fragmentation takes place.

Fights over economization

I observed an increasing acceptance of a neoliberal governing rationality, indicating the grip of economization on the critics. I have outlined how the moderator of the townhall catered to Lagarde by asking her to elaborate on why inclusive growth is "so important". This focus on inclusive growth has, however, received suspicion among the critics, who were annoyed not only by the uncritical style of the question but also by the agenda itself.

I participated in conversations where activists debated what they saw as a general trend towards the upgrading of the private sector in development. Many understood this to be the consequence of the IMF's agenda around inclusive growth, arguing that in the past, private companies had been used as an instrument for such an agenda because these were portrayed as "closer to the people" than government agencies. The activists thus attached this trend especially to a revival of PPPs. The IMF, during the meeting, made clear that PPPs are high on its agenda. Activists were worrying about this trend and had also published a brochure on PPPs which they distributed on the CSPF.[6]

In an email list of advocacy organizations, a well-known activist generally diagnosed "a new window for private sector finance [in development lending], prioritizing investments in the private sector as a key development strategy for fragile and conflict affected states like Myanmar". In the days around the CSPF, a joint letter had been discussed and several NGOs sent it to the European Council shortly after, problematizing its new development strategy with its method of "ramping up the use of official development assistance for guarantees to leverage in more investment". It is argued in the letter that "the proposal seems to make some challenging and perhaps unsubstantiated claims assuming a necessary link between investment, job creation, growth, and development. Investment and economic growth do not automatically lead to human or social development. ... It is especially difficult to establish such links in fragile states".[7] Although this letter was directed at the European Council, it shows that during the time of investigation, the term inclusive growth was not at all seen as unproblematic among the critics, and they felt accordingly frustrated during the townhall meeting when Lagarde was invited to outline her agenda.

At the CSPF, especially the question of water privatization was a hot topic among advocates. They complained about the abstract and number-driven logic that the institutions pursue and the lacking reference to the people's lifeworlds: 'Throughout the meeting, President Kim consistently failed to acknowledge that people's questions were rooted in their lived experiences and reflected legitimate concerns about Bank-funded projects'.[8] But not only the institutions were the targets of critique, also Nwadishi was perceived as a facilitator of their agenda. This constellation, a 'peer' who provides the stage for the institutional representatives who then argue in favour of water privatization and call opposition "ideological", was perceived by my conversation partners as "tragic".

Fights over participation or non-participation

The incorporation of critique is observable in a taming of critics, as well as in the elevation of individuals. Yet these practices are also countered by

---

[6] Maria José Romero, *What Lies Beneath? A Critical Assessment of PPPs and Their Impact on Sustainable Development* (Brussels: European Network on Debt and Development, 2015).

[7] Letter to the European Council by an NGO coalition led by Oxfam.

[8] See Ciel's report, available at: {http://www.ciel.org/world-bank-president-snubs-commun ity-concerns-public-forum/}.

other practices, again contributing to fragmentation. These are a conscious non-participation in the meeting and the utterance of critique towards the individuals who are seen as 'coopted'. This latter practice can only be reported in anecdotal evidence from the CSPF, where one critical activist told me that the moderator's performance was "a disgrace", and several were complaining about her serving the institutions. They, however, also were expressing a certain confusion as in how to act against this tendency, because they generally welcomed the institution's openness towards having someone from civil society take on the job as moderator: hence they continued to feel that Nwadishi was 'on their side'. They did not, furthermore, plan to actively counter this problem. I rather perceived them as perplexed, tired, and frustrated. This frustration also led to gossip and some derogatory terms in informal conversations. When I asked critical NGOs whether they felt like partners to the World Bank Group (as insinuated by Hartwig Schäfer, discussed previously), I often received answers like the following:

> 'No! [laughs]. It's a good question. That's so funny. Well, maybe, you know, some other groups do. Like World Resources Institute, or World Vision. Those are the ones I put on the [political] right. Or even Oxfam, which might be just that way removed from them. … Yeah, maybe some groups feel like they're real partners.' (Interview, US activist)

Regarding general non-participation at the meeting, many chose this option, thus rejecting the procedural opening-up of the institutions. Since this decision strongly overlaps with the content-based practice of arguing or declining to argue inside the institutional setup, I will, instead of repeating the aforementioned, focus on the reception of these decisions within the advocacy network. At one panel, where a big NGO had invited an activist from an 'affected community' in Fiji, a World Bank manager asked why this community would not make use of the participation mechanisms with a stronger vigour. The man from Fiji answered: "Our communities live from two to three dollars a day. How do you expect them to engage with you?".

This question was also discussed among the activists. Those who see themselves as brokers for the affected people are aware of their difficult position in-between the "locals" and the "bankers" as they put it.[9] They constantly reflect on the best strategy, being aware of their own privilege. This privileged position also inhibits them from engaging in a more radical form of protest. A German activist told me, for instance: "The only ones

---

9   See also Kristina Hahn and Anna Holzscheiter, 'The ambivalence of advocacy: representation and contestation in global NGO advocacy for child workers and sex workers', *Global Society* 27, 4 (2013), pp. 497–520.

who are organizing real protest are the Asians. But they don't come here anymore." In general, I heard several stories of earlier annual meetings when the activist coalition had been more diverse, and the CSPF had not yet been so 'boring' and consensual. The activists hence reflected on their part quite actively. Others have a more radical approach and feel failed by their fellow activists being incorporated, as an interviewee said about an influential NGO which at one point started to join the CSPF: "I was so shocked. What is [NGO] doing in the IMF? Cause, we used to protest outside the IMF" (Interview, US activist).

I thus observed at the CSPF an irritation about those activists who are perceived by others as 'coopted'. Deviating from my theoretical expectation, I did not observe active discussions or even fights about participation or non-participation. In later interviews, I gathered critique from activists who decided to stay away. Referring to the criticized (those advocating 'inside'), I could observe a process of active reflection. They asked themselves whether they were 'right here' and expressed a certain sadness about the absence of other, more radical, groups.

Estrangement between 'weak' reformists and 'irresponsible' maximalists

The mechanism receiving least attention in this analysis is legitimation because its observable – arguing with the institutions on their terms – is so self-evident in this case: if you do not want to argue with them, you do not attend. And this is exactly what happened for large parts of the critical spectrum. Now, this finding would not be sufficient if it were only based on non-attendance of some actors (even if many), because absence itself can have many reasons. Yet, my observations and conversations with activists make me confident in stating that this practice is a conscious political decision, again bolstering the argument on fragmentation: in conversations with several of the engaged activists portrayed before, they told me that the townhall was "not worth the time", "useless", or "only a show". They drew on their experiences in previous years and concluded that their attendance was not necessary. I only spotted a couple of 'critical' NGO activists, attending without raising their voice, and one actively participating.

The townhall meeting took place on Wednesday, 5 October. On the following day, the Inspection panel hosted an open house with drinks and finger food. Many NGOs were attending and used the opportunity to network, gather with friends, have a glass of wine, and discuss politics. On this occasion, I was introduced to one of the most experienced activists from a Belgian organization. The person introducing me had attended the townhall meeting and was quite angry about it (as he told several of his colleagues and also World Bank staff). When we met the activist who had not attended the townhall, he was already sick of talking about the issue and so he asked me to describe the atmosphere at the townhall meeting.

After my report, the two men discussed what this meant for their activism, asking me for my opinion. When I asked them in turn what they would expect from such a meeting, they took it as a provocative, rhetorical question (which it was not intended to be) and answered: "Yes, you are right, we have to be more radical again", thereby implying a greater degree of disruptive action. They told me about "the good old days" when they blocked or disturbed meetings and staged walkouts if they felt that certain basic standards had been violated. Nowadays, they felt, the institutions could play with them and did not have to be afraid any longer.[10]

While I reported a far-ranging internalization of the style of arguing within large parts of the activist coalition, I also detected a scepticism towards this deliberative approach at the townhall meeting by some of the advocates present in Washington DC, and a shift away from the whole CSPF by those ones not present. One such individual, for instance, said: "They organize circuses. We can have these roundtables and discussions, every spring meeting and every fall meeting and they get us space to have a meeting and they provide us with lunches, and they give us a reception. So, they keep us occupied the whole damn time" (Interview, US activist).

Decreasing trust levels between professionals and activists

The professionalization of critics is visible in the way they organize as 'CSOs'. Furthermore, they even take responsibility for organizing the CSPF together with the institutions. Previously, I have outlined what a professionalized approach to advocacy looks like at the CSPF: 'Civil society' takes responsibility in the organization and smooth running of the interaction, and advocacy is conducted in a way accessible to the institutions rather than by antagonizing them. BIC, for instance, posed a question by appealing to the institutional logic and personal legacy of its President rather than condemning its action. Fragmentation takes place when other parts of the activist network distance themselves from this form of professionalization and stress the need for spontaneity and the advantages of less formalized — more direct — forms of action.

After the townhall session, I spoke to some activists about BIC, referring to the aforementioned tactic of appealing to the President's legacy as well as about the organization's director who, on a different panel, had called for progressive networks *across* civil society and the institutions. Asking

---

[10] There is a video snippet putting together the answers that activists found appalling, available at: {https://www.youtube.com/watch?v=eEyQuO5VeSg}.

them about their opinion, they smiled mildly, and one said: "He came from World Vision, what else would you expect?" This refers to BIC's new General Director (at the time), the successor of Chad Dobson, a veteran in the scene of advocacy. The new Director arrived at the NGO just before the CSPF in 2016 and was widely seen as a proponent of a 'soft' approach. World Vision is a charity not known as an advocacy organization, much less a critical one.

The condescending statement about him shows the fragmentation of the network in terms of approaches. While some organizations try to professionalize their work, others perceive this as a dilution. Such a mutual estrangement is often visible, although not verbalized, when for instance the moderator of the session 'The Future of the CSPF' stated: "We are here by the grace of the World Bank and the IMF" and others in the room are shaking their heads in disbelief.

Although I have illustrated some examples of the fragmentation of critics through professionalization, this section is the weakest in terms of confirming the theoretical argument. This is not surprising since all the present advocates subscribe to the professionalized approach at least to a certain degree. Direct action groups, anarchists, and other non-professionalized critics of the institutions would not see this attendance as worthwhile, which essentially prevents systematic access to them and their practices. Therefore, the fragmentation caused by professionalization (if any) should be visible between those ones who attend and those ones who do not, a process that I could only vaguely hint at here. This also shows the limits of participant observation in an institutional setting.

Forced or self-induced exclusion of groups and their claims that are 'external' to rules of the game

The regulation of the World Bank Group's and the IMF's interaction with critics was shown previously in the critics' endorsement of institutional rules and the respective self-policing. If this tendency is challenged by a neglect of regulated approaches in that, for instance, parts of the critical network refuse to abide by the rules their peers have approved of, this leads to fragmentation.

In the case of the townhall meeting, this happened quite extensively, and even publicly. The head of Oxfam US, for instance, criticized the rule-based approach and its restrictive implementation on Twitter, calling this 'heavy moderation'.[11] Oxfam is not known to be among the radical NGOs but rather one oriented towards compromise. Therefore, this critique is even more significant than the ones I observed to be issued by the usual suspects.

---

[11] Available at: {https://twitter.com/nadiadaar/status/783794376384413701}.

It is interesting, however, that some observers mentioned an increase in regulation in this particular year in comparison to the years before and complained about this:

> In years past, the town-hall style meetings have featured people asking questions, providing testimonies and comments, and sometimes even protesting the decisions made by those who wield tremendous power and influence over their communities' lives and livelihoods. This year, however, participation was tightly and unnecessarily controlled, questions were disallowed, and President Kim's responses suggested a callous disregard for community concerns.[12]

First, this implies a general increase in regulation of what can be said and how. Since this is coorganized by a 'civil society representative', it confirms the regulation as theorized previously. Second, however, these complaints also show that other parts of the advocacy coalition are far from convinced that these rules are to the advantage of "all of us" as it was argued by Nwadishi. In the same report of CIEL, the NGO also complains about a "limiting structure of the discussion" highlighting that the possibility to say *something* does not equal a good exchange and that the growing regulation applied in the session is to the disadvantage of critics. These critics complained that "if the townhall is any indication, President Kim's (and by extension the World Bank's) understanding of 'inclusive' is still missing the point".

---

[12] See the CIEL report, available at: {http://www.ciel.org/world-bank-president-snubs-community-concerns-public-forum/}.

Conclusion

When protesters of the Global Justice Movement stormed the annual meeting of the World Bank Group in 2000, forcing its President to integrate activists and affected people into the institutional decision making, I was 13 years old. How could I blame my students to whom this episode – and what followed from it – seems like distant history? I started research for this book in 2014, and even since then, international politics has changed enormously. Transnational solidarity ties have been further strained, not least by a global pandemic. Euphoria around transnational activism has sharply declined, and in many countries, repression has re-emerged as the ruling tool of choice. Finishing this book, the activist who inspired its guiding question has already retired and moved to the countryside.

So why bother? After seven years, about a hundred interviews, and uncountable pages of documents that I consulted for this study, I think that his question is still absolutely crucial for building a progressive social movement that sustains solidarity beyond the single event: bemoaning the broken solidarities of the Global Justice Movement, he noticed that the grievances had not changed significantly, and that social movements were still alive and kicking around the world but "nowadays we don't manage to bring those local struggles together anymore; the movement is so fragmented. How has that happened?" I do hope that I will make my way to his country house someday to tell him that his question has been pestering my brain for such a long time. But mainly, I would like to tell him that I have found an answer to his question. It is not a simple answer, because the ways in which the movement has been divided are produced not by a simple ruler, but by a dynamic constellation ('complex rule'). Understanding how this constellation works, in turn, is the basic precondition for strategizing in the future. Nevertheless, I'll try to be brief and tell him this:

Complex rule

It is important to understand that institutions like the World Bank Group are contributing to the establishment and unceasing re-inscription of international structures of rule. They are not rulers themselves; it is within institutions that specific normative frameworks, ways of negotiation and forms of respectable organization are sedimented as 'reality'. The World Bank Group, the institution that was antagonized most fiercely by the Global Justice Movement, has changed its character significantly over the years. Especially, it started to invite critique in instead of shutting it out. This is neither good nor bad. It is an observable property of a changing way in which super- and subordination is organized; a constellation that, following Boltanski, I have termed *complex rule*. The character of complex rule is that its institutions offer opportunities to their critics. Academics have noticed this change and dubbed it the 'opening up of international organizations'.[1] Below a certain 'threshold of tolerance', or what Daase and Deitelhoff call 'within the applicable rules of the game', deviance can be practiced within open global governance.[2] What I have observed over the years, then, was an increasing self-limitation of critics to the space within these rules of the game. This serves institutions to 'preserve the appearance of an agreement'[3] – they institutionalize the rules of the game as 'reality' – while deviation is marked as irresponsible or 'crazy', as a World Bank manager put it in one of my interviews.

This constellation is driven by (1) a *neoliberal governing rationality* which legitimizes itself according to (2) a *reflexive order of justification* and is organized as (3) a *managerial bureaucracy*. These three dimensions are aspects of an increasing institutionalization of super- and subordination that is realized not by repression but, to the contrary, by its openness towards, responsibilization of, and incorporation of critique. Critique struggles with this managerial mode of rule because the latter 'can avoid the accusation of deriving from a will to domination'.[4] Critics are confronted with 'partners' instead of enemies and receive invitations to join consultations and other opportunities. Parts of the critics (tactically or by conviction) co-constitute this networked form of interaction and subscribe to its normative premises. Others, in effect, feel increasingly alienated from their former peers. A contestation emerges among the critics about the right form of critique. During these contestations, critique becomes fragmented and the social movement, which had cohered around this critique, declines as a result. Its solidarity is broken.

But this story of fragmentation is not an automatism; it is furthermore not a one-directional causal process. Rather, the constellation of complex rule is established and reproduced by practices both on the side of the institution as

---

[1] Tallberg et al., *The Opening Up of International Organizations*.
[2] Boltanski, *On Critique*, p. 65; Daase and Deitelhoff, 'Reconstructing global rule by analyzing resistance', p. 14.
[3] Boltanski, *On Critique*, p. 65.
[4] Boltanski, *On Critique*, p. 129.

well as on the side of critique. Therefore, the five mechanisms of complex rule which I have theorized can be observed in practices on both sides while these practices are heavily contested on the side of the critics: parts of them are (1) normatively in line with the neoliberal governing rationality; (2) generally willing to use the newly won opportunities and to talk with the institution in its grammar of justification; and (3) organize in accordance with a professionalized setting, endorsing institutionalization and respecting the 'rules of the game'.

These tendencies are sometimes resulting from a strategic appropriation of the opponent's logic and are in other cases driven by a general belief in the benevolence of the system. Either way, these processes are fiercely disputed internally – with other parts of the movement rejecting all the aforementioned – which leads to a general fragmentation of critique: the movement is divided into a professionalized transnational activist network, heavily integrated into institutionalized politics, and other parts of the (former) movement that refocus their attention on local problems (a particular finding for many Asian activists), or they move into other contexts. In effect, the social movement declines, for it has lost the ability to mobilize critique alongside a common frame. In the case of the interaction between the World Bank Group and the social movement opposing it, I observed these processes in five mechanisms: economization, incorporation, legitimation, professionalization, and regulation.

These processes have multiple causes and pathways. I inductively reconstructed the mechanisms of this history of interaction (Chapter 5) and then systematically traced them in Chapters 6–9. I found that, first, the social movement has fragmented in light of the open institutional interaction, and, second, those parts that remained were yet again being fragmented during these interactions under complex rule (through the same mechanisms). The overall fragmentation of the movement after the Millennium had its origins in the institutionalization of complex rule in the 1990s. Furthermore, those parts of the movement that stuck together as a critical transnational activist network during the 2000s (the diverse set of movement-actors in the Extractive Industries Review in Chapter 6 and 7, as well as the rather moderate mix of CSOs in the Civil Society Policy Forum in Chapter 8 and 9) were again being fragmented during these interactions, leading to an ever-more institutionalized and de-mobilized practice of critique which, through this practice, co-stabilized complex rule.

Sure?

How can I be sure that the proposed processes, and not entirely different ones, are responsible for the phenomenon of fragmentation? *Equifinality*, the possibility that a multitude of causal paths end up with the same result, rightly receives a big deal of attention in the process tracing literature.[5] And indeed, when I presented my hypotheses in the past, many came up with an alternative answer to the activist's question that I call the *success-hypothesis*. It explains the fragmentation of critique with the lack of need for further critique, because the movement was so successful and triggered reforms via institutional learning.[6] The World Bank Group has established binding environmental and social standards for project evaluation and an inspection procedure to verify compliance with these guidelines. Through this institutional innovation, a more balanced project allocation has emerged. Many World Bank Group employees whom I interviewed explicitly made this argument. One high ranking IFC manager told me that

> 'the level of confrontation really declined a lot. I think civil society saw that we made some substantial changes, improvements ... of course they didn't get everything they wanted, but I think they felt: well, let's at least work with these guys, let's use them to influence the industry. That's what I think happened.'

There were big successes of the Global Justice Movement in the 1990s, especially the introduction of the Inspection Panel and the CAO. Also, the introduction of the safeguards and performance standards were decisive institutional adaptations. As was shown in the many reports on resettlements, circumvented guidelines, parochial practices and risk-taking at the cost of locals, these standards and institutional changes have not fundamentally changed the development-practice 'on the ground' though.[7] Schettler has found that even if we accept the adoption of accountability mechanisms as a 'success', persuasion through conventional channels is a rare occurrence. His comparative study of social movement tactics suggests that "social movement researchers are well advised to adopt a broader conception of 'counter mobilization' as a scope condition for movement success".[8] Based on the horrific findings in these reports, I personally draw the conclusion

---

[5]   Bennett and Checkel, *Process Tracing*, p. 21.
[6]   Park, 'Changing the international rule of development to include citizen driven accountability'.
[7]   Inclusive Development International, 'Outsourcing development: lifting the veil on the World Bank Group's lending through financial intermediaries', 2016, available at: {http://www.inclusivedevelopment.net/wp-content/uploads/2016/09/Outsourcing-Developmnet-Introduction.pdf}; Oxfam, 'The suffering of others: the human cost of the international finance corporation's lending through intermediaries' (Oxford, 2015), available at: {https://www.oxfam.org/en/research/suffering-others}.
[8]   Leon Valentin Schettler, *Socializing Development: Transnational Social Movement Advocacy and the Human Rights Accountability of Multilateral Development Banks* (Bielefeld: Transcript, 2020), p. 225.

that there still is a 'development debacle' and that changes were mainly made with regard to packaging, not so much in practice.[9] However, *my* take on what 'objectively' happened is irrelevant in this regard. What matters for proving or disproving the success hypothesis is whether the critics at the time perceived the changes as success.

None of my activist interview partners felt that they had succeeded. Now, this is a weak test, for it could be the case that I only sampled those ones for interviews who continued to criticize the World Bank Group, because those who felt that they succeeded may be difficult to find when looking for critics of the institution. Yet, I also talked to several radical activists who left the movement and concentrated on different topics or organized outside the transnational activist network. For them, it was not a success but too soft an approach to critique that drove them away. I have reconstructed in Chapters 7 and 9 how these activists accused the people in NGOs of being too professional: allegedly, the latter's main interest was to be respected by the institutional counterparts, while they were too afraid of "go to the throat activism" (Interview, US activist).

These veteran activists were frustrated by the countless meetings, ridiculed the soft advocates who thought that one could change the world "by the grace of the World Bank" and decided to use their energy for something else. This holds true even more in the Southeast Asian context, where activists were heavily concerned about the local populations exposed to extractive industries projects. From their perspective, the EIR has shown that institutional deliberation processes were useless and that they needed to fight locally at the side of the affected people rather than with NGOs in Washington DC.

The interpretation of the 'success' was highly contested inside the movement. In fact, this was one of the two questions that led to the anti-debt movement's separation (see Chapter 5). Success/failure was by far not the only dividing line, though. Furthermore, even within those who stayed (the more institutionalized critics in the global North), this question remained contested. The ensuing discussions as to whether one should demobilize because of some successes, or whether one should double-down because of the rhetorical cladding of similar practices, contributed to the overall fragmentation of critique.

9/11 and the war in Iraq

While the success hypothesis is mostly prevalent among academics and World Bank Group staff, many activists also disagreed with my narrative, arguing instead that the terror attacks of 9/11 and the consecutive American

---

[9]   Catherine Weaver, *Hypocrisy Trap*.

war in Iraq were the decisive factors. They argue that the movement was at its peak when the World Trade Centre in New York was attacked. This led to the demobilization in the years to come because it was perceived as disrespectful to protest in the light of this catastrophe. Furthermore, because the 9/11 attacks were directed against a symbol of American-driven global capitalism, to also attack American-driven capitalist organizations seemed misplaced. After that, when George W. Bush Jr. started the war in Iraq, the mobilization concentrated on this issue, hence shifting the focus to peace instead of economic exploitation. A trade union organizer told me that the protests against development institutions

'here in the US were really broken apart with 9/11. Many of the groups that were mobilizing on the financial institutions shifted to peace issues, I guess, and the trade union movement, which was an important part of it ... didn't really mobilize a lot of people for that, for those demos. They focused on other stuff, and I would say they were not part of the big peace wave.'

To tackle such alternative explanations, it is a common practice in process tracing to use 'hoop tests'.[10] Failing a hoop test provides strong evidence about the alternative explanation being false. Van Evera's example for a hoop test is: 'Was the accused in the state on the day of the murder?'.[11] Now, the fragmentation of critique and the resulting decline of social movements is not a single event, like a murder. Nevertheless, Van Evera's metaphor is helpful in elaborating why I think the narrative around 9/11 does not disprove my argument: the mechanisms of fragmentation could be detected already around the millennium. With the example of the North/South division over the question of debt, I have shown that the fragmentation was already in full swing in the year 2000. I furthermore analysed that NGOs like Friends of the Earth publicly distanced themselves from street protests at the World Bank Group/IMF spring meetings to secure their elevated position created by incorporation, a stab in the back of the movement's dissident parts which had not occurred in comparable situations like in 1994. I have traced these new developments to institutional incorporation and its indicators of NGOization and the elevation of individuals, as well as the economization of the European Jubilee Debt Campaign (see Chapter 5). 9/11 was not yet 'in the state' at that time, and I am therefore confident that this incident did not cause the fragmentation of critique.[12]

---

[10] Bennett and Checkel, *Process Tracing*, p. 17.
[11] Van Evera, *Guide to Methods for Students of Political Science*.
[12] See also Tarrow and Hadden, 'Spillover or spillout?'

Nevertheless, 9/11 was an amplifying external factor for the demobilization of the movement, especially in the US. This shows, however, that the fragmentation of critique is not equivalent to the demobilization on the streets but rather, as I have argued, important as its structural basis. Complex rule is a deeper constellation of super- and subordination that fragments critique against its own institutionalization. The demobilizing effect of 9/11 and the Iraq War were accelerating this process.

Protest cycle theory

Another, more academic, objection can be derived from the 'cycles of protest' argument.[13] Cycles of protest occur when multiple movement groups engage in sustained protest across time and space.[14] During a cycle of protest, many sectors of society can be expected to participate in the protest (workers and church groups for example) and employ increasingly confrontational tactics. A cycle of protest can hence be defined as a rapid expansion of a social movement and its practices in terms of geographical spread, diversity of its groups and disruptiveness of protest. Yet, the theory also predicts that, over time, 'protest eventually descends through a mixture of institutionalization, government reform, state repression, and/or participant exhaustion'.

As with 9/11, I do not want to refute the idea of a protest cycle. To the contrary, I think that the description that social movements usually descend after a few years, combined with the additional factor of 9/11, is helpful in explaining the movement's decline after the millennium. The question of this book was not whether these processes happened but *how*. This is important because the quasi-automatic explanation of protest cycle theory makes it hard to understand what the mechanisms were. The descend of street protest, furthermore, is not equal to the fragmentation of critique. The focus on protest only is a specificity of the discipline of social movement studies which, by defining its essence over the attention to one specific practice, often overlooks constellational processes and more structural political changes that require more complex social-theoretical arguments.[15]

---

[13] Sidney Tarrow, *Democracy and Disorder: Protest and Politics in Italy, 1965–1975.* (Oxford: Clarendon Press, 1989).

[14] Paul Almeida, 'Cycles of protest', Oxford Bibliographies Online, 2016, available at: {http://www.oxfordbibliographies.com/view/document/obo-9780199756223/obo-9780199756223-0086.xml}.

[15] Britta Baumgarten and Peter Ullrich, 'Discourse, power and governmentality: social movement research with and beyond Foucault', in Jochen Roose and Hella Dietz (eds) *Social Movements in Social Theory. Mutual Inspirations* (Wiesbaden: Springer, 2016), pp. 13–38.

I have shown in Chapters 8 and 9 that the five mechanisms of complex rule were still effective in 2016, dividing the remains of a movement whose cycle of protest was, undisputedly, long over at that time. The transnational activist network that embodies the critique until this day is thus under pressure despite its highly institutionalized form of organization and style of advocacy. This means that complex rule did not only have the effect to split the movement into radical dissidents and moderate oppositionists. Rather, its mechanisms can be observed until this day and even within the moderate faction. While the end of the GJM could hence be explained by protest cycle theory, the fragmentation that I traced goes deeper for (1) it even has an effect on the two already divided factions, and (2) it contributes to further stabilizing complex rule, a theoretical argument that goes beyond the generic approach of 'protest cycles'. While 'the suspect' 9/11 had not yet 'been in the state' when the fragmentation began in 2000, the second suspect (the protest cycle) had long left it when I still observed fragmentation taking place in 2016. This highlights that the agency of the critics is vital to understand these processes, for there is a choice – if not always an informed and conscious one – behind most of the described practices of critique. Movements are not simply determined by cycles or external events. That is why focusing on the 'how' is so valuable for social inquiry.

Implications for international theory

As I have emphasized throughout this book, complex rule is not a new model for IR in general but a theorization of a particular constellation in global governance. Already in the late 1980s, I detected practices contributing to its development. Starting in the mid-1990s, the constellation has become, I argued, the ordering principle of open global governance. I have reconstructed that complex rule was instantiated by a multiplicity of actors, and by a number of – partly contradictory – motivations and practices. It emerged in the context of increasing autonomy and power of IOs on the one hand, and the critique of their practices by a plethora of (mainly) non-state actors on the other. These two sides of complex rule were extensively traced and theorized via mechanisms in this book. Complex rule as a constellation, emerges *in the process* of this back-and-forth between institutional practices of economizing the world; incorporating critique and legitimating the self vis-à-vis critics; as well as professionalizing the discourse, and regulating the potential avenues of practice.

These processes were partly provoked, partly accepted, and partly criticized by the critics of the World Bank Group, who – as a consequence of their own (divided) contributions to complex rule – fragmented substantially. It may be provocative to many critics to read the word *contribution* here. However, I have shown in detail that, in fact, these practices of critique played significantly into the production and reproduction of what could later be called complex rule.

Complex rule thus emerged in the process of interaction itself and cannot be explained by an external reason, much less by the power of a third actor. In contrast, I have put great emphasis on the operationalization of complex rule as a constellation emerging in this process of interaction. It is hence not an 'object', and it is not understandable outside the power-relations that I traced. It would therefore be a mistake to objectify complex rule as something 'independent of the actions by which it is produced'.[16]

Nevertheless, these processes have something to say about other contexts in global governance, too. The World Bank Group has been a model for all the other development banks. As one insider put it: "The Bank is snow-white and the other MDBs are the seven dwarfs". They model themselves explicitly after the World Bank Group. This even holds for the Chinese-led AIIB, and it certainly applies to other regional development banks. It is no coincidence, hence, that the opening scene of this book played at the Asian Development Bank's Annual Meeting. To the activists observed, these are simply different institutions representing the same problem. This is in line with the understanding of institutions promoted here: rather than being rulers of their own, they embody a structure of rule.

It is plausible to assume that this structure is also embodied by other institutions of open global governance. I observed the same mechanisms in the IMF (Chapter 8 and 9), and I have good reasons to suspect that similar processes happened in the WTO. In fact, in a different study, Nicole Deitelhoff, Regina Hack and myself found a 'divide and rule' process at play in the WTO's treatment of critics – even though in that case we focused on two mechanisms only (incorporation and legitimation) – and were therefore forced to speculate whether the division of critics was only a coincidental effect.[17] Building on my process tracing in the World Bank Group, and others' participant observation in the WTO,[18] I will suggest to my co-authors that in future work on the WTO, we can confidently delete the question mark which we had cautiously put behind the 'divide and rule'.

---

[16] Douglas Maynard and Thomas Wilson, 'On the reification of social structure', in Scott M. McNall and John Wilson (eds) *Current Perspectives in Social Theory: A Research Annual* (Greenwich: JAI Press, 1980), p. 287.

[17] Felix Anderl, Nicole Deitelhoff, and Regina Hack, 'Divide and rule? The politics of self-legitimation in the WTO', in *Rule and Resistance beyond the Nation State: Contestation, Escalation, Exit* (London: Rowman & Littlefield International, 2019), pp. 49–68.

[18] Tucker, 'Participation and subjectification in global governance'; Regina Hack, 'Deliberation als Reaktion auf Protest? Das zivilgesellschaftliche Dialogforum der WTO', *Zeitschrift Für Internationale Beziehungen* 24, 1 (2017), pp. 37–67.

The future of complex rule and its critique

The institutional actors and their critics under investigation here share one core feature: they are normative globalists. By now, it seems almost bizarre to analyze the critique of global governance and to focus on those actors who opposed it within a framework of *global justice*. Global governance is currently under attack from a very different, anti-globalist, direction. Nationalist, authoritarian forces are dominating the sphere of critique and issue their attacks on IOs not based on a vision of a progressive 'justice for all' but a revisionist 'back to the future'.

While both forms of critique have been heavily directed against IOs, in the former case these organizations were able to incorporate parts of the critique. In the case of the revisionist critique of global governance, it remains to be seen how IOs will react to it. However, since the reactionary forces behind this agenda are not only against international organizations (plural) but also against international organization (singular), IOs will hardly be able to incorporate them sustainably. Therefore, a repetition of the process that I theorized – reproducing a form of transnational rule in which institutions subordinate critique by way of its incorporation – is unlikely. Since global governance institutions are embedded in a geopolitical framework which is arguably becoming increasingly 'simple' through these revisionist interventions by right-wing critics of global governance, their differentiated governing mechanisms, which were created as a response to progressive critique, are increasingly at odds with the current trajectory of international politics.

More interestingly, the question that follows from this is: why did this happen? This book did not directly tackle this question. I have studied the emergence of complex rule as a constellation. That means that the flaws of this order can explicitly not be blamed on 'one side', much less on a single actor. In its emergent character, complex rule is an effect of its underlying interactions, and structures future practices accordingly. Yet, since I excavated a number of pathologies of this system, two initial extrapolations shall be made in order to signal that things could have been different.

First, IOs like the World Bank Group misrepresented the underlying reasons for the critique of their practice, hence treating large parts of their critics like 'crazies'. Although the institution changed some of the rules, especially in terms of access and transparency, the underlying substantial problems were not addressed. Today, the World Bank Group still resettles local populations by force, finances extractive industries through financial intermediaries, measures development on economistic scales, and preaches austerity policies. It hence took the reasons of critique to be solely a cry for recognition instead of a fundamental disagreement with its policies and practices. The resulting 'opening-up' may have calmed down and demobilized the protests by leading to the fragmentation of critique in combination with the other mechanisms of complex rule, but it did so at the cost of destroying the belief in 'global solutions' that the World Bank Group still proposes. 'The globalists' are nowadays almost perceived as synonymous to 'neoliberals'.[19] While Marx would turn in his grave, this tendency has alienated the many from global governance. No wonder they seek their salvation in nationalist, parochial projects.

Second, the solidarities of the Global Justice Movement were not simply broken from above. Their fragmentation was not inevitable. Rather, as I have shown in detail, the activists themselves contributed to the five mechanisms alongside which critique became fragmented. Of course, there were factions and different political outlooks in the movement all along, but the fragmentation that I reconstructed goes beyond the political, economic, and geographical differentiation of a movement. It is precisely the essence of a successful social movement to organize solidarity across these differences. Consequently, the fragmentation is neither the fault of the transnational activist network's too light-hearted belief in institutionalized lobbying, nor the radicals' persistence in anti-institutional protest. It is their common shortcoming not to have continuously cohered around a shared critique despite their different levels of radicalism.

While this work of cohering was executed exemplarily well during the 1990s, the emergence of complex rule made this more difficult as I have shown in detail. Propelling the critique's fragmentation, some critics bought into the neoliberal premise of so called 'global knowledge': they settled in a localized bubble of an elitist network of experts clustered around Washington DC, lightly criticizing its politics while inhabiting its institutions, and showcasing their own elevated status, thereby undermining the movement's anti-capitalist, anti-authoritarian, and pluralist roots. Many other critics, in turn, localized as well: reorienting towards so-called 'local issues' they retreated to their nation states, thereby undermining the very foundation of the movement's critique, namely that capitalism operates transnationally and hence solidarity, and critique, must be thought and practiced across borders, too.

During the mutual dissociation of these different factions that occurred in the wake of institutional opening-up, they were not able to organize solidarity with each other any longer. The resulting divisions are the effect of as well as constitutive for the further institutionalization of complex rule. This does not mean that the movement would have 'won', had they acted otherwise. It means that in a constellation such as open global governance, it is easy to

---

[19] Quinn Slobodian, *Globalists: The End of Empire and the Birth of Neoliberalism* (Boston: Harvard University Press, 2018).

forget that solidarity is a movement's most important currency. Rule keeps critique in fragmentation. In the specific case of open global governance, this fragmentation is achieved not through authoritarian measures but through a combination of mechanisms that each hold genuine promises for social movements. A constellation that endorses critique and invites critics to become an active part of the governance process is not *a ruler*. But as the movement is divided, it is also ruled.

References

Acharya, Amitav (2004) 'How ideas spread: whose norms matter? Norm localization and institutional change in Asian regionalism', *International Organization* 58, 2, pp. 239–75.

Adorno, Theodor W (2008) *Lectures on Negative Dialectics: Fragments of a Lecture Course 1965/1966* (Cambridge: Polity).

Agné, Hans, Lisa Maria Dellmuth, and Jonas Tallberg (2015) 'Does stakeholder involvement foster democratic legitimacy in international organizations? An empirical assessment of a normative theory', *The Review of International Organizations* 10, 4, pp. 465–88.

Alexander, Nancy, Sara Grusky, and Sameer Dossani (2001) 'News & notices for IMF and World Bank watchers', Vol. 2, Washington DC.

Alimi, Eitan Y., Lorenzo Bosi, and Chares Demetriou (2012) 'Relational dynamics and processes of radicalization: a comparative framework', *Mobilization* 17, 1, pp. 7–26.

Almeida, Paul (2016) 'Cycles of protest', Oxford Bibliographies Online, http://www.oxfordbibliographies.com/view/document/obo-9780199756223/obo-9780199756223-0086.xml

Amenta, Edwin, Neal Caren, Elizabeth Chiarello, and Yang Su (2010) 'The political consequences of social movements', *Annual Review of Sociology* 36, pp. 287–307.

Amenta, Edwin and Michael P. Young (1999) 'Making an impact: conceptual and methodological implications of the collective goods criterion', in Marco G. Giugni, Doug McAdam, and Charles Tilly (eds) *How Social Movements Matter* (Minneapolis: University of Minnesota Press), pp. 22–41.

Anderl, Felix (2018) 'Entwicklung als Motiv für Herrschaft und Widerstand. Kohärenz und Fragmentierung während des Zivilgesellschaftsforums der Weltbankgruppe', *Peripherie: Zeitschrift für Politik und Ökonomie in der Dritten Welt* 38, 150/151, pp. 219–44.

Anderl, Felix (2021) 'Kontestation, Politisierung, Herrschaft: Bewegungsforschung und Internationale Beziehungen', *Forschungsjournal Soziale Bewegungen* 34, 1, pp. 122–37.

Anderl, Felix and Philip Wallmeier (2019) '"Institution" als Scharnierkonzept zwischen Herrschaft und Widerstand', *Forschungsjournal Soziale Bewegungen* 32, 2, pp. 192–206.

Anderl, Felix, Nicole Deitelhoff, and Regina Hack (2019) 'Contestation: Introduction to the section', in Felix Anderl, Christopher Daase, Nicole Deitelhoff, Victor Kempf, Jannik Pfister, and Philip Wallmeier (eds) *Rule and Resistance beyond the Nation State: Contestation, Escalation, Exit* (London: Rowman & Littlefield International), pp. 23–26.

Anderl, Felix, Nicole Deitelhoff, and Regina Hack (2019) 'Divide and rule? The politics of self-legitimation in the WTO', in Felix Anderl, Christopher Daase, Nicole Deitelhoff, Victor Kempf, Jannik Pfister, and Philip Wallmeier (eds) *Rule and Resistance beyond the Nation State: Contestation, Escalation, Exit* (London: Rowman & Littlefield International), pp. 49–68.

Anderl, Felix, Priska Daphi, and Nicole Deitelhoff (2021) 'Keeping your enemies close? The variety of social movements' reactions to international organizations' opening up', *International Studies Review* 23, 4, pp. 1273–99.

Anderl, Felix, Christopher Daase, Nicole Deitelhoff, Victor Kempf, Jannik Pfister, and Philip Wallmeier (2019) 'Introduction', in Christopher Daase, Nicole Deitelhoff, Felix Anderl, Victor Kempf, Jannik Pfister, and Philip Wallmeier (eds) *Rule and Resistance beyond the Nation State: Contestation, Escalation, Exit* (London: Rowman & Littlefield International), pp. 1–21.

Arrighi, Giovanni (2010) 'The world economy and the cold war, 1970–1985', in Melvyn P. Leffler and Odd Arne Westad (eds) *The Cambridge History of the Cold War*, Vol. 3 (Cambridge: Cambridge University Press), pp. 23–44.

Avant, Deborah, Martha Finnemore, and Susan Sell (2010) *Who Governs the Globe?* (Cambridge: Cambridge University Press).

Bacevic, Jana (2019) 'Knowing neoliberalism', *Social Epistemology* 33, 4, pp. 380–92.

Bachrach, Peter and Morton S. Baratz (1962) 'Two faces of power', *The American Political Science Review* 56, 4, pp. 947–52.

Balaton-Chrimes, Samantha, and Fiona Haines (2015) 'The depoliticisation of accountability processes for land-based grievances, and the IFC CAO', *Global Policy* 6, 4, pp. 446–54.

Bank Information Center (2006) 'EIR implementation status report: World Bank Group commitments on revenue and contract transparency', Washington DC, http://www.bankinformationcenter.org/wp-content/uploads/2013/01/EIR_Implementation_Status_Report.pdf

Barnett, Michael (2017) 'Hierarchy and paternalism', in Ayşe Zarakol (ed) *Hierarchies in World Politics* (Cambridge: Cambridge University Press), pp. 66–94.

Barnett, Michael (2020) 'Change in or of global governance?', *International Theory* 13, 1, pp. 131–43.

Barnett, Michael and Martha Finnemore (1999) 'The politics, power, and pathologies of international organizations', *International Organization* 53, 4, pp. 699–732.

Barnett, Michael and Martha Finnemore (2004) *Rules for the World: International Organizations in Global Politics* (Ithaca: Cornell University Press).

Barnett, Michael N. and Raymond Duvall (2005) 'Power in global governance', in Michael N. Barnett and Raymond Duvall (eds) *Power in Global Governance* (Cambridge: Cambridge University Press), pp. 1–32.

Baumgarten, Britta and Peter Ullrich (2016) 'Discourse, power and governmentality. Social movement research with and beyond Foucault', in Jochen Roose and Hella Dietz (eds) *Social Movements in Social Theory: Mutual Inspirations* (Wiesbaden: Springer), pp. 13–38.

Beach, Derek and Rasmus Brun Pedersen (2013) *Process Tracing Methods: Foundations and Guidelines* (Ann Arbor: University of Michigan Press).

Beaumont, Paul and Ann E. Towns (2021) 'The rankings game: a relational approach to country performance indicators', *International Studies Review* 23, 4, pp. 1467–94.

Bello, Walden (1982) *Development Debacle: The World Bank in the Philippines* (Manila: Institute for Food and Development Policy).

Bennett, Andrew and Jeffrey T. Checkel (2015) *Process Tracing: From Metaphor to Analytic Tool* (Cambridge: Cambridge University Press).

Bernstein, Steven (2011) 'Legitimacy in intergovernmental and non-state global governance', *Review of International Political Economy* 18, 1, pp. 17–51.

Bexell, Magdalena, Kristina Jönsson, and Nora Stappert (2020) 'Whose legitimacy beliefs count? Targeted audiences in global governance legitimation processes', *Journal of International Relations and Development* 24, 2, pp. 483–508.

Bexell, Magdalena, Jonas Tallberg, and Anders Uhlin (2010) 'Democracy in global governance: the promises and pitfalls of transnational actors', *Global Governance* 16, 1, pp. 81–101.

Bhaskar, Roy (1978) *A Realist Theory of Science* (Brighton: Harvester).

Bially Mattern, Janice and Ayşe Zarakol (2016) 'Hierarchies in world politics', *International Organization* 70, 3, pp. 623–54.

Biebricher, Thomas and Eric Vance Johnson (2012) 'What's wrong with neoliberalism?', *New Political Science* 34, 2, pp. 202–11.

Blichner, Lars C. and Anders Molander (2008) 'Mapping juridification', *European Law Journal* 14, 1, pp. 36–54.

Boltanski, Luc (2008) 'Individualismus ohne Freiheit: Ein pragmatischer Zugang zur Herrschaft', *Westend: Neue Zeitschrift Für Sozialforschung* 5, 2, pp. 132–49.

Boltanski, Luc (2011) *On Critique: A Sociology of Emancipation* (Cambridge: Polity).

Boltanski, Luc and Laurent Thévenot (2006) *On Justification: Economies of Worth* (Princeton: Princeton University Press).

Bosi, Lorenzo, Marco Giugni, and Katrin Uba (2016) *The Consequences of Social Movements* (Cambridge: Cambridge University Press).

Bosi, Lorenzo and Katrin Uba (2009) 'Introduction: the outcomes of social movements', *Mobilization* 14, 4, pp. 409–15.

Bossche, Peter Van den (2008) 'NGO involvement in the WTO: a comparative perspective', *Journal of International Economic Law* 11, 4, pp. 717–49.

Brand, Ulrich (2005) 'Order and regulation: global governance as a hegemonic discourse of international politics?', *Review of International Political Economy* 12, 1, pp. 155–76.

Bräutigam, Deborah A and Monique Segarra (2007) 'Difficult partnerships: the World Bank, states, and NGOs', *Latin American Politics and Society* 49, 4, pp. 149–81.

Bretton Woods Project (2001) 'PRSPs just PR', Bretton Woods Update 23. London, http://www.brettonwoodsproject.org/publications/23-2/

Bröckling, Ulrich (2017) *Gute Hirten führen sanft: Über Menschenregierungskünste* (Berlin: Suhrkamp).

Brown, Wendy (2015) *Undoing the Demos: Neoliberalism's Stealth Revolution* (New York: Zone Books).

Brundtland, Gro Harlem (1987) *Our Common Future* (New York: United Nations Organization).

Buchanan, Allen and Robert O. Keohane (2006) 'The legitimacy of global governance institutions', *Ethics & International Affairs* 20, 4, pp. 405–37.

Buchanan, Ian (2010) 'Constellation', in *Oxford Dictionary of Critical Theory* (Oxford: Oxford University Press), p. 96.

Buckley-Zistel, Susanne (2020) 'Spatializing memory and justice in transformation processes', in Rachid Ouaissa, Friederike Pannewick, and Alena Strohmaier (eds) *Re-Configurations: Contextualising Transformation Processes and Lasting Crises in the Middle East and North Africa* (Heidelberg: Springer), pp. 25–35.

Burchell, Graham (1996) 'Liberal government and techniques of the self', in Andrew Barry, Thomas Osborne, and Nikolas Rose (eds) *Foucault and Political Reason* (London: University College London).

Callison, William (2014) 'Sovereign anxieties and neoliberal transformations: an introduction', *Qui Parle: Critical Humanities and Social Sciences* 23, 1, pp. 3–34.

Callison, William and Zackary Manfredi (2020) 'Theorizing mutant neoliberalism', in William Callison and Zachary Manfredi (eds) *Mutant Neoliberalism: Market Rule and Political Ruptur* (New York: Fordham University Press) pp. 1–38.

Celikates, Robin (2018) *Critique as Social Practice: Critical Theory and Social Self-Understanding* (London: Rowman & Littlefield International).

Choudry, Aziz and Dip Kapoor (2013) *NGOization: Complicity, Contradictions and Prospects* (London: Zed Books).

Clark, Dana (2003) 'Understanding the World Bank Inspection Panel', in Dana Clark, Jonathan Fox, and Kay Treakle (eds) *Demanding Accountability: Civil-Society Claims and the World Bank Inspection Panel* (Lanham, MD: Rowman & Littlefield), pp. 1–24

Clark, Dana, Jonathan A. Fox, and Kay Treakle (2003) *Demanding Accountability: Civil-Society Claims and the World Bank Inspection Panel* (Lanham, MD: Rowman & Littlefield).

Clark, John D. (2002) 'The World Bank and civil society: an evolving experience', in Jan Aart Scholte and Albrecht Schnabel (eds) *Civil Society and Global Finance* (London: Routledge), pp. 111–27.

Clark, John D. (2003) *Worlds Apart: Civil Society and the Battle for Ethical Globalization* (Bloomfield: Kumarian Press).

Colchester, Marcus and Emily Caruso (2005) *Extracting Promises: Indigenous Peoples, Extractive Industries and the World Bank* (Baguio City: Tebtebba Foundation).

Compliance Advisor Ombudsman (2003) 'Extracting sustainable advantage? A review of how sustainability issues have been dealt with in recent IFC & MIGA extractive industries projects'. Washington DC, http://documents.worldbank.org/curated/en/886741478094865899/A-review-of-how-sustainability-issues-have-been-dealt-with-in-recent-IFC-MIGA-extractive-industries-projects

Coy, Patrick G. and Timothy Hedeen (2005) 'A stage model of social movement co-optation: community mediation in the United States', *Sociological Quarterly* 46, 3, pp. 405–35.

Daase, Christopher and Nicole Deitelhoff (2014) 'Reconstructing global rule by analyzing resistance'. Dissidence Working Papers 1/2014, https://dissidenz.net/wp-content/uploads/2013/03/wp1-2014-daase-deitelhoff-en.pdf

Daase, Christopher and Nicole Deitelhoff (2015) 'Jenseits der anarchie: widerstand und herrschaft im internationalen system', *Politische Vierteljahrsschrift* 56, 2, pp. 299–318.

Daase, Christopher and Nicole Deitelhoff (2019) 'Opposition and dissidence: two modes of resistance against international rule', *Journal of International Political Theory* 15, 1, pp. 11–30.

Dany, Charlotte (2013) *Global Governance and NGO Participation: Shaping the Information Society in the United Nations* (London: Routledge).

Dany, Charlotte and Katja Freistein (2016) 'Global governance and the myth of civil society participation', in Berit Bliesemann de Guevara (ed) *Myth and Narrative in International Politics: Interpretive Approaches to the Study of IR* (London: Palgrave Macmillan), pp. 229–48.

Daphi, Priska (2014) 'International solidarity in the global justice movement: coping with national and sectoral affinities', *Interface: A Journal for and about Social Movements* 6, 2, pp. 164–79.

Daphi, Priska (2017) *Becoming a Movement: Identity and Narratives in the European Global Justice Movement* (London: Rowman & Littlefield Intl).

Daphi, Priska (2019) 'The global justice movement in Europe', in Christina Flesher-Fominaya and Ramon Feenstra (eds) *Routledge Handbook of Contemporary European Social Movements: Protest in Turbulent Times* (London: Routledge), pp. 142–54.

Daphi, Priska (2020) 'Politisierung und soziale Bewegungen: zwei Perspektiven', *Leviathan Sonderband* 35, pp. 97–120.

Daphi, Priska and Felix Anderl (2016) 'Radicalization and deradicalization in transnational social movements: a relative and multi-level model of repertoire change', Dissidence Working Papers. Frankfurt am Main, https://dissidenz.net/wp-content/uploads/2013/03/wp1-2016-daphi-anderl.pdf

Daphi, Priska, Felix Anderl, and Nicole Deitelhoff (2019) 'Bridges or divides? Conflicts and synergies of coalition building across countries and sectors in the global justice movement', *Social Movement Studies*, 21, 1–2, pp. 8–22.

Davies, Thomas R. and Alejandro M. Peña (2021) 'Social movements and international relations: a relational framework', *Journal of International Relations and Development* 24, 1, pp. 51–76.

Dean, Mitchel (1999) *Governmentality: Power and Rule in Modern Society* (London: Sage).

Deitelhoff, Nicole (2006) *Überzeugung in der Politik – Grundzüge einer Diskurstheorie internationalen Regierens* (Frankfurt am Main: Suhrkamp).

Deitelhoff, Nicole (2009) 'The discursive process of legalization: charting islands of persuasion in the ICC case', *International Organization* 63, 1, pp. 33–65.

Deitelhoff, Nicole and Christopher Daase (2020) 'Rule and resistance in global governance', *International Theory* 13, 1, pp. 1–9.

Deitelhoff, Nicole and Lisbeth Zimmermann (2020) 'Things we lost in the fire: how different types of contestation affect the robustness of international norms', *International Studies Review* 22, 1, pp. 51–76.

Della Porta, Donatella (1995) *Social Movements, Political Violence and the State* (Cambridge: Cambridge University Press).

Della Porta, Donatella and Marco Diani (2006) *Social Movements: An Introduction* (Oxford: Blackwell).

Della Porta, Donatella, Massimiliano Andretta, Lorenzo Mosca, and Herbert Reiter (2007) *Globalization from Below: Transnational Activists and Protest Networks* (Minneapolis: University of Minnesota Press).

Delbridge, Rick and Tim Edwards (2013) 'Inhabiting institutions: critical realist refinements to understanding institutional complexity and change', *Organization Studies* 34, 7, pp. 927–47.

Dellmuth, Lisa Maria, and Jonas Tallberg (2015) 'The social legitimacy of international organisations: interest representation, institutional performance, and confidence extrapolation in the United Nations', *Review of International Studies* 41, 3, pp. 451–75.

Dellmuth, Lisa Maria and Jonas Tallberg (2017) 'Advocacy strategies in global governance: inside versus outside lobbying', *Political Studies* 65, 3, pp. 705–23.

Desrosieres, Alain (2001) 'How "real" are statistics? Four possible attitudes', *Social Research* 68, 2, pp. 339–55.

Deutscher Bundestag (2004) 'Antrag: für eine nachhaltige Rohstoff- und Energiepolitik der Weltbank' (Berlin: Deutscher Bundestag), http://dipbt. bundestag.de/doc/btd/15/034/1503465.pdf

Dhawan, Nikita (2007) *Impossible Speech: On the Politics of Silence and Violence* (Leeds: Academia).

Dingwerth, Klaus (2005) 'The democratic legitimacy of public-private rule making: what can we learn from the World Commission on Dams?', *Global Governance* 11, pp. 65–83.

Dingwerth, Klaus (2007) *The New Transnationalism: Transnational Governance and Democratic Legitimacy* (London: Palgrave Macmillan).

Dingwerth, Klaus and Philipp Pattberg (2006) 'Global governance as a perspective on World Politics', *Global Governance* 12, 2, pp. 185–203.

Dingwerth, Klaus, Dieter Kerwer, and Andreas Nölke (2008) *Die Organisierte Welt: Internationale Beziehungen und Organisationsforschung* (Baden-Baden: Nomos).

Dingwerth, Klaus, Henning Schmidtke and Tobias Weise (2020) 'The rise of democratic legitimation: why international organizations speak the language of democracy', *European Journal of International Relations* 26, 3, pp. 714–41.

Dingwerth, Klaus, Antonia Witt, Ina Lehmann, Ellen Reichel, and Tobias Weise (2019) *International Organizations under Pressure: Legitimating Global Governance in Challenging Times* (Oxford: Oxford University Press).

Donnelly, Jack (2016) 'Beyond hierarchy', in Ayşe Zarakol (ed) *Hierarchies in World Politics* (Cambridge: Cambridge University Press), pp. 243–65.

Duncan, Jessica (2015) *Food Security Governance: Civil Society Participation in the Committee on World Food Security* (Abingdon: Routledge).

Dyke, Nella van (2003) 'Protest cycles and party politics: the effects of elite allies and antagonists on student protest in the United States, 1930–1990', in Judith Goldstein (ed) *States, Parties, and Social Movements* (Cambridge: Cambridge University Press), pp. 226–45.

Eagleton-Pierce, Matthew (2016) *Neoliberalism: The Key Concepts* (London: Routledge).

Earl, Jennifer (2000) 'Methods, movements and outcomes: methodological difficulties in the study of extra-movement outcomes', in Patrick G. Coy (ed) *Research in Social Movements, Conflicts and Change* (Bingley: Emerald), pp. 3–25.

Ecker-Ehrhardt, Matthias (2018) 'Self-legitimation in the face of politicization: why international organizations centralized public communication', *Review of International Organizations* 13, 4, pp. 519–46.

Eckl, Julian (2021) 'Zooming in dissolves the taken-for-granted: towards a political anthropology of international organisations', in Sarah Biecker and Klaus Schlichte (eds) *The Political Anthropology of Internationalized Politics* (Lanhham MD: Rowman & Littlefield), pp. 67–94.

Eitan, Alimi, Bosi Lorenzo, and Demetriou Chares (2012) 'Relational dynamics and processes of radicalization: a comparative framework', *Mobilization* 17, 1, pp. 7–26.

Engelkamp, Stephan, Katharina Glaab, and Judith Renner (2014) 'Office hours: how (critical) norm research can regain its voice', *World Political Science Review* 10, 1, pp. 61–89.

Epstein, Charlotte. 'Stop telling us how to behave: socialization or infantilization?', *International Studies Perspectives* 13, 2 (2012), pp. 135–45.

Epstein, Charlotte, Ayşe Zarakol, Julia Gallagher, Robbie Shilliam, and Vivienne Jabri (2014) 'Forum: interrogating the use of norms in international relations: postcolonial perspectives', *International Theory* 6, 2, p. 293.

Eschle, Catherine and Bice Maiguashca (2005) *Critical Theories, International Relations and 'the Anti-Globalisation Movement': The Politics of Global Resistance* (Abingdon: Routledge).

Eschle, Catherine and Bice Maiguashca (2010) *Making Feminist Sense of the Global Justice Movement* (Lanham: Rowman & Littlefield).

Eschle, Catherine and Bice Maiguashca (2014) 'Reclaiming feminist futures: co-opted and progressive politics in a neo-liberal age', *Political Studies* 62, 3, pp. 634–51.

Espeland, Wendy N. and Mitchell L. Stevens (1998) 'Commensuration as a social process', *Annual Review of Sociology* 24, 1, pp. 313–43.

Espeland, Wendy N. and Mitchell L. Stevens (2008) 'A sociology of quantification', *Archives Europeennes de Sociologie* 49, 3, pp. 401–36.

Espeland, Wendy N. and Berit Vannebo (2008) 'Accountability, quantification, and law', *Annual Review of Law and Social Science* 3, pp. 21–43.

European Parliament (2004) 'European parliament resolution on the World Bank-commissioned Extractive Industries Review – B5-0171/2004, 29 March 2004' (Brussels: European Parliament), http://www.europarl.europa.eu/sides/getDoc.do?pubRef=-//EP//TEXT+MOTION+B5-2004-0171+0+DOC+XML+V0//EN

Fehl, Caroline and Katja Freistein (2020) 'Organising global stratification: how international organisations (re)produce inequalities in international society', *Global Society* 34, 3, pp. 285–303.

Ferguson, James (1994) *The Anti-Politics Machine: 'Development', Depoliticization, and Bureaucratic Power in Lesotho* (Minneapolis: University of Minnesota Press).

Forst, Rainer (2011) *Kritik der Rechtfertigungsverhältnisse: Perspektiven einer kritischen Theorie der Politik* (Berlin: Suhrkamp).

Forst, Rainer (2012) *The Right to Justification: Elements of a Constructivist Theory of Justice* (New York: Columbia University Press).

Forst, Rainer (2015) *Normativität und Macht: Zur Analyse Sozialer Rechtfertigungsverhältnisse* (Berlin: Suhrkamp).

Foucault, Michel (1978) *Discipline and Punish: The Birth of the Prison* (New York: Vintage Books).

Foucault, Michel (1988) 'Technologies of the self', in Luther H. Martin, Huck Gutman, and Patrick H. Hutton (eds) *Technologies of the Self: A Seminar with Michel Foucault* (Amherst: University of Massachusetts Press).

Foucault, Michel (1991) 'Governmentality', in Graham Burchell and Colin Gordon (eds) *The Foucault Effect: Studies in Governmentality* (Chicago: Chicago University Press), pp. 87–104.

Foucault, Michel (1994) 'Politik und Ethik', *Deutsche Zeitschrift für Philosophie* 42, 4, pp. 703–8.

Foucault, Michel (2004) *The Birth of Biopolitics: Lectures at the Collège de France, 1978–79* (New York: Picador).

Foucault, Michel (2006) *Sicherheit, Territorium, Bevölkerung: Geschichte der Gouvernementalität – Vorlesungen am Collège de France 1977–1978* (Berlin: Suhrkamp).

Fox, Jonathan A. (2005) 'Advocacy research and the world bank: propositions for discussions', in Marc Edelman and Angelique Haugerud (eds) *The Anthropology of Development Organizations: From Classical Political Economy to Contemporary Neoliberalism* (Malden, MA: Blackwell), pp. 306–33.

Fox, Jonathan A. (2003) 'Introduction: framing the inspection panel', in *Demanding Accountability: Civil-Society Claims and the World Bank Inspection Panel* (Lanham: Rowman & Littlefield), pp. xi–xxxi.

Fox, Jonathan and David L. Brown (1998) 'Assessing the impact of NGO advocacy campaigns on World Bank projects and policies', in Jonathan A. Fox and David L. Brown (eds) *The Struggle for Accountability: The World Bank, NGOs and Grassroots Movements* (Cambridge, MA: MIT Press), pp. 485–551.

Fox Piven, Frances and Richard Cloward (1977) *Poor People's Movements: Why They Succeed, How They Fail* (New York: Vintage).

Freistein, Katja (2018) 'Quantification as bureaucratic ritual'. Paper written for the ECPR General Conference, Hamburg (23 August).

Gamson, William A. (1990) *The Strategy of Social Protest* (Belmont, CA: Wadsworth).

Gamson, William A. and David. S. Meyer (1996) 'Framing political opportunity', in Doug McAdam, John D. Mccarthy, and Mayer N. Zald (eds) *Social Movements. Political Opportunity Structures, Mobilizing Structures, and Cultural Framings*, Cambridge: Cambridge University Press, pp. 275–90.

George, Alexander L. and Andrew Bennett (2005) *Case Studies and Theory Development in the Social Sciences* (Cambridge, MA: MIT Press).

Giugni, Marco, Marko Bandler, and Nina Eggert (2006) 'The global justice movement: how far does the classic social movement agenda go in explaining transnational contention?', Civil Society and Social Movements: UNRISD Working Papers, Geneva, http://www.unrisd.org/unrisd/website/document.nsf/(httpPublications)/8647C951DCB7E800C12571D1002D7BE4?OpenDocument

Giugni, Marco G. (1998) 'Was it worth the effort? The outcomes and consequences of social movements', *Annual Review of Sociology* 24, pp. 371–93.

Goede, Marieke de, Anna Leander, and Gavin Sullivan (2016) 'Introduction: the politics of the list', *Environment and Planning D: Society and Space* 34, 1, pp. 3–13.

Goodwin, Jeff and James Jasper (2004) 'Caught in a winding, snarling vine: the structural bias of political process theory', in Jeff Goodwin and James Jasper (eds) *Rethinking Social Movements* (Lanham, MD: Rowman and Littlefield), pp. 3–30.

Graeber, David (2009) *Direct Action: An Ethnography* (Oakland: AK Press).

Grande, Edgar and Swen Hutter (2016) 'Beyond authority transfer: explaining the politicisation of Europe', *West European Politics* 39, 1, pp. 23–43.

Gronau, Jennifer and Henning Schmidtke (2016) 'The quest for legitimacy in world politics – international institutions' legitimation strategies', *Review of International Studies* 42, 3, pp. 535–57.

Großklaus, Matthias (2015) 'Appropriation and the dualism of human rights: understanding the contradictory impact of gender norms in Nigeria', *Third World Quarterly* 36, 5, pp. 1253–67.

Guzzini, Stefano (2012) 'Social mechanisms as micro-dynamics in constructivist analysis', in Stefano Guzzini (ed) *The Return of Geopolitics in Europe? Social Mechanisms and Foreign Policy Identity Crises* (Cambridge: Cambridge University Press), pp. 251–77.

Habermas, Jürgen (1979) *Communication and the Evolution of Society* (Boston: Beacon Press).

Habermas, Jürgen (1979) *The Philosophical Discourse of Modernity* (Cambridge MA: MIT Press).

Hack, Regina (2017) 'Deliberation als Reaktion auf Protest? Das zivilgesellschaftliche Dialogforum der WTO', *Zeitschrift für Internationale Beziehungen* 24, 1, pp. 37–67.

Hahn, Kristina and Anna Holzscheiter (2013) 'The ambivalence of advocacy: representation and contestation in global NGO advocacy for child workers and sex workers', *Global Society* 27, 4, pp. 497–520.

Hamati-Ataya, Inanna (2013) 'Reflectivity, reflexivity, reflexivism: IR's 'reflexive turn' – and beyond', *European Journal of International Relations* 19, 4, pp. 669–94.

Hannah, Erin, Holly Ryan, and James Scott (2017) 'Power, knowledge and resistance: between co-optation and revolution in global trade', *Review of International Political Economy* 24, 5, pp. 741–75.

Hanrieder, Tine (2008) 'Moralische Argumente in den internationalen Beziehungen: Grenzen einer verständigungstheoretischen "Erklärung" moralischer Debatten', *Zeitschrift Für Internationale Beziehungen* 15, 2, pp. 161–86.

Hanrieder, Tine (2014) 'Gradual change in international organisations: agency theory and historical institutionalism', *Politics* 34, 4, pp. 324–33.

Harvie, David, Keir Milburn, Ben Trott, and David Watts (2005) *Shut Them Down! The G8, Gleneagles 2005 and the Movement of Movements* (West Yorkshire: Dissent! and Autonomedia).

Heupel, Monika, Gisela Hirschmann, and Michael Zürn (2018) 'International organisations and human rights: what direct authority needs for its legitimation', *Review of International Studies* 44, 2, pp. 343–66.

Hintjens, Helen (2006) 'Appreciating the movement of the movements', *Development in Practice* 16, 6, pp. 628–43.

Hobson, John M. (2014) 'The twin self-delusions of IR: why 'hierarchy' and not 'anarchy' is the core concept of IR', *Millennium: Journal of International Studies* 42, 3, pp. 557–75.

Holdo, Markus (2019) 'Cooptation and non-cooptation: elite strategies in response to social protest', *Social Movement Studies* 18, pp. 444–62.

Hutter, Swen (2019) 'Exploring the full conceptual potential of protest event analysis', *Sociological Methodology* 49, 1, pp. 58–63.

Hutter, Swen and Edgar Grande (2016) *Politicising Europe: Integration and Mass Politics* (Cambridge: Cambridge University Press).

Inayatullah, Naeem and David L. Blaney (2017) 'Constructivism and the normative: dangerous liaisons?', in Charlotte Epstein (ed) *Against International Relations Norms: Postcolonial Perspectives* (London: Routledge), pp. 23–37.

Inclusive Development International (2016) 'Outsourcing development: lifting the veil on the World Bank Group's lending through financial intermediaries', http://www.inclusivedevelopment.net/wp-content/uploads/2016/09/Outsourcing-Developmnet-Introduction.pdf

Janis, Irving L. (1983) *Groupthink: Psychological Studies of Policy Decisions and Fiascoes* (Boston: Houghton Mifflin).

Jasper, James (2012) 'Introduction: from political opportunity structures to strategic interaction', in Jeff Goodwin and James M. Jasper (eds) *Contention in Context. Political Opportunities and the Emergence of Protest* (Stanford: Stanford University Press), pp. 1–36.

Jasper, James *The Art of Moral Protest: Culture, Biography, and Creativity in Social Movements* (London: University of Chicago Press).

Jasper, James M. and Jan W. Duyvendak (eds) (2015) *Players and Arenas: The Interactive Dynamics of Protest* (Amsterdam: Amsterdam University Press).

Johnson, Tana (2016) 'Cooperation, co-optation, competition, conflict: international bureaucracies and non-governmental organizations in an interdependent world', *Review of International Political Economy* 23, 5, pp. 737–67.

Jolly, Richard, Louis Emmerij and Thomas G. Weiss (2009) *UN Ideas that Changed the World* (Bloomington: Indiana University Press).

José Romero, Maria (2015) *What Lies Beneath? A Critical Assessment of PPPs and Their Impact on Sustainable Development* (Brussels: European Network on Debt and Development).

Junk, Julian and Frederik Trettin (2014) 'Internal dynamics and dysfunctions of international organizations — an introduction to the special issue', *Journal of International Organizations Studies* 5, 1, pp. 8–11.

Karimasari, Nadya (2011) 'Transnational environmental and agrarian movements influencing national policies: the case of palm oil plantation in Indonesia', MA Thesis (The Hague: International Institute of Social Studies).

Kauppi, Niilo and Mikael R. Madsen (2014) 'Fields of global governance: how transnational power elites can make global governance intelligible', *International Political Sociology* 8, 3, pp. 324–30.

Keck, Margaret E. and Kathryn Sikkink (1998) *Activists Beyond Borders: Advocacy Networks in International Politics* (Ithaca: Cornell University Press).

King, Gary, Robert O. Keohane, and Sidney Verba (1994) *Designing Social Inquiry. Scientific Inference in Qualitative Research* (Princeton: Princeton University Press).

Kitschelt, Herbert (1986) 'Political opportunity structures and political protest: anti-nuclear movements in four democracies', *British Journal of Political Science* 16, pp. 57–85.

Klabbers, Jan, Anne Peters, and Geir Ulfstein (2009) *The Constitutionalization of International Law* (Oxford: Oxford University Press).

Klein, Naomi (2007) *The Shock Doctrine: The Rise of Disaster Capitalism* (New York: Picador).

Klein, Thomas (2007) *'Frieden und Gerechtigkeit!' Die Politisierung der unabhängigen Friedensbewegung in Ost-Berlin während der 80er Jahre* (Köln: Böhlau).

Kortendiek, Nele (2021) 'How to govern mixed migration in Europe: transnational expert networks and knowledge creation in international organizations', *Global Networks* 21, 2, pp. 320–38.

Kortendiek, Nele and Jens Steffek (2018) 'Participatory governance in international organizations', in Hubert Heinelt (ed) *Edward Elgar Handbook on Participatory Governance* (Cheltenham: Edward Elgar), pp. 203–24.

Kriesi, Hanspeter (2011) 'Political context and opportunity', in David A. Snow, Sarah A. Soule, and Hanspeter Kriesi (eds) *The Blackwell Companion to Social Movements* (Malden, MA: Blackwell), pp. 67–90.

Krisch, Nico (2012) 'Global governance as public authority: an introduction', *International Journal of Constitutional Law* 10, 4, pp. 976–87.

Lake, David A. (2009) *Hierarchies in International Relations* (Ithaca, NY: Cornell University Press).

Lake, David A. (2010) 'Rightful rules: authority, order, and the foundations of global governance', *International Studies Quarterly* 54, 3, pp. 587–613.

Lavelle, Kathryn C. (2011) *Legislating International Organisation: The US Congress, the IMF and the World Bank* (Oxford: Oxford University Press).

Lemke, Thomas (2001) 'Max Weber, Norbert Elias und Michel Foucault. Über Macht und Subjektivierung', *Berliner Journal für Soziologie* 11, 1, pp. 77–95.

Lemke, Thomas (2002) 'Foucault, governmentality, and critique', *Rethinking Marxism: A Journal of Economics, Culture & Society* 14, 3, pp. 49–64.

Lemke, Thomas (2007) 'An indigestible meal? Foucault, governmentality, and state theory', *Distinktion: Scandinavian Journal of Social Theory* 8, 2, pp. 43–64.

Lenz, Tobias and Lora Anne Viola (2017) 'Legitimacy and institutional change in international organisations: a cognitive approach', *Review of International Studies* 43, 5, pp. 1–23.

Lie, Jon Harald Sande (2015) 'Developmentality: Indirect governance in the World Bank–Uganda partnership', *Third World Quarterly* 36, 4, pp. 723–40.

Liebenthal, Andrés, Roland Michelitsch, and Ethel Tarazona (2005) 'Extractive industries and sustainable development: an evaluation of World Bank Group experience' (Washington DC: World Bank Group).

Liese, Andrea (2010) 'Explaining varying degrees of openness in the Food and Agricultural Organization of the United Nations (FAO)', in Christer Jönsson and Jonas Tallberg (eds) *Transnational Actors in Global Governance. Patterns, Explanations, and Implications* (Basingtoke: Palgrave Macmillan), pp. 88–109.

Liste Philip (2021) 'In-between juridification and politicisation: zooming in on the everyday politics of law', in Claudia Wiesner (ed) *Rethinking Politicisation in Politics, Sociology and International Relations* (London: Palgrave), pp. 245–65.

Louis, Marieke and Lucile Maertens (2021) *Why International Organizations Hate Politics: Depoliticizing the World* (London: Routledge).

Lukes, Steven (1974) *Power: A Radical View* (London: Palgrave Macmillan).

Maiguashca, Bice (2005) 'Globalisation and the "politics of identitiy": IR Theory through the looking glass of women's reproductive rights activism', in Catherine Eschle and Bice Maiguashca (eds) *Critical Theories, International Relations and 'the Anti-Globalisation Movement'* (London: Routledge), pp. 117–36.

Martínez-Torres, María Elena, and Peter M. Rosset (2010) 'La Vía Campesina: the birth and evolution of a transnational social movement', *Journal of Peasant Studies* 37, 1, pp. 149–75.

Maynard, Douglas and Thomas Wilson (1980) 'On the reification of social structure', in Scott M. McNall and John Wilson (eds) *Current Perspectives in Social Theory: A Research Annual* (Greenwich: JAI Press), pp. 287–322.

McCarthy, Thomas (2009) *Race, Empire, and the Idea of Human Development* (Cambridge: Cambridge University Press).

McMichael, Philip (2017) *Development and Social Change: A Global Perspective* (London: Sage).

Mehta, Praadeep S. (1994) 'Fury over a river', in Kevin Danaher (ed) *50 Years Is Enough: The Case Against The World Bank and the International Monetary Fund* (Boston: South End Press), pp. 117–20.

Menke, Christoph (2015) *Kritik der Rechte* (Berlin: Suhrkamp).

Merry, Sally Engle (2011) 'Measuring the world: indicators, human rights, and global governance', *Current Anthropology* 52, S3 (April), pp. 83–95.

Meyer, David. S. (2003) 'How social movements matter', *Contexts* 2, 4, pp. 30–35.

Meyer, David. S. (2005) 'Social movements and public policy: eggs, chicken, and theory', in David. S. Meyer, Valerie Jenness, and Helen Ingram (eds) *Routing the Opposition: Social Movements, Public Policy, and Democracy* (Minneapolis: University of Minnesota Press), pp. 1–26.

Meyer, David S. (2012) 'Protest and political process', in Edwin Amenta, Kate Nash, and Alan Scott (eds) *The Wiley-Blackwell Companion to Political Sociology* (Oxford: Blackwell), pp. 395–407.

Meyer, David S. (2004) 'Protest and and political opportunity', *Annual Review of Sociology* 30, pp. 125–45.

Meyer, David S. and Debra C. Minkoff (2004) 'Conceptualizing political opportunity', *Social Forces* 82, 4, pp. 1457–92.

Mitchell, Timothy (2002) *Rule of Experts. Egypt, Techno-Politics, Modernity* (Berkeley: University of California Press).

Moghadam, Valentine M. (2009) *Globalization and Social Movements: Islamism, Feminism, and the Global Justice Movement*. (Lanham, MD: Rowman & Littlefield).

Morcillo Laiz, Álvaro and Klaus Schlichte (2016) 'Another Weber: state, associations and domination in international relations', *Cambridge Review of International Affairs* 29, 4, pp. 1448–66.

Morcillo Laiz, Álvaro and Klaus Schlichte (2016) 'Special section: international organizations, their staff and their legitimacy: Max Weber for IR', *Cambridge Review of International Affairs* 29, 4, pp. 1441–519.

Morcillo Laiz, Álvaro and Klaus Schlichte (2016) 'Rationality and international domination: revisiting Max Weber', *International Political Sociology* 10, 2, pp. 168–84.

Morgan, Rhiannon (2007) 'On political institutions and social movement dynamics: the case of the United Nations and the global indigenous movement', *International Political Science Review* 28, 3, pp. 273–92.

Morse, Bradford and Thomas R. Berger (1992) 'Sardar Sarovar – Report of the Independent Review' (Ottawa: Resource Futures International), http://www.ielrc.org/content/c9202.pdf

Motta, Renata (2014) 'Transnational discursive opportunities and social movement risk frames opposing GMOs', *Social Movement Studies* 14, 5, pp. 576–95.

Müller, Birgit (2013) 'Introduction – lifting the veil of harmony: anthropologists approach international organizations', in Birgit Müller (ed) *The Gloss of Harmony: The Politics of Policy-Making in Multilateral Organisations* (New York: Pluto Press), pp. 1–20.

Mundy, Karen (2010) '"Education for all" and the global governors', in Deborah Avant, Martha Finnemore, and Susan Sell, (eds) *Who Governs the Globe?* (Cambridge: Cambridge University Press), pp. 222–355.

Murray Li, Tania (2007) *The Will to Improve: Governmentality, Development, and the Practice of Politics* (Durham, NC: Duke University Press).

Nakamura, Karen (2002) 'Resistance and co-optation: The Japanese Federation of the Deaf and its relations with state power', *Social Science Japan Journal* 5, 1, pp. 17–35.

Nelson, Paul J. (2001) 'Transparency mechanisms at the multilateral development banks', *World Development* 29, 11, pp. 1835–47.

Ness, Gayl D. and Steven R. Brechin (1988) 'Bridging the gap: international organizations as organizations', *International Organization* 42, 2, pp. 245.

Neumann, Iver B. and Ole Jacob Sending (2007) '"The international" as governmentality', *Millennium: Journal of International Studies* 35, 3 (September 24), pp. 677–701.

Niemann, Holger and Henrik Schillinger (2016) 'Contestation "all the way down"? the grammar of contestation in norm research', *Review of International Studies*, 43, 1, pp. 1–21.

O'Brien, Robert, Anne Marie Goetz, Jan Aart Scholte, and Marc Williams (2000) *Contesting Global Governance* (Cambridge: Cambridge University Press).

Offe, Claus (2009) 'Governance – an "empty signifier"?' *Constellations* 16, 4, pp. 550–62.

Onuf, Nicholas G. (2013) *World of Our Making: Rules and Rule in Social Theory and International Relations* (London: Routledge).

Onuf, Nicholas G.(2018) *The Mightie Frame: Epochal Change and the Modern World* (Oxford: Oxford University Press).

Onuf, Nicholas G. and Frank F. Klink (1989) 'Anarchy, authority, rule', *International Studies Quarterly* 33, 2, pp. 149–73.

Ouchi, William G. and Alan L. Wilkins (1985) 'Organizational culture', *Annual Review of Sociology* 11, 1, pp. 457–83.

Oxfam (2015)'The suffering of others: the human cost of the international finance corporation's lending through intermediaries' (Oxford: Oxfam), https://www.oxfam.org/en/research/suffering-others

Oxfam International (2000) 'Towards global equity: Oxfam International's strategic plan, 2001–2004', (Melbourne: Oxfam International).

Pallas, Christopher L. and Anders Uhlin (2014) 'Civil society influence on international organizations: theorizing the state channel', *Journal of Civil Society* 10, 2, pp. 184–203.

Park, Sung-Joon (2015) '"Nobody is going to die": an ethnography of hope, indicators and improvizations in HIV treatment programmes in Uganda', in Richard Rottenburg, Sally Engle Merry, Sung-Joon Park, and Johanna Mugler (eds) *The World of Indicators: The Making of Governmental Knowledge through Quantification* (Cambridge: Cambridge University Press), pp. 188–219.

Park, Susan (2010) *World Bank Group Interactions with Environmentalists: Changing International Organisation Identities* (Manchester: Manchester University Press).

Park, Susan (2017) 'Accountability as justice for the multilateral development banks? Borrower opposition and bank avoidance to US power and influence', *Review of International Political Economy* 24, 5, pp. 776–801.

Park, Susan (2019) 'Changing the international rule of development to include citizen driven accountability – a successful case of contestation', in Felix Anderl, Christopher Daase, Nicole Deitelhoff, Victor Kempf, Jannik Pfister, and Philip Wallmeier (eds) *Rule and Resistance beyond the Nation State: Contestation, Escalation, Exit: Contestation, Escalation, Exit* (London: Rowman & Littlefield International), pp. 27–49.

Peluso, Nancy, Suraya Afiff, and Noer Rachman (2008) 'Claiming the grounds for reform: agrarian and environmental movements in Indonesia', *Journal of Agrarian Change* 8, 2–3, pp. 377–407.

Perkins, John (1997) *Geopolitics and the Green Revolution: Wheat, Genes, and the Cold War* (Oxford: Oxford University Press).

Petry, Martin (2003) *Wem gehört das Schwarze Gold? Engagement für Frieden und Gerechtigkeit in der Auseinandersetzung mit dem Erdölprojekt Tschad-Kamerun – Erfahrungen eines internationalen Netzwerks* (Frankfurt am Main: Brandes & Apsel).

Piper, Nicola and Anders Uhlin (2004) 'New perspectives on transnational activism', in Nicola Piper and Anders Uhlin (eds) *Transnational Activism in Asia* (London: Routledge), pp. 1–25.

Porter, Theodore (1995) *Trust in Numbers: The Pursuit of Objectivity in Science and Human Life* (Princeton: Princeton University Press).

Pruijt, Hans and Conny Roggeband (2014) 'Autonomous and/or institutionalized social movements? Conceptual clarification and illustrative cases', *International Journal of Comparative Sociology* 55, 2, pp. 144–65.

Reitan, Ruth (2007) *Global Activism* (New York: Routledge).

Rhodes, R.A.W. (1996) 'The new governance: governing without government', *Political Studies* 44, 4, pp. 652–67.

Rhodes, R.A.W. (1997) *Understanding Governance: Policy Networks, Governance, Reflexivity and Accountability* (Buckingham: Open University Press).

Rich, Bruce (1994) *Mortgaging the Earth: The World Bank, Environmental Impoverishment, and the Crisis of Development* (London: Earthscan).

Rich, Bruce (2013) *Foreclosing the Future: The World Bank and the Politics of Environmental Destruction* (New York: Island Press).

Rone, Julia (2016) 'The people formerly known as the oligarchy: the co-optation of citizen journalism', in Mona Baker and Bolette Blaagaard (eds) *Citizen Media and Public Spaces* (London: Routledge), pp. 208–24.

Rone, Julia (2018) 'Contested international agreements, contested national politics: how the radical left and the radical right opposed TTIP in four European countries', *Review of International Law* 6, 2, pp. 233–53.

Rosenau, James and Ernst Otto Czempiel (1992) *Governance without Government: Order and Change in World Politics* (Cambridge: Cambridge University Press).

Rottenburg, Richard and Sally E. Merry (2015) 'The world of indicators. The making of governmental knowledge through quantification', in Richard Rottenburg, Sally E. Merry, Sung-Joon Park, and Johanna Mugler (eds) *The World of Indicators. The Making of Governmental Knowledge through Quantification* (Cambridge: Cambridge University Press), pp. 1–33.

Rucht, Dieter (2011) 'Studying movement outcomes: a skeptical view', Draft Paper, Conference Outcomes of Social Movements and Protest WZB, June 23–25.

Rucht, Dieter (2012) 'Globalisierungskritische proteste als herausforderung an die internationale politik', in *Die Politisierung Der Weltpolitik* (Frankfurt am Main: Suhrkamp), pp. 61–83.

Saeed, Raza (2009) 'Conceptualising success and failure for social movements', *Law, Social Justice & Global Development Journal* 9, 2, pp. 1–13.

Salim, Emil (1997) 'Recollections of my career', *Bulletin of Indonesian Economic Studies* 33, 1, pp. 45–74.

Salim, Emil (2003) 'Striking a better balance: Vol. 1: The World Bank and extractive industries – the final report of the Extractive Industries Review', Jakarta.

Salim, Emil (2003) 'Striking a better balance: Vol. 2: Stakeholder inputs: Converging Issues and Diverging Views of the World Bank Group's involvement in extractive industries', Jakarta.

Salim, Emil (2003) 'Striking a better balance: Vol. 3: The World Bank and extractive industries – The final report of the Extractive Industries Review: Annexes', Jakarta.

Sarfaty, Galit (2012) *Values in Translation: Human Rights and the Culture of the World Bank* (Stanford: Stanford University Press).

Schemeil, Yves (2013) 'Bringing international organization in: global institutions as adaptive hybrids', *Organization Studies* 34, 2, pp. 219–52.

Schettler, Leon Valentin (2020) *Socializing Development: Transnational Social Movement Advocacy and the Human Rights Accountability of Multilateral Development Banks* (Bielefeld: Transcript).

Schlichte, Klaus (2012) 'Der Streit der Legitimitäten: Der Konflikt als Grund einer historischen Soziologie des Politischen', *Zeitschrift für Friedens – Und Konfliktforschung* 1, 1, pp. 9–43.

Schlichte, Klaus (2015) 'Cubicle land – bürokratie und demokratie in der regierung der welt', in *Ordnungsbildung Und Entgrenzung* (Wiesbaden: Springer), pp. 175–97.

Schlichte, Klaus (2017) 'Max Weber in Mosambik: Bürokratische Herrschaft in der Weltgesellschaft', in Christopher Daase, Nicole Deitelhoff, Ben Kamis, Jannik Pfister and Philip Wallmeier (eds) *Herrschaft in den Internationalen Beziehungen* (Wiesbaden: Springer), pp. 73–93.

Schlichte, Klaus (2018) 'Warum zahlen nicht reichen: Plädoyer für eine erweiterte Erfahrung der internationalen Beziehungen', *Zeitschrift Für Internationale Beziehungen* 25, 2, pp. 155–66.

Scholte, Jan Aart (2008) 'Civil society and IMF accountability', CSGR Working Paper, Warwick.

Scholte, Jan Aart (2012) *Building Global Democracy? Civil Society and Accountable Global Governance* (Cambridge: Cambridge University Press).

Scholte, Jan Aart (2020) 'Beyond institutionalism: toward a transformed global governance theory', *International Theory* 13, 1, pp. 1–13.

Schwarzmeier, Jan (2001) Die Autonomen. Zwischen Subkultur und Sozialer Bewegung. Dissertation (Göttingen: Universität Göttingen).

Scott, James (1987) *Weapons of the Weak: Everyday Forms of Peasant Resistance* (New Haven: Yale University Press).

Sending, Ole Jacob (2015) *The Politics of Expertise: Competing for Authority in Global Governance* (Ann Arbor: University of Michigan Press).

Sending, Ole Jacob and Iver B. Neumann (2006). 'Governance to governmentality: analyzing NGOs, states, and power', *International Studies Quarterly* 50, 3, pp. 651–72.

Shihata, Ibrahim F. (2000) *The World Bank Inspection Panel: In Practice* (Oxford and Washington DC: Oxford University Press/The World Bank).

Shore, Cris and Susan Wright (2015) 'Audit culture revisited', *Current Anthropology* 56, 3, pp. 421–44.

Shore, Cris and Susan Wright (2015) 'Governing by numbers: audit culture, rankings and the New World Order', *Social Anthropology* 23, 1, pp. 22–28.

Slobodian, Quinn (2018) *Globalists: The End of Empire and the Birth of Neoliberalism* (Boston: Harvard University Press).

Sondarjee, Maïka (2020) 'Change and stability at the World Bank: inclusive practices and neoliberal technocratic rationality', *Third World Quarterly* 42, 2, pp. 348–65.

Spivak, Gayatri (1988) 'Can the subaltern speak?' in Patrick Williams and Laure Chrisman (eds) *Colonial Discourse and Postcolonial Theory. A Reader* (New York: Columbia University Press), pp. 66–111.

Spivak, Gayatri (1993) *Outside the Teaching Machine* (New York: Routledge).

Srivastava, Swati (2013) 'Assembling international organizations', *Journal of International Organization Studies* 3, 1, pp. 72–83.

Steffek, Jens (2000) 'The power of rational discourse and the legitimacy of international governance', EUI Working Papers. Florence, RSC No. 2000/46.

Steffek, Jens (2009) 'Discursive legitimation in environmental governance', *Forest Policy and Economics* 11, 5–6, pp. 313–18.

Steffek, Jens (2016) 'Max Weber, modernity and the project of international organization', *Cambridge Review of International Affairs* 29, 4, pp. 1502–19.

Steffek, Jens (2017) 'International organizations and bureaucratic modernity', in Richard Ned Lebow (ed) *Max Weber and International Relations* (Cambridge: Cambridge University Press), pp. 119–42.

Steffek, Jens (2021) *International Organization as Technocratic Utopia* (Oxford: Oxford University Press).

Steffek, Jens, Claudia Kissling and Patrizia Nanz (2008) *Civil Society Participation in European and Global Governance: A Cure for the Democratic Deficit?* (Basingtoke: Palgrave Macmillan).

Steinhilper, Elias (2015) 'From "the rest" to "the West"? Rights of indigenous peoples and the western bias in norm diffusion research', *International Studies Review* 17, 4, pp. 536–55.

Straßenberger, Grit (2013) 'Autorität: Herrschaft ohne Zwang – Anerkennung ohne Deliberation', *Berliner Journal Für Soziologie* 23, 3, pp. 494–509.

Suh, Doowon (2011) 'Institutionalizing social movements: the dual strategy of the Korean women's movement' *Sociological Quarterly* 52, 3, pp. 442–71.

Susen, Simon (2015) 'Towards a critical sociology of dominant ideologies: an unexpected reunion between Pierre Bourdieu and Luc Boltanski', *Cultural Sociology* 10, 2, pp. 195–246.

Tallberg, Jonas, Thomas Sommerer, Theresa Squatrito, and Christer Jönsson (2013) *The Opening Up of International Organizations* (Cambridge: Cambridge University Press).

Tallberg, Jonas, Thomas Sommerer, Theresa Squatrito, and Christer Jönsson (2014) 'Explaining the transnational design of international organizations'. *International Organization* 68, 4, pp. 741–74.

Tarrow, Sidney (1989) *Democracy and Disorder: Protest and Politics in Italy, 1965–1975* (Oxford: Clarendon Press).

Tarrow, Sidney (2001) 'Transnational politics: contention and institutions in international politics', *Annual Review of Political Science* 4, 1, pp. 1–20.

Tarrow, Sidney (2011) *Power in Movement: Social Movements and Contentious Politics* (Cambridge: Cambridge University Press).

Tarrow, Sidney, and Jennifer Hadden (2007) 'Spillover or spillout? The global justice movement in the United States after 9/11', *Mobilization: An International Quarterly* 12, 4, pp. 359–76.

Tauli-Corpuz, Victoria (2005) 'Preface to the second edition', in Marcus Colchester and Emily Caruso (eds) *Extracting Promises: Indigenous Peoples, Extractive Industries and the World Bank* (Baguio City: Tebtebba Foundation).

Taylor, Verta and Nella van Dyke (2004) 'Get up, stand up: tactical repertoires of social movements', in David A. Snow, Sarah A. Soule, and Hanspeter Kriesi (eds) *The Blackwell Companion to Social Movements* (Oxford: Blackwell).

The World Bank (2017) 'Environmental and social framework', (Washington DC: The World Bank), http://documents.worldbank.org/curated/en/383011492423734099/pdf/114278-WP-REVISED-PUBLIC-Environmental-and-Social-Framework-Dec18-2017.pdf

The World Commission on Dams (2000) *Dams and Development: A New Framework for Decision-Making – the Report of the World Commission on Dams* (London: Earthscan).

Tilly, Charles (1978) *From Mobilization to Revolution* (Reading: Addison-Wesley).

Tilly, Charles (1995) *Popular Contention in Great Britain, 1758–1834* (Cambridge, MA: Harvard University Press).

Tilly, Charles, Doug McAdam, and Sidney. G. Tarrow (2001) *Dynamics of Contention* (Cambridge: Cambridge University Press).

Tilly, Charles and Sidney Tarrow (2015) *Contentious Politics* (New York: Oxford University Press).

Tsing, Anna L. (2005) *Friction: An Ethnography of Global Connection* (Princeton: Princeton University Press).

Tucker, Karen (2014) 'Participation and subjectification in global governance: NGOs, acceptable subjectivities and the WTO', *Millennium: Journal of International Studies* 42, 2, pp. 376–96.

Uhlin, Anders and Sara Kalm (2015) *Civil Society and the Governance of Development: Opposing Global Institutions* (London: Palgrave).

Van Evera, Stephen (1997) *Guide to Methods for Students of Political Science* (Ithaca, NY: Cornell University Press).

Veit, Alex (2011) 'Social movements, contestation and direct international rule: theoretical approaches', *Stichproben: Wiener Zeitschrift für Kritische Afrikastudien* 20, 20, pp. 17–43.

Vestena, Carolina (2019) 'Rechtliche Institutionen als Vermittlungsort der "Politik der Straßen": eine Auseinandersetzung mit der Rechtsprechung der Krise in Portugal', *Forschungsjournal Soziale Bewegungen* 32, 3, pp. 248–61.

Vrasti, Wanda (2013) 'Universal but not truly "global": governmentality, economic liberalism, and the international', *Review of International Studies* 39, 1, pp. 49–69.

Waltz, Kenneth (1979) *Theory of International Politics* (Long Grove: Waveland Press).

Weaver, Catherine (2009) *Hypocrisy Trap: The World Bank and the Poverty of Reform* (Princeton: Princeton University Press).

Weaver, Catherine and Stephen C. Nelson (2017) 'Organizational culture', in Jacob Katz Cogan, Ian Hurd, and Ian Johnstone (eds) *The Oxford Handbook of International Organizations* (Oxford: Oxford University Press), pp. 920–40.

Weber, Max (1978) *Economy and Society. Vol. 1, Part 2* (Los Angeles: University of California Press).

Weber, Max (1930) *The Protestant Ethic and the Spirit of Capitalism* (T. Parsons, trans) (New York: The Citadel Press).

Wendt, Alexander (1992) 'Anarchy is what states make of it: the social construction of power politics', *International Organization* 46, 2, pp. 391–425.

Wendt, Alexander (1998) 'On constitution and causation in international relations', *Review of International Studies* 24, pp. 101–17.

Wiener, Antje (2004) 'Contested compliance: interventions on the normative structure of world politics', *European Journal of International Relations* 10, 2, pp. 189–234.

Wiener, Antje (2014) *A Theory of Contestation* (Heidelberg: Springer).

Wiener, Antje (2018) *Contestation and Constitution of Norms in Global International Relations* (Cambridge: Cambridge University Press).

Wiesner, Claudia (2021) 'Introduction: rethinking politicisation in politics, sociology and international relations', in Claudia Wiesner (ed) *Rethinking Politicisation in Politics, Sociology and International Relations* (London: Palgrave), pp. 1–15.

Wilde, Pieter De and Michael Zürn (2012) 'Can the politicization of European integration be reversed?' *Journal of Common Market Studies* 50, 1, pp. 137–53.

Wolfensohn, James (2004) 'Letter from James Wolfensohn to Emil Salim' (Washington DC: World Bank), http://siteresources.worldbank.org/INTOGMC/Resources/eirfaq.pdf

Wolfensohn, James D. (2010) *A Global Life: My Journey among Rich and Poor, from Sydney to Wall Street to the World Bank* (New York: Public Affairs).

Wood, Lesley J. (2007) 'Breaking the wave: repression, identity, and Seattle tactics', *Mobilization: An International Quarterly* 12, 4, pp. 377–88.

World Bank (1985) 'Directive on disclosure of information' (Washington DC: The World Bank).

World Bank (1998) 'The Bank's relations with NGOs: issues and directions', *Social Development Papers* (Washington DC: The World Bank).

World Bank (2002) 'The World Bank Policy on disclosure of information', http://www1.worldbank.org/operations/disclosure/documents/disclosurepolicy.pdf

World Bank (2004) 'World Development Report 2004: making services work for poor people' (Washington DC: The World Bank), https://doi.org/10.1093/jae/ejh019

World Bank (2007) 'Strengthening World Bank group engagement on governance and anticorruption' (Washington DC: The World Bank).

World Bank (2013) 'World Bank– civil society engagement: review of fiscal years 2010–2012' (Washington DC: The World Bank).

World Bank Administrative and Civil Service Reform Thematic Group (2001) 'The World Bank's Poverty Reduction Support Credit (PRSC) – a new approach to support policy and institutional reforms in low income countries', *Working on Administrative & Civil Reform*, Vol. 1. (Washington DC: The World Bank).

World Bank Group (2004) 'Comments received on the Draft Management Response to the Final Report of the Extractive Industries Review: staff report by the Oil, Gas and Chemicals Department' (Washington DC: The World Bank).

World Bank Group (2004) *Striking a Better Balance: The World Bank Group and Extractive Industries – the Final Report of the Extractive Industries Review. World Bank Group Management Response* (Washington DC: The World Bank).

World Bank Group (2010) 'The World Bank Access to Information Policy' (Washington DC: The World Bank).

World Bank Group (2014) 'Strategic framework for mainstreaming citizen engagement in World Bank Group' (Washington DC: The World Bank), https://consultations.worldbank.org/Data/hub/files/consultation-template/engaging-citizens-improved-resultsopenconsultationtemplate/materials/finalstrategicframeworkforce_4.pdf

Zarakol, Ayşe (2016) *Hierarchies in World Politics* (Cambridge: Cambridge University Press).

Ziai, Aram (2009) 'Development: projects, power, and a poststructuralist perspective', *Alternatives: Global, Local, Political* 34, 2, pp. 183–201.

Ziai, Aram (2013) 'The discourse of "development" and why the concept should be abandoned', *Development in Practice* 23, 1, pp. 123–36.

Ziai, Aram (2015) *Development Discourse and Global History: From Colonialism to the Sustainable Development Goals* (London: Routledge).

Ziai, Aram (2017) 'Can the subaltern file claims? The World Bank inspection panel and subaltern articulation', *Momentum Quarterly: Journal for Societal Progress* 5, 4, pp. 255–64.

Zimmermann, Lisbeth, Nicole Deitelhoff, and Max Lesch (2017) 'Unlocking the agency of the governed: contestation and norm dynamics', *Third World Thematics: A TWQ Journal* 2, 5, pp. 691–708.

Zürn, Michael (2004) 'Global governance and legitimacy problems', *Government and Opposition* 39, 2, pp. 260–87.

Zürn, Michael (2012) 'Autorität und Legitimität in der postnationalen Konstellation', in *Der Aufstieg der Legitimitätspolitik*, pp. 41–63.

Zürn, Michael (2017) 'From constitutional rule to loosely coupled spheres of liquid authority: a reflexive approach', *International Theory* 9, 2, pp. 261–85.

Zürn, Michael (2018) *A Theory of Global Governance: Authority, Legitimacy & Contestation* (Oxford: Oxford University Press).

Zürn, Michael, Martin Binder, and Matthias Ecker-Ehrhardt (2012) 'International authority and its politicization', *International Theory* 4, 1, pp. 69–106.

Zürn, Michael and Matthias Ecker-Ehrhardt (2013) *Die Politisierung der Weltpolitik: Umkämpfte Internationale Institutionen* (Berlin: Suhrkamp).

Index